ECONOMIC DEVELOPMENT
IN THE TROPICS

Economic Development in the Tropics

B. W. HODDER

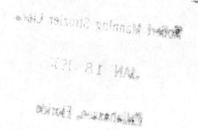

METHUEN
LONDON AND NEW YORK

First published in 1968 by
Methuen & Co. Ltd
11 New Fetter Lane, London EC4P 4EE
Second edition 1973
Third edition 1980
Published in the USA by
Methuen & Co.
in association with Methuen, Inc.
733 Third Avenue, New York, NY 10017
© *1968, 1973 and 1980 B. W. Hodder*
Printed in Great Britain by
Richard Clay (The Chaucer Press) Ltd, Bungay, Suffolk

British Library Cataloguing in Publication Data

Hodder, Bromwell William
Economic development in the tropics. –
3rd ed.
1. Tropics – Economic conditions
I. Title
330.9′172′4   HC695   80-40446

ISBN 0-416-74250-5
ISBN 0-416-74260-2 Pbk

Contents

Figures

Tables

Preface

No one concerned with the study of any part of the developing world today can fail to consider in his analysis at least some of the problems and manifestations of economic development. Explicit or implicit in much of his work is likely to be some attempt to understand the nature and causes of poverty, backwardness, or underdevelopment, and to make some objective comment on the lines along which successful development might most logically be pursued. In so doing, however, he becomes aware of two distinct sets of problems. First, there are those practical problems which arise from the existence in a specific areal setting of a unique combination of natural and human resources, considered both quantitatively and qualitatively; for all applied problems of development are in part regional or local problems. Secondly, there are those problems of a more theoretical nature, relating to the aims, methods, and processes of development, which have received a good deal of attention from economists and other social scientists over the last forty years or so. Both types or sets of problems seem to demand full consideration in any specific applied case of development. Just as there are dangers in the indiscriminate application of theoretical models and procedures to a particular case study, so any attempt to comment on development in an area without at least some acquaintance with economic development theory is likely to be both ingenuous and misleading.

I have tried in these pages to deal briefly, simply, and in a very preliminary way with some of the more important practical and theoretical problems of development in the tropical sectors of the developing world and, more specifically, to emphasize those issues which seem to me best able to provide the necessary interdisciplinary background for the study by geographers of economic development in these areas. I have therefore included at least some discussion of all material, whether 'geographical' or not, that seems to be relevant to an understanding of the problems of tropical development. The more theoretical material, however, has been treated very briefly and introduced only where absolutely necessary; and on many occasions I have done little more than simply to refer to the theoretical discussion in the literature and to indicate the more significant areas of disagreement and intellectual controversy. Any reader wishing to delve more deeply into the theoretical material or requiring a more rigorous treatment of any particular line of inquiry will find this possible by following up the relevant literature referred to in the text. As for the detailed factual and descriptive material, this is most conveniently to be found in those major regional geographical texts – by, for instance, Blakemore and Smith (1971) Hance (1964), Spate and Learmonth (1967) and Fisher (1964).

In writing this introductory book on tropical development I have kept in mind the needs of undergraduates concerned regionally or systematically with any part of the tropical world, and the rapidly increasing number of graduates studying in the various Area Study Programmes for Latin America, Africa, South Asia, and Southeast Asia. Much of the material and most of the ideas presented here have grown out of a number of lecture and seminar courses, and are set against my own experience in living and working in various parts of the Asian and African tropics over a continuous period of some twelve years. My first-hand experience of the American tropics, however, has been limited to brief visits to Central America, the Caribbean and Venezuela since 1965, so that a good deal of what I have to say is highly selective and possibly even more biased by my own tropical contacts than I realize. Certainly I am aware that much of what I have written here is controversial, especially where I seem to have taken a perhaps unusually optimistic standpoint over the potentialities for development in tropical countries.On a subject so vast and ultimately so practical a good deal of what one says must necessarily involve questionable hypotheses and over-simplifications. Yet I have thought it best to give my own views on tropical development, finding this practice to be more successful in stimulating discussion than is any attempt to provide a comprehensive or systematic academic analysis of the geography of tropical areas. And it is above all to stimulate further thought, discussion, and field work in tropical lands that this book has been written.

My chief debt is to former undergraduates and colleagues of the University of Malaya (Singapore) and University of Ibadan (Nigeria), with whom I lived and worked from 1952 to 1963 and from whom I learned much of what I know about the tropics. The authorities of both universities also made it possible for me to travel in various other parts of South-east Asia and Africa. I also owe a great deal to the encouragement and help given to me over many years by Professor R. W. Steel, Professor C. A. Fisher, and Professor A. E. Smailes. A number of experts have been kind enough to read and comment on parts of the typescript; and for this I am particularly grateful to Dr B. W. Atkinson, Dr D. R. Harris, Dr N. Harris, Mr D. C. Ledger, and Dr A. Warren. Responsibility for any errors of fact or interpretation, however, remains mine alone. To the Central Research Fund of the University of London I am indebted for a grant enabling me to visit the American tropics during the summer of 1965. Much of the work of typing was undertaken by Mrs C. Hartley, Miss L. Bull and, in the final stages, by Miss J. Storric. The line diagrams were drawn by Mr G. Brannon, Senior Draughtsman in the Department of Geography, Queen Mary College, University of London.

Queen Mary College,   B. W. HODDER
University of London, 1967

Note to Revised Edition. In this revised edition I have taken the opportunity not only to bring the bibliography and tables up to date, but also to incorporate some of the more important ideas and attitudes now current in the debate on development problems. I am grateful to all those who have discussed with me many of the points raised in these pages and, in so doing, have helped me to clarify and, in some cases, substantially to change my earlier views. To Mr. P. O'Keefe I am particularly indebted for his help in bringing some of the material up to date and for helping me to draft the new chapter fourteen, in which the political context is given explicit attention. The new Fig. 1 has been drawn by Mr. A. de Souza, Cartographer of the Department of Geography, School of Oriental and African Studies, University of London.

School of Oriental and African Studies,   B. W. HODDER
University of London, 1972

Preface to Third Edition. Apart from bringing some of the material and most of the bibliography up to date, this new edition incorporates three case studies in a new chapter fourteen. As the most populous and, in many senses, the most important countries in their respective sectors of the tropics, Brazil, Nigeria and India reflect most of the characteristics, issues and problems examined in the preceding chapters.

I am grateful to many people for their comments on and criticisms of this little book over many years. In preparing this new edition, however, I must record my special thanks to two of my colleagues – Philip Stott and Richard Wiltshire – who made detailed suggestions for improving sections of the book. Where expense has precluded making substantial changes in the text, the more important trends in the literature are referred to briefly in the appendix – 'Notes on some recent trends'.

School of Oriental and African Studies,   B. W. HODDER
University of London, 1980

Introduction: Some Definitions

Although there is still no generally accepted theory of *economic development*, all definitions imply that it involves raising living standards: it is, for example, 'a social process which results in a cumulative increase in levels of consumption' (Belshaw, 1956: XV). Other definitions include as a necessary element in development the more equitable distribution of wealth, economic development in this sense involving a perceptible and cumulative rise in the material standard of living for an increasing proportion of the total population. Another definition refers to a more equitable *spatial* distribution of wealth in a country, while others make the 'quality of life' an important, even crucial, consideration. Clearly, economic development, however defined, can occur in all countries, including those already highly developed. Yet though many of the theories and applied problems of economic development may be the same for economically advanced as for developing countries, important differences of approach or attitude seem to be needed. The difference between the economics of developed and developing countries 'lies not so much in the problems which confront them (after all, both types are actively trying to raise real income per head) as in the assumptions which one "naturally" makes in considering the problem – and all too often fails to specify explicitly ... For understanding the economic problems of underdeveloped countries one needs to develop a new set of instinctive assumptions' (Reddaway, 1963: 1–2). Again, the results of any analysis made of an economy in which the subsistence sector is negligible are likely to need modification when applied to those economies, common in the tropics, in which subsistence production is important. For a number of reasons, indeed, it may well be desirable to distinguish between economic development (associated with economically and socially backward societies) and economic growth (associated with advanced or developed societies).

These pages will deal solely with economic development applied to countries at a relatively low level of development and in an environment – the humid tropics – which many writers believe to contain obstacles likely to complicate and even to frustrate the application of measures for economic development.

By *underdevelopment* is meant that condition, characteristic of developing countries, in which levels and growth rates of real income and capital per head of population are low by comparison with Western Europe, North America and Australia. However, there are a number of weaknesses in using *per capita* income measures. National income and population data are themselves often no more than the crudest of estimates. Furthermore, *per capita* income normally refers to standard of living defined only in a quantitative sense: it takes no account at all of qualitative aspects of life. Then *per capita* data are perhaps not fully relevant in a situation where subsistence production is important, perhaps dominant; nor can *per capita* income data show the distribution of national income among classes or groups (Bauer and Yamey, 1957: 16–24) – a consideration of some importance in a country like Venezuela where the extremes of income are very widely separated. Again, *per capita* figures cannot reveal serious inequalities in the spatial distribution of wealth, either between regions or between the rural areas and large metropolitan centres. Low *per capita* income figures for developing countries, moreover, are not to be thought of as always static, declining or only very slowly increasing. As Myint (1964) has noted, this viewpoint has affected most current theories of economic development and arises from notions about 'vicious circles', the need for the 'big push', from the Malthusian spectre of population pressure in developing countries, and from popular notions of developing countries as closed, traditional societies. But in many developing countries – especially in Latin America – *per capita* income growth rates are very high indeed.

Other definitions of a developing country emphasize the potentialities for development, while another describes a developing country as one 'characterized by (i) mass poverty which is chronic and not the result of some temporary misfortune, and (ii) by obsolete methods of production and social organization, which means that the poverty is not entirely due to poor natural resources and hence could presumably be lessened by methods already proved in other countries' (Staley, 1954: 13). It is also possible to define underdevelopment on the basis of occupational structure, a developing country being said to have at least 50 per cent of its gainfully employed males engaged in agriculture, fishing, and forestry.

Perhaps the most satisfactory way of defining underdevelopment for the purposes of the present study, however, is simply to refer to certain characteristics which are commonly, though not invariably, found in a developing country in the tropics:

(i) low life expectancy at birth, high infant mortality rates, poor health, and illiteracy;

(ii) low *per capita* output, together with poverty and indebtedness;

(iii) subsistence production generally important;

(iv) economies non-diversified and geared to primary production;

(v) little manufacturing industry;

(vi) no large-scale application of scientific and technological methods to agriculture or industry;

(vii) narrowness of markets.

Many of these and other variables have been discussed in a volume by Ginsberg (1960) and mapped in an atlas which aims at casting some light on the meanings of the terms 'development' and 'underdevelopment' by 'analysing them into some commensurable components and showing the world pattern of distribution of these components by countries' (Ginsberg, 1961:5). In the former volume Berry illustrates the complexity of any attempt to classify or categorize countries by levels of development: he demonstrates that while it may be true that most developing countries appear to be high on the demographic scale and low on the technological scale, there is no clear break in the spectrum between the less developed and more developed countries. Certainly it is easy to over-generalize about developing countries, ignoring differences between densely populated and highly populated countries and between countries at widely differing levels of economic achievement. Perhaps the first thing to bear in mind about developing countries, indeed, is that 'beyond the broad common fact of poverty it is rarely safe to make generalizations about them without first specifying the type of underdeveloped country one is considering' (Myint, 1964: 14); in such circumstances there is clearly no point in looking for a single theory to cover all developing countries.

With these reservations in mind, it is worth noting that developing countries cover much of Asia, Africa, and Latin America, as well as many parts of eastern and southern Europe well outside the tropics. Covering rather more than half the world's land surface, developing countries contain over two-thirds of the world's population.

Within the developing world, the area with which this study is concerned is for the sake of brevity termed the *tropics*, but is in fact restricted to the *humid tropics*, defined for the purposes of this study as in Table 3 which shows those countries whose populations lie wholly or substantially within the humid tropics, so that a country like Niger is included (most of its population living in the southern humid tropical parts of the country) while Sudan is excluded (most of the population there living in the northern desert or semi-desert areas). There was considerable discussion in the 1960s about the precise limits of the humid tropical region (Fosberg *et alia*, 1961; Garnier, 1961; Gaussen and Legris, 1963; Gourou, 1966). One way of defining the humid tropics is to refer to the *A* type climates of Köppen (1936). Gourou (1966) takes the mean temperature of 64·4° F (18° C) for the coolest month and the boundaries of those areas where 'cultivation is possible without irrigation' to delimit his humid tropical region, though he emphasizes the need to accept these limits cautiously and not always to adhere to them rigidly.

While these limits are perfectly satisfactory for all working purposes, more recent attempts have understandably been made to express the latter part of Gourou's definition – 'agriculture possible without irrigation' – more precisely. This is admittedly a rather unsatisfactory phrase because the need to irrigate is clearly dependent upon so many variables, such as choice of crop and methods of cultivation. Garnier (Fosberg *et alia*, 1961) has suggested criteria involving air moisture content and temperature. Garnier's view, briefly stated, is that humid tropical conditions may be identified by reference to a climatic situation in which the mean monthly temperature for at least eight months of the year equals or exceeds 68° F (20° C); the vapour pressure and relative humidity for at least six months of the year average at least 20 millibars and 65 per cent respectively; and the mean annual rainfall totals at least 40 inches (1,016 mm), precipitation being at least 2·95 inches (75 mm) for each of six months during the year. In the same paper Küchler puts forward his views based upon vegetation criteria.

The differences between the many suggested limits to the humid tropics are least in West Africa and America and greatest along the northern boundary of the Asian tropics, especially in India, and to a lesser extent in East Africa. These areal differences in the degree of coincidence of the various limits are explained partly by the contrasts between climatic patterns on the western and eastern margins of continents, and partly by the complications introduced by position and elevation. Whether or not to include the tropical highlands in the humid tropical area is arguable. Garnier excludes elevations of over about 3,300 feet (1,000 m) because such areas are not strictly 'humid tropical' in his sense. On the other hand, there does appear to be some justification for including at least the tropical uplands of intermediate altitudes, for it is usually inconvenient in practice to exclude the many upland enclaves such as those found in South-east Asia and Central America.

Much of the current discussion about the precise limits of the humid tropics is admittedly academic and of no relevance to the present study except in so far as it helps to clarify notions about the region and affects the possibilities of generalization. The environmental variations within the tropics are immense; and one of the chief conclusions arising from a comparative study of the tropical world is that it is rarely possible to formulate useful generalizations which are valid both for a country like Malaya, within the tropical rain forest or equatorial region, and for a country like Nigeria, most of which lies within the savanna tropics where differences between the wet and dry seasons profoundly affect the life and welfare of the people.

CHAPTER 1

Natural Resources and Tropical Development

The significance of natural resources. In assessing the role of natural resources in economic development, a number of writers strongly criticize the 'geographical school' (by which is meant the 'natural resource' school) of economic development studies for its crude determinism, its tendency to discuss physical factors at length but non-physical and especially economic factors hardly at all, and for appearing to ignore altogether the theoretical framework of economic development studies. Examples of this 'natural resource' school of thought can be found in the work of Semple (1911), Huntington (1915) and Parker (1961).

Some authorities would go so far as deliberately to disregard the role of natural or physical resources in economic development. It is argued, for instance, that economic growth is determined by capital – 'the engine of growth' – and is thus largely the result of an interaction between savings and the capital–output ratio (Harrod, 1948). Analyses such as this leave nature out of explicit consideration and give little if any attention to the role of natural resources, either qualitatively or quantitatively. While natural resources may receive some mention in theoretical analyses, their explicit consideration is commonly believed to be unnecessary (Kuznets, 1959; Meade, 1955). It is argued not only that land is a fixed factor but also that the old Ricardian model in which economic growth is limited by land – and especially by the poverty of natural resources – has been completely disproved by the experiences of nineteenth-century Europe and North America. Increasing returns and technical progress have always upset the Ricardian model. Even where countries have resource deficiencies, it should be possible for them to draw upon the resources of other countries, for instance by trade. Trade clearly opens up the possibility of breaking through any constraints imposed by natural resource deficiencies and links growth more intimately and directly to population and capital accumulation, both of which leave a continuing potential for economic expansion (Barnett and Morse, 1963). Again, it is possible to compensate for lack of natural resources by the substitution of capital or labour skills and by social and economic improvements, including education – 'investment in human capital' – managerial capacity, and economies of scale.

Even the most cursory glance at natural resources – water, forests, soils, minerals, or power – reveals that there is indeed little correlation between the occurrence of these resources and the level of economic development in any particular tropical country. The presence or absence of naturally occurring material resources in no way immutably determines the economic development of a country. 'Since the changing fortunes of many countries and regions have not been connected with the discovery or exhaustion of natural resources within their territories, the fortuitous distribution of these resources certainly does not provide the only, and probably not even the principal, explanation of differences in development and prosperity' (Bauer and Yamey, 1957: 46–7). High productivity and prosperity can be achieved without abundant natural resources. While their possession may give certain initial advantages, plentiful natural resources are not necessarily associated with prosperity, nor are they a precondition for economic development.

It is true that many analyses grossly exaggerate the role of natural resources in economic development; and this is perhaps especially true of the work of geographers. In spite of his interest in the physical environment and in the broader aspects of man–environment relationships in specific areal settings, the geographer cannot afford to argue the overriding importance of the physical factors in development; he cannot associate himself with the school of thought which puts the emphasis upon natural resources and claims that the level of economic development in a country is somehow causally connected with its natural resource endowment; nor can the geographer afford to view economic development simply in terms of how far the natural resources in a country are developed or utilized. To abstract the purely physical factors in applied development studies is to falsify as surely as is to abstract the purely economic, political, or social factors.

On the other hand, it can be argued that there is no justification for ignoring natural resources altogether in any development analysis, and that there are real dangers in any tendency to underestimate the role of natural resources in tropical development. That any analysis of the applied problems of economic development cannot afford to accept natural resources as 'given' or 'fixed' is clear from the widely accepted need for the conservation of resources, both exhaustible and renewable: the problems of soil erosion and forest degeneration, for example, vividly illustrate the consequences of neglecting the utilization and conservation of resources. In recent years, too, a great deal of public attention has been focused on the dangers of exhausting many of the world's mineral, power and water resources; and considerable concern is being expressed over the way in which ecological systems are being disturbed or destroyed. Again, the theoretical arguments for giving scant attention to natural resources in tropical development studies may fall down in practice; for while in theory tropical low-income countries can make up for the lack of certain natural resources by trade, capital, and skills substitution, in practice most of these countries do not have the external trading potential, capital, or labour skills to enable them to make up for limited natural resources in this way (Barnett and Morse, 1963). Furthermore, a good deal of the available empirical evidence supports the contention that natural resources are by no means an irrelevance, especially in the early stages of development. In Venezuela the *per capita* income is higher than in most other tropical countries, and this fact is clearly and causally connected with the exploitation of rich oil resources in that country.

Thus while the relative lack or abundance of natural resources is never a determining factor in economic development, and while the natural endowment is usually less important to this process than is the human contribution, natural resources may constitute an important factor in planning and decision-making as far as economic development in low-income tropical countries is concerned. This, at least, is the standpoint taken in subsequent chapters. The importance of natural resources to developing countries is relatively greater than to the developed countries of the world. In low-income tropical countries rich natural resources can have great significance as sources of exports and foreign investments, while poor resources may form some limitation to growth. The quantity and character of natural resources may well have an important initial effect on patterns of production and levels of income.

The study of natural resources. Perhaps the most striking impression received from any study of the natural resources of the tropical world is the urgent need for more information about those resources. Such an impression remains true, not only for the assessment of mineral and power resources but also for the quantitative and qualitative analysis of moisture resources, vegetation, and soils. This point will be made several times in the following pages and is underlined by the reading of the current development plans of any tropical country. It is now widely realized that not enough is known about most of the natural resources of countries in the tropics, and that topographical, geological, hydrological, soil, and ecological surveys are vital prerequisites to any successful attempt at resource utilization. Though precise, accurate data are often very difficult and expensive to obtain, and though, also, it is true that these resources cannot easily acquire commercial value, further research into the various natural resources and their utilization is an immediate and basic need everywhere. Without such information, as has been abundantly proved on a number of occasions over the last two decades or so, all development schemes can be undertaken only with a serious risk of failure.

Yet while it is clearly convenient for the purposes of analysis to treat particular natural resources separately, it is perhaps worth pointing out that this is a somewhat arbitrary and misleading procedure. In any particular applied problem of economic development the interdependence of natural resources may be so close that it is impossible ever to single out any one factor or element as the crucial one for study. Water supply and hydro-electric power;

forests, soils, and vegetation: these are particularly obvious cases where the various kinds of natural resources are intimately dependent on one another. Furthermore, in any consideration of the applied problems of development of any of these natural resources, non-physical elements – human resources, economic factors or political considerations of one kind or another – are necessary to any full understanding. While it is convenient to write of the natural environment and natural resources associated with that environment as being quite distinct from the non-physical environment and resources, the truth is that all applied problems of economic development demand the examination of the 'total' environment, with its complex of resources and factors – natural, human, and capital.

Again, the quantity and quality of natural resources vary considerably from place to place, and it is perhaps not too much to say that every natural resource or group of resources poses a unique problem within the context of a specific area. This question of regional variation is of considerable geographical interest and is of great importance to development planning. The non-physical elements in the utilization of any natural resource are numerous, and may well be determining, but they operate within the limits and possibilities set by the nature and location of that resource. Mineral exploitation may be limited by difficulties of access. And in developing hydro-electric power potential, many of the best areas from the point of view of rainfall régime – that is, with rain all the year round – are associated in the tropics with the most difficult forest vegetation, the lowest population densities and low economic activity generally; many of the best potential sites from the physical point of view are therefore limited by their location.

Such areal differentiation in natural resource distribution is relevant not only to a continent or region but also to the political state within which the natural resources lie. In practice, the development of natural resources normally operates only within the context of a nation state, and the uneven distribution of mineral and power potential among different states is a matter of serious concern to those charged with planning. Many tropical developing countries, notably in West Africa and Central America, encompass only very small areas, and so may possess a narrow range and, perhaps, some important omissions in their pattern of natural resources. The territorial state context is also of importance here because some natural resources may be partly or even wholly private property: in the case of minerals, it may well be that the country in which the mineral lies will receive little or no financial benefit from its exploitation by concerns operating from another country.

It is, indeed, an important principle in the relationship between natural resources on the one hand and economic development on the other, that standards of world comparison are not necessarily relevant to the level of or prospects for economic development in a country. In this sense a map of the distribution over the world of any natural resource is almost an irrelevance in economic development planning. What matters more to a particular country is the occurrence of these resources relative to its own size, population, and economy. This is most clearly illustrated in the case of mineral and power resources. In Asia, Brunei's economic development has been overwhelmingly the result of her production of petroleum which, though small by world standards, provides a large part of her national income. Similarly, although the production of natural phosphates in Togo (West Africa) is small by world standards, the discovery and exploitation of phosphates in Togo has proved to be probably the most important single event in that country's economic history, making it possible to add some 50 per cent to the value of its export trade within a few years.

· · · · ·

While it is to some extent arbitrary to treat natural resources separately from the other factors of production in any analysis of the applied problems of economic development, there is perhaps more justification for doing this in the tropical world about which we still know very little and where the implications of natural resources for economic development have not yet been fully worked out. Yet even though it is necessary to emphasize our ignorance rather than our knowledge about the physical factors and natural resources of the tropics, it is also necessary to emphasize that there are no grounds for assuming that natural resources are anywhere a limitation to economic development or an excuse for the present relatively low standard of living in any part of the tropics: 'the Creator has not divided the world into two sectors, developed and underdeveloped, the former being more richly blessed with natural resources than the latter' (Bauer and Yamey, 1957: 46). The early traditional viewpoint of the tropics as having exceptionally rich natural resources and the 'modern' view of the tropics as poor or inferior in natural resources are equally false. The problem of natural resources is not that they are especially poor or inadequate in tropical countries but rather that the facts about these resources are little known and that their significance for economic development in any specific area is not fully understood. The standpoint adopted in the pages that follow is that any realistic analysis of an applied situation in tropical economic development must start from the assumption that the natural resource base is potentially adequate for substantial development, given sufficient knowledge about these resources and a ready adaptation of planning to the opportunities and limitations set by them. The next two chapters carry this point a little farther by discussing some of the characteristics and implications for development of the major natural resources of the tropical world.

CHAPTER 2

Natural Resources: Climate and Water Supply

Climatic types. The term 'tropical climate' popularly conjures up a picture of high temperature and humidity, constant rainfall, and unrelieved monotony. But of few parts of the tropics is this an accurate picture. Indeed, it is impossible to make any useful generalizations about the climate of the tropical world as a whole, not only because of the sheer size of the area but also because of complications introduced by the unequal distribution of land and sea, by great regional variations in relief and aspect, and by important positional differences in relation to extra-tropical areas.

At least three broad climatic types may be distinguished – the equatorial lowland, tropical monsoon, and tropical savanna climates (Table 1). The chief features of the true *equatorial lowland*

Table 1. *Three selected stations: rainfall and temperature*

	J.	F.	M.	A.	M.	J.	J.	A.	S.	O.	N.	D.	Year
Belem (Brazil)													
Temp., ° F	78	77	78	78	79	79	79	79	79	79	80	79	79
Temp., ° C	25·6	25	25·6	25·6	26·1	26·1	26·1	26·1	26·1	26·1	26·7	26·1	26·1
Rainfall, inches	7·6	13·4	17·0	17·8	11·8	9·0	2·3	2·8	0·6	0·5	0·6	2·6	89·6
Rainfall, mm	193	340	432	452	300	229	58	71	15	13	15	66	2,276
Bombay (India)													
Temp., ° F	75	75	79	82	85	84	81	80	80	82	81	78	80
Temp., ° C	23·9	23·9	26·1	27·8	29·4	28·9	27·2	26·7	26·7	27·8	27·2	25·6	26·7
Rainfall, inches	0·1	0·1	0·1	0·1	0·7	19·1	24·3	13·4	10·4	2·5	0·5	0·1	71·2
Rainfall, mm	3	3	3	3	18	485	617	340	264	64	13	3	1,809
Kano (Nigeria)													
Temp., ° F	71	75	83	88	87	83	79	78	79	81	77	72	80
Temp., ° C	21·7	23·9	28·3	31·1	30·6	28·3	26·1	25·6	26·1	27·2	25	22·2	26·7
Rainfall, inches	0·1	0·1	0·1	0·4	2·7	4·6	8·1	12·2	5·6	0·5	0·1	0	35·1
Rainfall, mm	3	3	3	10	69	117	206	310	142	13	3	0	892

climate are a mean annual rainfall of over 60 inches (1,594 mm), no true dry season, high relative humidities, and uniformly high temperatures. Belem (Brazil) is an example of a station with this kind of climate. It will be noted that the rainfall is by no means evenly distributed throughout the year. More commonly, definite double maxima occur, and there may even be a near approach to a short dry season. This kind of seasonal rhythm of rainfall is responsible for most variations within the type. In general, however, conditions are ideal for rain formation throughout most of the year in the equatorial lowlands. These are primarily areas of rising air, a fact which results in part from the lifting of trade-wind air masses along the inter-tropical convergence zone, and in part from local convection in the warm, humid, unstable doldrums air. Yet this climatic type is not solely a reflection of latitude, for several places on the equator, such as parts of East Africa and the coastal fringes of Equador and Peru, do not experience these conditions, whereas other places some way from the equator, notably the east coast of Malagasy, experience typically equatorial lowland climatic conditions.

In the *tropical monsoon climate*, rainfall seasonality is very well marked, though annual total amounts of rainfall may be even greater than in the equatorial lowlands, and this to some extent makes up for the rainfall's restricted duration throughout the year. This climatic type may be looked upon as resembling the equatorial lowland type in that the total amount of rainfall is large, though in its annual distribution the pattern of rainfall more nearly resembles the tropical savanna, or tropical wet-and-dry climate. As for temperatures, these commonly reach higher maximum figures than in the equatorial lowland zone, but the mean annual range is much greater, reaching to as much as 15° F (8° C). The tropical monsoon climate occurs chiefly in Asia on the Malabar coast, the coast of Burma, southern Ceylon, and in much of the Philippines, but is also significant on part of the western Guinea coast of Africa and in the lower Amazon valley.

Bombay experiences a tropical monsoon climate, but it will be noted that there is no simple division of the year into a wet, cooler season and a dry, hotter season. It is, in fact, more accurate to talk of the tropical monsoon of the Malabar coast as having four seasons. From December to March the south-east monsoon winds are blowing off the coast, rainfall is slight and temperatures relatively low; April and May comprise the transitional hot period when rainfall is slight, but temperatures and relative humidities are very high; from June to September the south-west monsoon is blowing, rainfall is heavy, relative humidities are high, but temperatures are reduced; and finally, during October and November, when the monsoon is retreating, rainfall is slight, humidities remain high, and temperatures increase.

Taken together, the equatorial lowland and tropical monsoon climatic types affect barely 10 per cent of the world's land surface, whereas the third main climatic type – the tropical savanna climate – alone covers over 10 per cent of the land surface of the world.

In the *tropical savanna climate*, illustrated in Table 1 by data for Kano (Nigeria), the rains, which are not of monsoonal origin, are concentrated into one or more parts of the year so that there is at least one definite dry season of variable duration, increasing in length and intensity with distance from the equator. The annual rainfall is less than in equatorial or monsoonal regions and may be as little as 20 inches (508 mm), though an average rainfall of 24 inches (610 mm) is sometimes taken as the minimum annual rainfall for the humid tropics. As for temperatures, the mean annual range is considerable, often exceeding 20° F (11° C).

This division of the humid tropical climate into three types is a useful conventional classification, but it tends to exaggerate the sharpness of the transition from the equatorial lowland type into the savanna or monsoon types. The transition is in fact gradual, sometimes complicated and often very difficult to describe. Furthermore, this three-fold classification of tropical climatic types tends to oversimplify the whole question of the extent and timing of the monthly humid and non-humid periods. In spite of the limitations of expressing seasonality in statistical terms, there is much to be said for using a classification like that of Lauer (1952), whose work depends upon the use of De Martonne's index of aridity in compounding the formula $20 \rightleftharpoons \dfrac{12p}{t + 10}$ to calculate indices for separate months, where 'p' represents the average monthly precipitation in millimetres and 't' represents the average monthly temperature in ° C. On this basis, Lauer classifies the humid tropical climates into five types: *equatorial*, in which there are 12 months with an index over 20; *equatorial with one dry period*, in which 7 months have an index over 20; *equatorial with two dry periods*, in which 5 months have an index over 20; *tropical dry winter*; and *tropical dry summer*. This classification indicates the diversity of climatic types within the tropics and emphasizes what is probably the most important criterion for any classification of tropical climates in economic development analyses – the length and timing of the humid period.

Climatic characteristics. Anomalies in rainfall seasonality are common throughout the tropics and the theoretical incidence of rainfall in relation to the movement of the overhead sun is in practice the exception rather than the rule. Thus in Guyana the two rainfall maxima coincide not with the highest but with the lowest altitudes of the noonday sun. Then there are local 'dry' areas in northern Venezuela, north-eastern Brazil, southern Burma, and in West Africa (southern Ghana and Togo). These anomalies are often explicable in terms of relief, the irregular distribution of land and sea, or the effects of ocean currents. Generally speaking, Africa's climate is modified in this way less than are the other two sectors because of the relatively small contrasts in relief, the compactness, and the relatively straight coastline of that continent.

The variation of rainfall from year to year may be considerable and unpredictable, and is of particular relevance to agriculture and water supply. As a general principle, annual reliability of rainfall decreases as the rainfall decreases, and this being so it is best illustrated from the drier fringes of the tropics. At Maiduguri in northern Nigeria the average rainfall for the forty-two years up to 1957 was 25·7 inches (653 mm), but it has in some years been less than 15 inches (381 mm) and in others over 35 inches (889 mm) – a significant degree of variation where the total rainfall is so critically low. Some of the most interesting work on rainfall reliability has referred to East and South-east Africa (Kenworthy and Glover, 1958; Kenworthy, 1964; and Gregory, 1964).

Another important characteristic of rainfall in the tropics is its high intensity, though really high degrees of intensity – over

2 inches (50 mm) an hour – are only common over short periods of less than one hour. In the humid tropics generally, local falls of 2–2·5 inches (50–64 mm) in one hour can be expected once in two years, and the maximum falls over a full hour recorded in Java and Singapore are 3·7 inches (94 mm) and 4·7 inches (119 mm) respectively (Beckinsale, 1957). Nevertheless, even very short periods of high intensity falls can have serious effects on water supplies, soils, and crops. Moreover, though rainfall intensities for periods of up to one hour may be no higher in tropical than in middle latitudes, intensities for longer periods are significantly higher (Mohr and van Baren, 1954).

As for temperatures, these are more striking in their uniformity than in their height, but everywhere plant growth is possible throughout the year. In the equatorial lowland tropics the mean monthly range of temperature is rarely more than 5° F (2·8° C). In the savanna tropics both the seasonal and diurnal ranges are much greater. Nevertheless, maximum temperatures are lower throughout the humid tropics than in the dry tropics or sub-tropics, especially near the coasts or where other water bodies, such as lakes or stretches of forest, act as thermal regulators and so limit temperature ranges.

The differences in relative humidity patterns between the equatorial lowland climate on the one hand and the tropical savanna and monsoon climates on the other are of great importance from the point of view of human energy, comfort, and health: relative humidities are continuously high in the former, but show strong seasonal variations in the latter. Diurnal variations are considerable everywhere, however, relative humidities usually being lowest in the early afternoon and highest in the very early morning, when they may reach 100 per cent.

Although it is a common belief that the tropics suffer from severe wind storms, such winds are confined to certain very localized areas; except under certain seasonal and local influences and in the neighbourhood of cyclones, wind speeds are generally under 10 mph (16 kph). The regions that suffer most from tropical cyclones are, in fact, largely outside or on the edge of the humid tropics; these cyclones normally form only outside the belt between

7° N and 7° S and are most common in the West Indies and Central America, Malagasy, the west and east coasts of India, the west coast of Burma, the east coast of the Indochinese peninsula, and in the northern Philippines. Apart from tropical cyclones, which are important here chiefly because of the damage to life and property they can inflict, there are other winds of local importance, such as the *harmattan* of West Africa, which blows as a cool, dry wind towards the Gulf of Guinea from the Saharan fringes during the November to February period, and brings cooler weather with very low relative humidities to much of the West African interior, and occasionally to as far south as the coast itself. Though the *harmattan* can affect the distribution of crops by exerting a marked desiccating effect, and may be one of the most important factors determining the nature of vegetation in any given area, its importance is more often seen in terms of human comfort.

In contrast to common notions, solar radiation is not necessarily greater in tropical than in temperate latitudes; indeed, near ground levels in the equatorial lowlands clouds may reflect over half the solar radiation incident upon them. Bernard (1945) has noted that in the central Congo Basin the mean and maximum values for total radiation seem to be no higher than those recorded in temperate regions during the summer months, and he ascribes the relatively low total radiation in this part of Africa to the high content of water vapour and to impurities such as smoke from bush fires in the lower atmosphere. Even where light intensity is greater in tropical than in temperate latitudes, this advantage is offset by the greater length of days in middle latitudes during the growing season.

Differences in the timing and total amount of solar radiation can affect the hardness and composition of grains and crop yields. Thus the highest yields of rice are produced not in the humid tropics but in such mid-latitude countries as Japan, Italy, and Spain. This is due partly to longer hours of sunshine, which greatly benefit the photosynthetic processes of rice plants. Even within the tropics rice yields produced in the rainy season may be lower than those produced during the dry season when the percentage of cloud is less.

The length of day varies but little within the tropics, but what variations there are can be most significant agriculturally, for even the smallest differences in length of day may be enough to provide stimulus for flowering. In Malaya the photosensitivity of padi varieties affects very much the suitability of any one variety for a particular area. Rice, in fact, provides an outstanding example of a crop affected by photoperiodism, and Jagoe (1952) shows that short periods of extra illumination, coincident with daylight, which maintain a daily light period of more than 21 hours 30 minutes, inhibit or very greatly delay inflorescence development in three typical and widely grown varieties of Malayan rice. Indeed, what evidence there is seems to suggest that tropical plants are more sensitive to small changes in the length of day than are plants of higher latitudes, though internal as well as environmental factors probably play some part in explaining other widely different types of behaviour found among tropical plants (Tempany and Grist, 1958).

The main climatic factors relevant to this study of tropical development are rainfall, atmospheric humidity, temperature, light intensity, and light duration. In the tropics, rainfall rather than temperature determines seasons, and it is the amount and timing of rainfall which forms the chief criterion for distinguishing the various tropical climatic types. On the other hand, it has been demonstrated that in the geographical distribution of crops, temperature determines the limits north and south of the equator within which particular crops can be grown; rainfall and atmospheric humidity determine the distribution of plants within particular zones; while light intensity and the duration of illumination profoundly influence plant behaviour. Moreover, much of the literature refers to climate considered as an abstraction, although the limitations of using average rainfall, temperature, and similar data as a basis for agricultural planning are now widely recognized. The local climate, or the actual meteorological conditions occurring in a particular year over a strictly limited area are of more agricultural significance than are the theoretical abstractions of climate. Finally, the micro-climate and eco-climate, referring to the conditions immediately surrounding a plant, are probably of especial importance under tropical conditions. Further applied research in micro-climate and eco-climate is urgently needed.

Water supply. At first sight, it might seem paradoxical that the tropics – at least the humid tropics as defined in this study – should suffer from difficulties in water supply: after all, the humid tropics are sometimes defined as hot, wet lands where agriculture is possible without irrigation (p. 4). Yet water is probably the most important single determinant of tropical land use. The supply of moisture for agriculture is commonly unsatisfactory – either too much or insufficient – and this is often due to some of the climatic characteristics already noted.

The unequal distribution of rainfall throughout the year is most obviously a problem in the savanna or monsoon tropics where there are distinct and sometimes prolonged dry seasons and where the moisture balance between rainfall and evapotranspiration losses is so crucial agriculturally. Yet even in the equatorial tropics, certain parts of the year are normally drier than others; and this seasonal fluctuation of rainfall is often the climatic variable of greatest agricultural significance. The variability of rainfall can also have serious effects locally, even in an equatorial country. In north-western Malaya, for example, rainfall variations resulted in a lean year for peasants in 1949; in Kedah only 25 per cent of the anticipated rice crop was realized, and in the Kota Star and Kuala Muda districts there was a mass exodus of padi planters searching for employment. In Perlis, too, the early onset of the seasonal dry spell caused the complete destruction of approximately 43,430 acres (17,590 ha) of padi (Hodder, 1959). This kind of disaster is very common and many examples could be cited from at least some part of the Indo-Pakistan subcontinent in most years. In many parts of the humid tropics croplands are unirrigated and so depend chiefly on the direct rainfall. What irrigation works there are have in many cases only a supplementary effect on water supply in conserving and distributing rain-water. If the rains come too soon or too late these irrigation works can do little to save the situation.

Problems in water supply are also caused by high rainfall intensities which have two main effects as far as water supply is concerned. In the first place, much of the water is lost by rapid run-off; and it is unfortunate that in many tropical areas the very rains which are sufficient in amount to contribute significantly to soil moisture are those in which rainfall intensities are high. Secondly, local variations in rainfall are great. Even within a small geographical area some districts may be short of water while others are adequately supplied or even suffering from a surplus of water.

Yet another factor affecting water supply in tropical countries is the tendency for rainfall to be interspersed between periods during which insolation is intense, so that rates of evaporation and transpiration are high and the balance of moisture available for agricultural purposes consequently reduced. And in many areas, as has been noted in Ceylon, the difficulties already inherent in a markedly seasonal rainfall are enhanced by the fact that 'drought comes in the hottest and windiest time of the year, so that loss by evaporation is very high' (Farmer, 1957: 46). Similarly, in the northern parts of West Africa the rainless months are frequently accompanied by the drying *harmattan* wind.

The limitations of using only rainfall data to measure moisture conditions have encouraged the search for formulae leading to moisture indices, and the importance of considering evaporation and transpiration in assessing moisture resources has been emphasized by Thornthwaite (1948) and others. Garnier (1958, 1960, 1961) has illustrated this for West Africa, making use of the concept of potential evapotranspiration, and from his work it is possible to obtain some idea of the problems involved in the utilization of moisture resources in West Africa, at least in so far as these problems are climatically derived. Without irrigation, Garnier concludes, full advantage of the favourable temperatures for growth cannot be taken anywhere in the region because there is some period of moisture deficit in all parts of West Africa. Over more than half of Nigeria, for instance, mean annual rainfall is less than mean annual water need, a fact which limits the possibilities of irrigating all the year round and suggests the need for careful selection of localities for irrigation schemes.

Finally, the supply of water may be affected by hydrological changes. This factor has been discussed for the Rima Basin of northern Nigeria where recent increases in flood heights in the lower Rima Valley were found to have been caused by a 'deterioration of channel conditions due to excessive aggradation, itself the result of an increase in the quantities of sediment carried by the major tributaries' (Ledger, 1960: 113).

Difficulties in the supply of water for the growing of crops, then, are due to the characteristics of the rainfall – seasonality, variability, high intensity; to evaporation; and to hydrological changes. But the significance of these factors depends to a large extent upon other physical considerations. The characteristics of the land on which the rain falls – its porosity and permeability, topography, soil, and vegetation – also influence the moisture balance and may be agriculturally more important than the characteristics of the rainfall itself. Thus in Malaya the choice of localities for vegetable growing is influenced not so much by climatic considerations as by the available sites suitable from the point of view of relief, drainage, accessibility, and soil type: a clay, for instance, is usually preferred to a lighter soil because although the clay may be more difficult to work it does retain water.

Analyses of the amount and depth of groundwater resources have as yet received little attention compared with the work devoted to surface water resources. In India it has been estimated that only about 20 per cent of the available underground water resources are at present being utilized. For West Africa, Archambault (1960) has shown that underground water resources may well be of vital significance in agricultural and settlement development planning. In particular, the pockets of deep weathering in the basement complex – so widespread in West Africa – have been found to contain relatively stable water levels that can be tapped by wells. This phenomenon also often explains the existence of subterranean water supplies beneath the bed of dried-up surface streams over basement complex, notably granite, rocks. Groundwater resources are not only associated with water-bearing sedimentaries.

The relationship between forest vegetation and rainfall is controversial, but is unlikely to be very close. On the other hand, forests do undoubtedly have a significant effect, particularly in areas of marked relief, on water supply by reducing the amount of water entering streams as direct runoff. The encouragement of indigenous forest is normally included in all recommendations for the conservation of water supplies, and some writers give this point much emphasis. There is little doubt that a change from natural vegetation to cultivation normally results in 'an increased run-off, higher peak flows, reduced dry season flow and more erosion, the extent of the change depending upon the method of cultivation' (Ledger, 1960: 115).

Finally, the development and utilization of water resources may depend as much on economic, social, and political factors as upon the amount of water available. The type of crop grown is a matter of some significance because the major tropical crops – rice, rubber, coconuts, oil palm, yams, bananas, maize, sugar-cane, peppers, millets, manioc, and vegetables – have widely differing moisture requirements in amount, distribution and reliability. Although tropical rainfall is not as effective in providing soil moisture as might be supposed from total precipitation figures, water supply is often a 'problem' in the tropics only because the crop chosen is not wholly suited to the particular set of climatic, edaphic, or topographical conditions under which it is grown. Shortage of water may also be simply an expression of unsuitable methods of cultivation. Lim (1954) has noted this in the Krian district of Malaya where there is a wasteful and inefficient use of irrigation water resulting from the attempt to simulate deep swamp conditions to which the Banjarese immigrants from Celebes are used; these farmers appear to regard such conditions as an essential precondition for cultivation. All crops, however, may suffer from an excess of moisture at times and from insufficient moisture at others. The ideal conditions, in which the right amount of water is available in the right place at the right time, are only rarely achieved under natural conditions in the humid tropics.

The scarcity of information on the water resources of the tropical world reflects in part these numerous and complicated variables. Very little research, moreover, has yet been devoted to the accurate assessment of water resources in most tropical countries, either on the surface (Ledger, 1964) or underground. It is now generally realized, however, that development planning depends so much upon this information being available that a number of countries are undertaking large-scale research into their surface and underground water resources and the problems of their utilization.

For the Third Five-Year Plan of India it was estimated that the annual rainfall is equivalent to about 3,000 million acre-feet of water for the whole country. Of this amount, one-third is lost immediately by evaporation. Of the remainder, 1,350 million acre-feet flow into the river systems; 350 million acre-feet stay in the top-soil, thereby contributing directly to soil moisture; and 350 million acre-feet move down through the soil into some form of underground water storage. It is recognized, however, that much of the theoretical potential of 2000 million acre-feet can never be utilized. Of the surface water flow into rivers, for instance, it has been estimated that only one-third can be harnessed for irrigation because of local topography, flow characteristics, climate, and soil conditions – all of which impose limits on its use. At present only about 36 per cent of the usable flow of surface water is being utilized. Of the 300 million acre-feet which percolate down into porous strata and represent the annual enrichment of underground water, under 20 per cent is being utilized; and the actual amount of underground storage of water at any particular time may well be several times the annual enrichment figure of 300 million acre-feet. Geophysical investigations are now being undertaken to determine the depth of the bed-rock in various parts of the country.

Even in tropical monsoonal and savanna India, clearly, potential water resources are far from being inadequate over the country as a whole. During the next twenty to twenty-five years it is hoped that the amount of water utilized for irrigation will go up to '350–400 million acre-feet or 60 per cent of the annual supply from both surface and underground resources. That will leave adequate quantities of water for meeting probable domestic supply, industrial needs and the requirements of more power generation' (Indian Govt., 1961: 189). Assuming further hydrological and geological survey work in India and assuming, also, continued research into the various factors in water supply noted earlier in this chapter, water resources need not form any insuperable barrier to agricultural development in India.

The same conclusion probably holds true for all humid tropical countries. Indeed, in certain areas, such as Bangladesh, it is not so much a question of whether there are sufficient water resources, but of whether there is not too much water, at least for part of the year. In all countries of the humid tropics, however, the real problem is not how much water is theoretically available, but how to utilise and control the water already known to exist. Water storage is commonly necessary, and everywhere there is an urgent need for more data on rainfall, river flow, evaporation, transpiration, seepage or leakage rates, and silt-carrying capacities in flood, in order to secure the greatest storage volume with the least possible loss of water. The effective improvement, development and utilization of land for agricultural development in the humid tropics is to a great extent dependent on the provision of adequate irrigation or water-control measures.

Methods of water control. Traditional indigenous methods of water control, though widespread in the tropics, often do very little to reduce the hazards of cultivation. In the small riverine areas of southern Asia, for instance, brushwood dams are built across rivers and a portion of the flow is directed to the adjoining padi fields. Elsewhere, peasants seek out swampy areas where losses of water are usually made good by seepage and surface run-off from higher ground. But brushwood dams are frequently swept away by floods, and habitually swampy areas are by their very nature subject to prolonged flooding which may result in the partial or total loss of crops. In the great alluvial deltas of southern and south-western Asia different indigenous forms of irrigation by inundation are common, and throughout the Asian and African tropics various forms of the *shadouf* are in use. Other indigenous irrigation works, of particular importance in peninsular India and in Ceylon, include the tank, described by a number of writers. Typically, the tank is a modest affair consisting of an earthern embankment, or *bund*, blocking the line of a stream, or closing the outlet of a natural depression in which rain collects; in places it may take the form of a hollow in the ground fed by a channel cut from a neighbouring stream. Tanks, old and modern, can be seen at their best in the dry south-east of peninsular India, especially in the Madura-Ramnad country, and in Ceylon. The essential function of the tank is simply 'to correct the vicissitudes in the rainfall of a given season and to husband it so that it may be used to best advantage' (Williamson, 1931: 87). A rainfall régime that tends to foster the growth of a semi-aquatic crop such as rice – namely, heavy seasonal rainfall – favours the use of the tank, so that next to the canal proper it is the preferred type of irrigation work among rice cultivators.

Although popular attention is often concentrated on the large-scale schemes for irrigation and water control, most of the control of water for irrigation is concerned with small, humble indigenous works, the great majority of which are constructed and maintained by the cultivators themselves with or without assistance from government authorities. Minor irrigation schemes of this kind require comparatively small capital outlays, yield quick results, and can be executed speedily with local materials and labour. On the other hand, the protection afforded by them is liable to be cut short in drought years when protection is needed most: for example, tanks cannot store water when there is a failure of rainfall in the locality. Major and medium schemes, though much more expensive, do benefit large and extensive areas, give much more assured protection in years of scarcity, and can also be designed to serve a multiplicity of purposes. Nevertheless, small works are and will for long continue to be of fundamental importance, and many reports have emphasized that governments should devote more attention to them. In his report on the water resources of parts of Africa, Debenham (1948) was concerned to recommend the small, generally inexpensive local scheme rather than the grandiose and costly plan, whether it be for water supply, drainage, or hydro-electricity; he also stressed the importance of securing the full co-operation of the African peoples themselves, and was especially anxious that more action be encouraged at the village level, whether or not more ambitious and large-scale water schemes are put in hand by the central government. Indeed, 'the physical conditions of Africa south of the Sahara offer little scope for the development of a series of large-scale projects of irrigation such as those which have produced so dramatic a change in the economy of India, Egypt, and the Sudan' (Hailey, 1957: 1010).

Of the large-scale schemes for water control, perhaps the greatest interest has focused on the method of irrigation by large-scale impounding. Examples of this are numerous – the Niger Bend (Sandsanding) Scheme in West Africa, the Limpopo Scheme in Mozambique, the Krian Scheme in Malaya, La Ferme and La Nicoline Schemes in Mauritius, and the recent huge Mangla and Tarbela dams project on the Jhelum and Indus rivers respectively – but the greatest development in recent times has undoubtedly been in the monsoon countries of India, Pakistan, and Ceylon, where the need for water control is so urgent. East Pakistan is a good illustration of an area where the water problem is normally one of too much water rather than too little. Annual floods ordinarily occur over a third of the cultivated area, some of them of severe proportions: the 1954 floods, for instance, damaged 10,000 square miles (25,900 km²), destroyed crops, houses and livestock and deeply affected the lives of 12 million people. In this and similar regions adequate drainage is necessary to prevent the deterioration of the land by a rising groundwater table and consequent waterlogging. Anti-waterlogging measures such as drain-lining of irrigation channels in selected reaches have been taken up in the various development plans in Pakistan.

Of growing importance in recent years has been the construction of multi-purpose rather than single-purpose schemes of water control: the Volta Scheme of Ghana, for instance, involves the drainage of swamps and the provision of irrigation water as well as hydro-electric power; and the Niger Dams Project of Nigeria (Ledger, 1963) is similarly designed for multi-purpose benefits. There has also been an emphasis in recent years on unified river basin development, as in the Brahmaputra Scheme of Bangladesh. Agriculture, drainage, water power for industry: all are in varying ways fundamentally dependent upon the supply of water and may well affect each other's needs and supplies. Whether for irrigation, water power or drinking water, the planned regional and integrated planning of water resources is essential to economic development.

. . . . .

Even an equatorial lowland country, with a heavy rainfall distributed over most of the year, may suffer from water shortages, both for agriculture and for drinking. Other areas may suffer from too much water at times, too little water at other times. The explanation of this characteristic lies chiefly in the way the rain falls – its seasonal variability, unreliability, and torrential nature; the high rate of evaporation and transpiration; and the characteristics of the land on which the rain falls. All these factors affect the moisture balance available for agriculture and the amount of water available for drinking. In the monsoonal and savanna tropics, water supply is often the most important single problem awaiting solution.

The difficulty of this problem, however, depends to some extent on human activities. A farmer may court disaster by making a bad choice of crops, or by adopting unsuitable farming methods. On the other hand, by intelligently adapting his activities to the local effective moisture conditions, the farmer can make the most of his natural resources. As for drinking water, the siting of wells is especially important in the equatorial lowland environment with its high water table and in the conditions of generally poor sanitation. The bulk of the rural population of the tropics must for long continue to depend upon wells and streams for its drinking water. In the sphere of water supply the intelligent co-operation of the individual must go hand in hand with attempts to deal with the problem by the construction of irrigation and water control works and the construction of reservoirs and pipe water units. Here again, as in so many aspects of tropical life, the crucial need is for more basic data about moisture resources and the problems of their utilization in any one specific development area. Everywhere, however, the provision of a more reliable supply of water for agricultural, industrial, and domestic purposes must be looked upon as one of the most important concomitants of social and economic progress.

CHAPTER 3

Other Natural Resources

Vegetation. The theoretical distribution of vegetation types in the tropics is based chiefly upon climate and suggests a progressive change from tropical rain forest to tree, bush and grass savanna as the dry season increases in length and intensity away from the equator. But other ecological factors – edaphic, physiographic, and biotic – confuse the picture everywhere, in some cases drastically.

Tropical rain forest is a most impressive vegetation type, but it covers a smaller area than is often supposed. Three separate formations – the American, African, and Indo-Malayan forests – may be distinguished and important differences exist between them. The most widespread development of tropical rain forest today is found in the Indo-Malayan forest region; the largest area of continuous forest is in South America, and the least in Africa. In any region where rain forest is potentially the climatic climax 'only a part of the area is actually covered by mature forest. There may be large expanses where it has not yet developed – swamps, lakes, river margins, and estuarine mudflats occupied by seral communities in process of development towards the climax. There may also be bare rock and young volcanic lava where soil is gradually forming, and here, too, stages in the development of mature forest are found. In some tropical regions there are areas where local peculiarities of soil or topography make the development of typical rain forest impossible, even though the climate is suitable' (Richards, 1952: 7). On the other hand, the rain forest may extend beyond the usual climatic limits where local soil or drainage conditions are favourable.

The true rain forest is remarkable in many ways, but perhaps its most important characteristic, on which many other features are directly dependent, is the richness of its tree flora. On average the height of trees is greater than in most temperate forests, but they vary widely and there is much stratification of the forest. The trunks of the main trees are normally clear until the canopy is reached, though many trees are massively buttressed and there is an abundance of woody climbers and epiphytes. The forest interior is gloomy and oppressive. Climatic conditions there vary very little, evaporation is only slight so that humidity is always high, and air movement may average as little as a mile (1·6 km) a day.

The tropical rain forest is often thought to limit development. Most important, it is believed to be a serious barrier to movement and settlement, but in fact 'it is the slippery clay soil and the abundance of fallen logs and branches which make progress in the forest slow and laborious, rather than the thickness of the vegetation' (ibid.: 5). In its primary state the rain forest is not difficult to penetrate, whereas in the secondary (second-growth) forest, movement is often very difficult indeed. One of the greatest problems of development in the tropical rain forest areas, in fact, is that as soon as the forest is cut down it begins vigorously to re-establish itself as jungle, with dense and often impenetrable undergrowth, especially along river banks or in clearings where a good deal of light reaches the ground. The suggestion that the rate of growth of vegetation in tropical lands is more rapid than elsewhere is not strictly correct, for true growth involves the accumulation of new material, and the conclusions of workers in this field suggest that the mean net assimilation rate is more or less constant everywhere. Where there is a difference – and this is most relevant there – is in the rate of regeneration after cutting or burning.

In the monsoon forests the vegetation is thinner, trees are generally smaller and there is less diversity of vegetation forms. There are many woody lianas and herbaceous epiphytes but fewer woody epiphytes. Deciduous species are common and there is a well-marked leaf fall from many trees, especially at the beginning of the dry period. Many of the same difficulties of utilization, movement, settlement, and control arise here as in the tropical rain forest. But the tropical monsoon lands are characteristically the longest settled and most densely populated areas of the tropics, so that the natural forest has been very severely disturbed by human activities.

In the tree, bush, and grass savanna lands of the tropics movement and settlement become easier. Tropical tree and bush savannas are most extensive in Africa, but the bulk of these are probably derived from former forest, a point which gives emphasis to the need for forest conservation. Most of the savannas are also probably man-induced by cutting and burning over a long period. Grassland is very rarely the climax vegetation in the wet tropics, except where elevation or water-logging prohibit tree growth. According to Richards (op. cit.), all lowland tropical grasslands and 'open' savannas are either biotic climaxes due to edaphic conditions unfavourable to trees, or stages in a hydrosere. Whereas the boundary between the rain forest and deciduous forest is probably a true climatic limit, and is determined mainly by seasonal drought, it is doubtful whether any tropical grassland is a true climatic climax.

The present economic value of tropical forests is not great. In 1938, the total world exports of timber amounted to 43 million cubic yards, of which the tropics contributed only 4·4 million (Asia 1·8 million, Africa 1·4 million, and America 1·2 million). Since then the relative importance of the tropics in timber exports has hardly changed at all, the tropics producing about the same proportion – 10 per cent – of the world's roundwood. The reasons for this include the predominance of hardwoods, often very difficult to cut and transport, and for which world demand is much less than for softwoods; the tendency towards a mixed species composition, pure stands rarely occurring naturally in the tropical rain forest; the slow rate of forest growth (as distinct from re-growth); and inaccessibility. Several writers have distinguished concentric zones of progressive exploitation in tropical forests, zones which are especially noticeable in the most highly populated regions of India, the Indochinese peninsula, and Malaya; the transport distance determines the zones in which the exploitation of each category of species remains profitable. As for the monsoon forests, the percentage of precious hardwoods is usually higher than in the rain forest and, in Asia, includes the teak (*Tectona grandis*). The chief value of this tree lies in its straight, branchless trunk, its hardness, and its durability, but it is peculiarly liable to the ravages of shifting cultivation by burning and in many areas has been almost removed from the landscape: in northern Thailand, for instance, only 45 per cent of the forest land is now productive because of such burning. The largest indigenous teak forests have been carefully preserved, extended or, as in West Africa, where teak is not native, planted on a very large scale. Finally, what forests there are in the savanna lands are for the most part not economically productive and are only of local importance for fuel.

Nevertheless, in many countries of the tropics the forest must be looked upon as potentially the chief natural resource, not only for timber but also for fuel, cellulose, resin, gums, camphor, and rattans. Moreover, many of the obstacles to the exploitation of tropical forests are likely to be overcome; and the future development of timber production in the tropics will probably involve the creation of 'artificial communities composed of relatively few valuable species either by planting or by sylvicultural treatment of existing primary, depleted, or secondary mixed forest' (Richards, op. cit.: 7). Aubreville (1937) has suggested schemes of cutting and planting to transform mixed rain forest into commercially useful stands in fifty to a hundred years. In these artificial or planned forests, inaccessibility is much less of a problem in that a definite network of outlet roads can be constructed. The problem of protecting felled logs against attacks by insects and fungi is also being tackled.

There is already a need for tropical forest conservation. The consequences of widespread forest destruction at the present rate are many: the loss of forest products, the loss of protection against soil erosion and excessive run-off, and the less well understood effect on moisture resources. Here is a great natural resource rapidly being wasted away through ignorance, though the importance of forest resources in economic development planning is now widely recognized. In India, for instance, the Third Five-Year Plan estimated that the annual requirements of industrial wood including pulp materials, which amounted to 4·5 million tons in 1970, had increased to about 9·5 million tons by 1975. The demand for paper and rayon grade pulp, in particular, is likely to expand considerably with the growing population, increasing literacy and rising standards of living. As new plantations take twenty-five to thirty years to develop, in the ordinary course of events annual production could not increase beyond 5·5 million tons by 1975, leaving a gap of as much as 4 million tons.

For many immediate and practical economic reasons, forest conservation and reafforestation projects are clearly very necessary elements in the economic development policy of most tropical countries. Furthermore, Richards and others claim that deforestation has adverse effects on the course of plant evolution in the world as a whole, because the tropical rain forest has always played a role as a source of supply of genetical material in the evolution of new forms of plant life (see Appendix).

Soils. According to many writers, soil poverty is a fundamental and often intractable limitation to economic development in the tropics. The luxuriant vegetation associated with rain forest for long suggested that tropical soils were rich. It has been found, however, that the lush virgin tropical rain forest exists partly because it has been able to take back from the humus and shallow topsoil the equivalent of the nutrients it sheds upon the surface in leaves, branches, and trunks. The yearly production of organic matter is indeed very great, possibly exceeding 100 tons an acre, and the turnover is rapid, being assisted by the elements of fungi, bacteria, termites, and animals. Moreover, the forests of the humid equatorial regions may have started when 'the soil was not so poor, when rocks had not weathered so deeply, so that there was not such a scarcity of plant nutrients in the surface soil within the reach of the roots of the forest trees and other plants' (Carter and Pendleton, 1956: 506).

The general scarcity of plant nutrients in the surface soil of humid tropical areas is usually the result of intensive and extensive leaching. Where rainfall is normally in excess of evaporation, as it is for at least part of the year in the humid tropics, there is a net downward movement of water in the soil. This sweeps plant food downwards and leaves the surface soil an impoverished mixture of altered mineral particles. In more precise terms, leaching involves leaving the sesquioxides of aluminium and iron at or near the surface and carrying downwards silica and some aluminium silicates; these are relatively soluble in rain-water, particularly in combination with organic compounds.

This whole process is aided by the rapid chemical action, notably oxidation, induced by high temperatures. Indeed, the main difference between temperate and tropical weathering may be said to be the stepping-up of tempo in the tropics: 'in hot climates temperatures are higher by 18°–36° F (10°–20° C) and all chemical reactions proceed at two to four times the speed usual in temperate climates . . . If one bears in mind that there is no interruption by winter, one will hardly err in estimating that over the whole year and in relation to temperate climates the intensity of weathering in the tropics is increased at least tenfold' (Vageler, 1953: 16). Another writer has shown that the seasonal renewal of groundwater movement is of equal importance in tropical areas of strictly seasonal rainfall; such areas 'may be described as subject for part of the year to equatorial soil processes where surface evaporation is nearly nil and for part to desertic soil processes in which soil evaporation is at a maximum' (Dobby, 1954: 74).

Insufficient is yet known of the chemical and physical characteristics of tropical soils for any classification to be wholly satisfactory. The tentative classifications of Robinson (1949) and Aubert (1954) emphasize the importance of soil moisture and soil drainage. Charter (Bramner, 1956) classifies tropical soils into orders based on the factors which predominantly determine soil characteristics. And D'Hoore (1960) provides a widely used·fivefold classification of tropical soils. There is a tendency now in the literature to replace the term 'laterisation' by 'ferrallitization' (Aubert, 1954; Bunting, 1967) to describe the process of leaching, and to call the fully developed tropical soil a ferralitic (Ft) soil. The term laterite is now perhaps best confined to those soils where an actual or incipient 'pan' or hard layer exists. The Fe oxides give tropical soils their typically reddish colour. Certainly the most common soil type in the tropics is the reddish savanna soil and tropical red earths, in which molecular ratios of silica to alumina are about 1.33–2.00.

Whichever classification of tropical soils is used, however, it must be emphasized that these soils are no more homogeneous than are the soils of temperate lands. Moreover, the degree of leaching depends very much upon the age and situation of the soil: immature soils formed from geologically recent volcanic material will be relatively little leached and may have an inherently high level of fertility. There is also a marked difference between, on the one hand, soils of upland regions and, on the other, the alluvial soils of valleys, coastal regions, and flood plains of rivers. The latter soils, being usually less leached and more fertile, have a wider range of agricultural possibilities. Upland soils, however, are often inherently poor, except where they consist of immature volcanic soils, and on this account their agricultural uses are limited. Only where the dry season is more defined or where slope characteristics and soil texture are favourable is the possibility of development really significant.

All ferrallitic soils of the humid tropics, moreover, are not necessarily infertile. Even true laterites may be fertile, as in parts of Uganda or in Cuba, where the richest soil – the red clay of Matanzas – is loose laterite (Dumont, 1966: 30). And although termites in the soil may have a bad effect in destroying organic matter such as humus in tropical soils, many writers have pointed out that termites have value and importance in the tropics in rapidly breaking down dead organic matter on and in the soil. In tropical regions termites may take the place of earth-worm in preserving fertility (Adamson, 1943); and though termite mounds are inconvenient and may be less fertile than their surroundings, on poor soil they may form patches of relative fertility. De Schlippe (1956) has noted this in Zandeland, where cowpeas and sorghum are often confined to old termite mounds and so may be classified among patches of ecologically specialized crops.

Furthermore, the texture of ferrallitic soils is often very good indeed – that of a loam: and the wide range of uses for true laterites has been recently summarized by Persons (1970). It is particularly important that this good structure, with its particles integrated into small crumbs permitting an adequate entry of air and water, should be preserved. Exposure of the organic matter in the surface to tropical conditions may lead to structural deterioration of a soil. It is for this reason that western methods of deep ploughing and turnover of soils may be found unsuitable.

Efforts to correct the earlier popular misconception that tropical soils are extremely fertile – a traditional opinion based on the luxuriance of tropical rain forest vegetation – are possibly in danger of going too far in the opposite direction. The popular view of tropical soils nowadays is that they are generally poor: 'the fertility of 8 or 9 square miles of average land south of the Sahara and north of the Union of South Africa is equivalent to that of 1 acre of Iowa soil' (Kindleberger, 1966: 64). But there is no evidence for postulating inferior fertility in tropical soils. Rather does it appear that many tropical soils are capable of being very productive as long as each type of soil and land is treated in the most effective manner. Moreover, what is meant by inherent fertility in temperate lands is of a different nature and may have less agricultural relevance in the tropics. Providing that two soils have all the elements of plant food in fair amounts, the superior richness of one may make but little difference. It is also worth noting that local methods of agriculture and means of usufruction of the soils have an influence in maintaining tropical soils at a certain degree of fertility. Conclusions based on investigations with temperate soils are not always readily applicable to tropical soils. For instance, one of the most important tropical crops – wet rice – does not require 'fertile' soil in any normal sense of the term: what it does require is a soil capable of holding standing water. Again, judged by European standards, and in terms of temperate crops, tropical soils are deficient in calcium. But most tropical crops do not need much calcium and in some cases tropical soils contain so much calcium that artificial acidification is required. Comparisons between tropical and temperate soils can only have validity if their relations to crops, local agricultural methods, and other environmental elements are fully considered.

There is already sufficient evidence to make it possible to refute the general contention that tropical soils are a serious or permanent limitation to the agricultural development of the tropical world. Yet much remains to be learned about tropical soils, and in particular about their significance in the ecological complex. In many situations it may be misleading to consider the soil factor in isolation; and in this connexion the work of Milne (1935) on soil catenas, of Charter (1957) on soil/crop relationships, and of Coulter (1964) on tropical agricultural and soil surveys, is of especial interest. Furthermore, as one geographer has demonstrated, there is a need for more study of the relationship between soils and land use, in which 'several facets of the bio-geographical system may be in such delicate equilibrium that disturbance of one may bring about the collapse of the whole structure . . . In order adequately to plan agricultural development some assessment of the impact of new crops and techniques upon the ecosystem must be made, an end which may be achieved by study of the relations of the ecosystems at present existing, and by detailed investigation of individual mechanisms within them' (Moss, 1963: 165).

Soil erosion. The partial or complete removal of the thin covering of living soil is a phenomenon that has profound effects upon potentialities for agricultural development in many tropical lands. But before discussing soil erosion, two points must be made. First, normal denudation, or geological erosion, is a beneficial and indeed important process in soil formation: most of the fertile alluvial plains in tropical countries, for instance, are the result of this kind of long-term process. In the second place, large areas of the tropics suffer only slightly if at all from soil erosion in its more serious manifestations, especially where the density of population is low and where large areas are still covered by forest.

Two main types of soil erosion may be distinguished here: soil erosion by water, common throughout the tropics, and wind erosion, which is much less important, being confined to the drier fringes of the humid tropics during the dry season. Soil erosion induced by water flow may take one of two forms: sheet erosion, in which water passes over a smooth slope and flows down in a sheet, irreparably removing a thin layer of topsoil over an area; and channel erosion, in which gullies develop. The latter is a more impressive kind of erosion, and may bring about local desiccation by lowering the water table; but agriculturally it may have less significance than sheet erosion.

The severity of soil erosion induced by water flowing down a slope is influenced not only by the degree of slope but also by the amount, distribution, and intensity of rainfall, the physical characteristics of the soil, and the vegetative cover; moreover it commonly occurs in association with one or more of a number of human activities, especially agriculture, stock rearing, and mining.

In relating agricultural activities to the intensity and extent of soil erosion, confusion may arise from the failure to distinguish clearly between the processes of soil deterioration – the *in situ* deterioration of soils – and those of soil erosion, or the actual physical removal of soil. Soil deterioration may occur in many irrigated areas where soil erosion is unknown – for instance, in many irrigated rice fields in India where waterlogging induces salinity and alkalinity. On the other hand, it is true that there is a distinct connexion between these two processes: 'the maintenance of soil fertility is always the *sine qua non* of soil conservation' (Tempany and Grist, 1958: 92). Moreover, the rate of soil erosion depends not only on the slope and on the duration and rate of flow of water but also upon the soil structure, which is itself part of the process of soil deterioration. As several authorities have observed, tropical soils are for the most part characterized by low silica-alumina ratios and appear to be less susceptible to erosion losses than do the soils of temperate climates.

Nevertheless, the clearing of land for agricultural purposes is always liable to initiate or aggravate erosion unless care is taken. Clearly, the amount of topsoil which is removed by water erosion – itself precipitated by the clearing of the natural vegetation – must depend upon several factors: the time interval between exposure of the soil and the establishment of a new vegetative covering; the slope of the ground; and the type of crop. It has been established that perennial tree crops are better than arable crops at preventing soil erosion, and that those arable crops which form a more or less continuous cover – such as grass, lucerne, leguminous crops, sugar-cane, sweet potatoes, and pineapples – are better at preventing erosion than are those arable crops, such as maize, cotton, tobacco, and cassava, which are characterized by separate stems readily permitting the passage of moving water (ibid.). Wet padi farming is normally very satisfactory in this respect, and those parts of tropical Asia with flooded rice fields are not commonly associated with severe erosion problems though, as noted above, soil deterioration may occur.

When fully established perennial tree cultivation may be good for protecting the soil, but severe erosion problems arose in the days when clean weeding between the trees was practised. In Malaya, for example, the early days of rubber planting led to the realization that clean weeding is not always desirable in a tropical context and may well precipitate soil erosion. Local reluctance to clean weed between trees is not an indication of laziness or backwardness. A tropical garden with its untidy jungle of mixed trees and shrubs around the house is satisfactory in that it does not leave the soil exposed to torrential rain and does imitate fairly successfully the natural rain forest ecology in which the soil is not too severely exhausted or subjected to erosion. As Pelzer (1957) has noted, the steady continuous use of unirrigated land offers one of the most difficult agronomic problems in the humid tropics because of the difficulty of preventing soil erosion or soil depletion. This arises more especially where high population density demands continuous cultivation, as has been demonstrated in south-eastern Nigeria by Grove (1951) and Floyd (1965). In connexion with tree crops, too, the early stages of growth afford little protection to the soil and similar precautions are required as for arable crops. When tree crops are fully grown the aim should be to imitate conditions in the natural forest by avoiding clean weeding and by maintaining ground covers and mulching. Much attention has been given to the establishment of protective cover crops; and a large number of creeping covers, some leguminous and others non-leguminous, have been developed for this purpose. During replanting on slopes, efforts are commonly made to reduce the risks of soil erosion by such practices as bench terracing. The cultivation practices of peasant cultivators have often been criticized by observers, and there is little doubt that improved methods of agriculture have a part to play in reducing erosion. But it is as well not to ignore the fund of experience which lies at the root of many indigenous practices. For example, mound cultivation in Africa has been frequently criticized; but in practice the erosion effects are slight and compensated for by the beneficial effects mounding has on moisture retention and root growth.

For arable crops the uses of rotation in controlling erosion are many and include the possibility of enabling erosion-conducing crops, such as cassava, to alternate with erosion-preventing crops like sugar-cane. Inclusion of most kinds of grass cover in rotation is desirable not only because of the direct protection it affords against soil movement but also on account of the effect it exercises in promoting soil structure. Rotations, however, are by themselves inadequate to effect complete control unless they are accompanied by measures to maintain fertility, suitable cultural methods and, where necessary, measures to protect the soil in other ways.

Stock rearing is responsible for soil erosion in many parts of the tropics. Where there is overstocking, sometimes together with over-cropping, the vegetative cover is not given a chance to establish itself, bare patches appear, and the soil is easily broken up by the hooves of the animals. In Kenya, the Ukamba and Kumasi reserves are so badly overgrazed that, as early as 1938, 37 per cent of their area was eroded down to the subsoil; and on a reserve capable of supporting a maximum of 60,000 cattle there were distributed some 250,000 cattle, 269,000 goats, and 60,000 sheep (Hailey, 1957). Africa is perhaps the classic instance of a continent suffering from soil erosion caused by overgrazing, and defective livestock management there is in general responsible for greater losses from erosion than is defective cultivation. The reduction of stock numbers has been tried in many territories – notably in Malawi, Zimbabwe, Tanzania, Lesotho, Uganda, and Swaziland. But the solution probably lies more with the 'substitution of mixed farming or alternate husbandry for purely arable farming or grazing, cultivation of soil-conserving crops, restrictions on the use of pastures or numbers of livestock, protection of forests and reafforestation' (Tempany and Grist, 1958: 100). As a later chapter will show, however, the whole problem of overstocking is in many areas intimately bound up with cultural habits.

Other ways in which soil erosion can be initiated or increased include mining. And here, especially, the problems of erosion and silting are seen to be only different facets of the same problem: for instance, muddy water containing eroded soil in suspension has a greater abrasive action than has clear water. In Nigeria, Grove (1952) has discussed the relationship between mining and soil erosion on the Jos Plateau, and Ooi (1955) cites mining as one of the chief causes of soil erosion and silting in the Kinta Valley of Malaya. By skinning the ground surface (lampanning), the exposed hillsides are easily eroded and large quantities of silt are discharged into the river systems, leading to sedimentation, the raising of river beds, and flooding. In a village a mile or so from the confluence of the Tumboh and Kinta rivers, mining activities followed by erosion led to the mouth of the Tumboh being silted, and the overflow from the river converted the padi lands of the 2,000 inhabitants of Kampong Bulan Bidai into a swamp. The steamer service between the village and Telok Anson had to be abandoned, the population began drifting away, and by 1937 only 400 people were left.

The dangers of soil erosion are real and serious in almost all tropical countries. In India it is estimated that about 200 million acres (81 million ha) of land, or almost a quarter of the country's land surface, is suffering from soil erosion; and it is argued that it will not be possible to maintain yields of crops on dry lands, much less to increase them, if the soil is allowed to deteriorate through soil erosion in this way. Erosion problems are likely to intensify everywhere in the tropics as the distribution of population widens and as more of the vegetative cover is interfered with.

Mineral and power resources. Of the minerals, iron ore is present in some form or another in most parts of the tropics, where there are in fact many instances of ancient iron (lateritic) workings and smelting. But today it is produced in large amounts in Liberia, Venezuela, India, and Brazil. Reserves, however, are believed to be considerable. Brazil at present produces increasing tonnages of ore a year from the south-eastern part of the country, where a great steel industry has been built at Volta Redonda, and reserves there are estimated at about one-quarter of the world's present consumption of iron ore. Reserves in Venezuela and India, too, are good. At present the Indian production comes from the northern Orissa and Raipur districts of the Central Provinces, but in the south-west (Singhbhum) there is an area with a continuous thickness of 700 feet (229 m) of haematite containing more than 60 per cent iron. As for Africa, recently discovered iron deposits in Zimbabwe are considered to be very great; and in Liberia, too, deposits are considerable. According to latest estimates, indeed, Africa may well have the largest total potential reserves of iron ore of all the continents.

Tropical Africa also has the greatest current production of copper; and if the south-central African copper belt, extending from Zambia into Katanga, is regarded as a whole, it is easily the second largest single source of world supply today. These African beds are unusually uniform in metallization, and some of the ore is fit for direct smelting. Of the many other minerals, the tropics have a wide range, notably of bauxite (Guyana and Surinam, with very large reserves elsewhere in Jamaica, Brazil, India, and Thailand); tin (Malaya, Indonesia, Bolivia, and Nigeria); cobalt (Katanga and Zambia); columbite (Nigeria); uranium (Katanga); chromite (Zimbabwe, India, and the Philippines); and lead and zinc (Burma).

Of the mineral fuels – coal, petroleum, and natural gas – anthracite and bituminous coal is produced in significant quantities only in India; and only 3·5 per cent of the total world production of coal occurs in tropical countries. For lignite the percentage is even lower – some 0·3 per cent. The reserves of anthracite and bituminous coal in India are believed to be fairly good, the most productive coalfields lying in west Bengal and east Bihar, and an annual production target of some 97 million tons has now been achieved. The most productive parts of the chief coalfield in India lie in the Damodar valley belonging to the basin of the Hooghly, where about nine-tenths of the coal raised in India is produced.

All the coal resources of the Indian subcontinent, with the exception of some Punjab lignites, lie in India and not in Pakistan. Elsewhere in the tropics, Zimbabwe and Brazil are the only other countries producing over 2 million tons a year, and nowhere are proved reserves great.

The tropics produce about 13 per cent of the world's crude petroleum, the four largest producers at present being Venezuela, Nigeria, Indonesia, and Mexico, in that descending order of importance. With the present world fuel crisis and the political implications of continued over-dependence on Middle East oil, the relative significance to the Western developed countries of supplies from tropical developing countries like Nigeria has already increased markedly. Oil exploration is continuing apace in all sectors of the tropics. However, with the exception of those countries which have already become oil suppliers on a world scale, most developments to date have simply given individual countries the hope, or at least the possibility, of becoming less dependent on the Middle East. At the moment most of the world's proved reserves of over 250,000 million barrels occur outside the humid tropics in the Middle East, and reserves in Indonesia, Venezuela, and Colombia are small by world standards of comparison. Nevertheless, in aggregate tropical countries contain some 30 per cent of the world's oil reserves, and recent experience in southern Nigeria emphasizes that the difference between actual and potential production is in no case more important than it is with petroleum. Natural gas normally occurs wherever oil is found, but has also been discovered elsewhere. At the moment Venezuela has a large and rapidly expanding production of natural gas, and prospects for developing this in Nigeria and Borneo also seem bright.

Any consideration of mineral resources seen in relation to economic development in the tropics must clearly take into account much more than the simple figures of production by countries or regions. In the first place the size of the reserves is of particular importance in any discussion of these capital or 'wasting' resources; and enough has been said to indicate that while actual production of many minerals may be small in tropical countries compared with temperate countries, the reserves are substantial, though basic geological and mineralogical survey work is often only just beginning. Secondly, technological developments and changes in the consumption and world price of minerals are continuously affecting both the current production and the possibilities of exploiting reserves, so that all prognostications about the value of mineral reserves must be viewed with caution.

As for power, while in temperate countries thermal sources of power are likely to dominate for the foreseeable future, in tropical countries most immediate industrial developments are likely to depend upon the supply of power from hydro-electric stations, many of which are included in multi-purpose schemes involving water-control, storage, and irrigation facilities.

Hydro-electric power forms potentially perhaps the greatest power resource of the tropical world. As far as present utilization is concerned, however, whereas the rate of utilization of potential water power is 60 per cent in Europe, it is only 3 per cent in South America, 5 per cent in Central America, 13 per cent in Asia, and as little as 0·1 per cent in Africa. Water power has advantages over other sources of power in that it is a renewable as distinct from a capital resource, and requires no storage of fuels, such as coal or oil. Its chief disadvantage is the high cost of capital installations.

Of the three sectors of the tropics, Africa is particularly well endowed, possessing some 40 per cent of the world's potential hydro-electricity. The continent is the only area with considerable stretches of internal drainage, and remarkably little of it is really low-lying, even in the Congo Basin. On the Congo River the most striking instance of modern hydro-electric power development could take place if the plans, initiated under the former colonial governments, are ever put into effect. Less than 100 miles (160 km) from the coast, at the Inga Rapids where the Congo falls 300 feet in a 15-mile 'awesome span of sustained violence', it is hoped to create an African Ruhr. It is believed that Inga could eventually produce 25 million kW – ten times the production of the Grand Coulee and as much power as is now consumed annually by the whole of Western Europe. Moreover this power could be produced at the cheapest rate of any large installation in the world. The Inga

Scheme could easily do for the Congo what the Owen Falls
(McMaster, 1956), Kariba (Reeve, 1960), Volta and Niger Dams
(Ledger, 1963) schemes are doing for other parts of the continent.
In tropical America a number of important hydro-electric schemes
have been begun, the largest being at Guri on the Caroni River
above its junction with the Orinoco in Venezuela. When completed, this will be the largest scheme in the humid tropics and
provide power not only for the programme of rapid industrialization in Guayana (eastern Venezuela) but also for most of the
Venezuelan industrial and domestic market. Again in South
America, mention must be made of the proposed Great Lakes
Plan to create five large, artificial lakes in the interior in order to
assist economic integration in the continent; the lakes would enable
timber and mineral exploitation to develop and provide hydro-
electric power for industry in the northern half of the continent.

The problems of developing hydro-electric power in a country
are many and complex, stretching far beyond such relatively simple
physical difficulties as irregular stream flow. Some of the factors
can be illustrated from the case of India. Many of the Indian projects, such as the river valley projects of Bhakra-Nangal, Hira-
kud, Chambal, Tungabhadra, and Nagarjunasagar, provide both
irrigation and power and are designed to help rebuild the agricultural economy as well as to pave the way for the rapid industrialization of the country. Over the country as a whole, however, a
total hydro-electric power potential of about 41 million kW has
been assessed as technically and economically feasible and the
additional generating capacity installed during the Second Five-
Year Plan averaged about 0·45 million kW per annum. By 1975–6
the aggregate installed generating capacity in the country was of
the order of 15 million kW. According to present estimates roughly
half this capacity can be provided from hydro-electric projects and
the balance now comes mainly from thermal stations. In order
to raise these targets, however, new hydro-electric sites will
need to be investigated speedily and work commenced in time to
take advantage of subsequent plans. The Indian Third Five-Year
Plan clearly appreciated the interdependence of natural and human
resources and their factors in power development. In deciding

upon particular methods of power generation for different areas, the key factors taken into account were: the capital cost per kilowatt of installed capacity; the foreign exchange component; the cost per kilowatt-hour generated; the period required for construction; the impact on other allied development activities such as coalmining, washeries, irrigation, and the exploitation of natural gas; and stimulus to the development of technological methods. In India the average production costs per kilowatt-hour of electricity for hydro, coal-fired, and diesel power stations are in the ratio of 1·2, 3, and 25 respectively.

A good deal of research is now being directed into the economics of large river-development projects. Serious doubts are now frequently cast on the wisdom of investing large sums of scarce capital in huge multi-purpose projects; and many authorities would now agree with Hanson that 'the creation and operation of a multi-purpose river project presents an under-developed country with the most difficult of all assignments in the sphere of public enterprise' (Hanson, 1960: 333).

.   .   .   .   .

There seem to be no grounds for assuming that the climatic, vegetation, soil, mineral, or power resources of the tropical world are not potentially adequate for greatly increased economic development. Certainly there can be no question of explaining the present generally low level of agricultural and industrial development in terms of inadequacies in these resources. Admittedly the problems of resource utilization are considerable, but in most cases they arise from insufficient basic information. In all countries there is an urgent need for an intensification of climatic, vegetation, soil, and geological survey and mapping, and for a much closer study of the relevance of all natural resources to the general processes of economic development.

CHAPTER 4

Human Resources: Qualitative Aspects

Much thinking and writing on the quality of tropical peoples in relation to prospects for economic development is riddled with prejudices and misconceptions. In the more extreme cases it is argued, either implicitly or explicitly, that many tropical peoples are innately incapable of participating fully in western-type economic life and even that they are inferior human types. Some writers argue that the enervating climate is such as to produce indigenous peoples who are lazy and both physically and mentally incapable of sustained effort. The standpoint taken here, however, is that all thinking and writing on the qualitative aspects of human resources in tropical lands must start from the assumption that there is no innate incapacity of the kind described above. The real problem, it is argued, is how to encourage the human skills, attitudes, and efficiency of economic organization which alone can provide the 'political, social and institutional framework which exploits the impulses to expansion' within an economy (Rostow, 1960).

At this stage it might be useful to look at a few examples of the issues and problems which need consideration and fuller study before any attempt can be made to induce the kind of change so frequently required.

Some social and institutional issues. A number of writers argue that existing institutional relationships and attitudes are inadequate in most tropical countries. Certainly, conventions and taboos of a number of kinds may restrict economic opportunity in many ways, including the use of resources. Probably the most striking prejudice of this kind hampering economic development concerns livestock, for both in Asia and in Africa there are some classes or communities which take a non-commercial attitude to livestock, fail to exploit their cattle to best advantage in terms of work, meat and milk, and carry excessive numbers of animals. Under Hindu laws, for instance, beasts of inferior quality cannot be killed or restrained from breeding, even though the numbers of animals may be so excessive as to be an obvious drain on the farmers' resources and on the land (Lewis, 1955: 43). There may be a similarly excessive accumulation of cattle in order to achieve social distinction or to discharge obligations, such as the bride price (Prescott, 1960). Then there are prejudices against manual work, against having economic relations with strangers, against changing occupations, and against migration. Other conventions include those relating to family life, especially the place of the woman in the economy, the control of agricultural practices by priests, and the caste system (Bailey, 1958).

The extended family, sometimes known as the joint family, is a common feature of the economic and social life of many tropical countries, especially in Africa and South Asia, and entails hospitality on a lavish scale to family members and the indiscriminate maintenance of distant relatives. Property and income are pooled and inherited as such; and expenditure is not accounted for individually. A man may thus have obligations towards a much larger number of people than in communities in which the concept of the family is more restricted. In appropriate circumstances, admittedly, the extended family system has many virtues. But at a later stage it can form an obstacle to economic progress in that a man is likely to be much less willing and able to rise in the income scale, and to save and invest, when he knows that he will have to distribute his gains among his relatives (Bauer and Yamey, 1957: 64–6).

In considering whether the attitudes to work of tropical peasants are restrictive on economic development, it is often pointed out that tropical peoples generally work shorter hours than do their counterparts in temperate latitudes. But the definition and measurement of the employed labour force in many tropical countries is complicated by several factors, including the place in the labour force of women and children, who sometimes make important, even decisive, contributions to economic activity. Again, and particularly in subsistence or semi-subsistence agriculture, the demands of labour vary greatly with the seasons. The study of daily and seasonal work cycles in tropical countries is as yet little advanced, but several interesting facts have already been revealed. Ooi (1959) shows that Malay padi planters work hard for only part of the year and that the rubber smallholder works in total only very short hours; for peasant smallholders and fishermen in Malaya the normal working hours per day are 3·5–5·1 hours. Similarly, in the West Indies it has been found that the individual agricultural labourer works 5 hours a day for 4 days a week on the average: that is, for some 20 hours a week. And A. Richards (1939) noted that the Bemba of Northern Rhodesia work for 5–6 months in an agricultural year, averaging only about 4 hours a day. This is a common enough feature of tropical countries, but should be taken to express endemic under-employment and simple agricultural systems rather than any inability or disinclination on the part of the farmer to work longer hours because of laziness, climate, or dietary deficiencies. Furthermore, the difficulty of getting tropical peasants to work very hard does not prevent them seizing opportunities to use better seeds, fertilizers, or more profitable crops: it has not 'prevented the Gold Coast farmer . . . from switching from subsistence production to creating the largest cocoa industry in the world, over a short space of time; or prevented the farmers of Uganda or of Indonesia from taking enthusiastically to cotton or rubber respectively' (Lewis, 1955: 41). All the evidence seems to suggest that changes in the attitudes of tropical peasants to work can only be effected by making the peasant want to work harder and giving him the opportunity to do so. This is very much a problem of changing his attitudes towards cash incentives. There are many instances of peasants responding to increases in the rate of earnings by producing or working proportionately less, because they need only a money income sufficient to pay for their fixed and limited wants. In economic terms this phenomenon is expressed in a backward-bending supply curve as distinct from the more normal upward-sloping curve of labour (Berg, 1961). In primitive societies, extra income beyond the conventional level may not be enjoyed as much as in more advanced societies because of the limited ranges of possible uses. Extra money has to be spent not so much in acquiring new goods of a type not owned before, as in buying more of the same – more drink, more cloth. As Bauer and Yamey (1957) conclude, however, there are no grounds for postulating a ceiling to economic development imposed by inflexibility in habits of consumption (p. 86). Imitation is doing its work, replacing the old forms of compulsion in labour which, while necessary to development by western entrepreneurs in tropical countries, was nevertheless not likely ever to cause any fundamental or radical change in indigenous attitudes to work. The tropical peasant is continually acquiring new wants, and is showing himself increasingly willing to work to satisfy them without compulsion.

In examining the role of social factors in tropical economic development emphasis is perhaps too often put on the limitations imposed by these factors, but though there is admittedly much in the attitudes of tropical peoples that may curb economic growth, there is also much in their social organization which can serve its cause. In Nigeria, for instance, the people have strong local loyalties; 'they are closely tied to the immediate family or clan; they support local "unions" (clubs); and they take pride in local achievements. The banding together of families, clans, and village communities in producers' co-operatives, in the savings clubs of the Yoruba and in the thrift societies' of the Ibo strangers in northern Nigeria: these are practical and promising illustrations of self-help. Furthermore, 'respect for elders and acceptance of their counsel, if not carried to the point of becoming an impediment to learning new ways, make for social restraint and stability. Respect for learning in any form and the authority enjoyed by *mallams* (learned men) of the northern parts of Nigeria, and by teachers and even students in southern Nigeria, suggest a 'key role which the teaching profession can play in developing new attitudes, and in the adoption of new institutions and techniques'. Many Nigerian social traditions, attitudes, and institutions, indeed, have positive value in a period of rapid change and advancement, and the same holds true for probably all tropical countries. The real problem is how to make use of these existing and powerful forces in any particular line of development, and how to ensure that they assist rather than obstruct its cause. Thus the International Bank report on Nigeria recommends that full support should be given to the co-operative movement as a vehicle for economic development in the country, 'for it is a form of economic organization fully compatible with Nigerian tradition and social sentiment' (International Bank, 1954: 10–11).

As for the role of education in the economic development of tropical countries, on which there is already a substantial literature, a good deal of controversy exists over the form such education should take. Balogh (1966: 90) argues that the input of conventional education is fatal from the point of view of balanced progress; and certainly the experience of India and several African independent countries would seem to give strong support to this view. According to Balogh three commonsense principles need to be adopted: that education should be in close harmony with the technical and administrative requirements of the country; that education should not create a disaffected intellectual proletariat; and that education should be in close touch with the life of the community as a whole.

There is a wide range of opinion about the role of social or cultural factors in economic development. While some writers believe their role to be negligible or only marginal, others, like Hagen (1962), regard social and cultural factors as causal and decisive; and Balogh (1966) claims that these social factors often do not provide a framework in which the profit and price mechanisms can operate so effectively as in developed societies. For this reason economic models based on the assumption of an efficiently working price mechanism are dangerous. Other less extreme viewpoints are expressed by Rostow (1953; 1956), Hoselitz (1952), and many others, who regard social and cultural factors as but two of the many variables affecting economic development. The question as to which of these points of view is correct is clearly of real practical significance for planning and policy-making in those countries of the tropical world where social and cultural forces appear to play a relatively substantial role in human life and activity. Case studies to support each of the various viewpoints can no doubt be found. Yet it may be unwise to try to make general conclusions about so diffuse and complex an issue. On *a priori* grounds, as Kindleberger has urged, it seems difficult not to reject both of the extreme points of view: 'sociocultural determinism is no more likely an explanation of the course of economic development than is economic determinism of social history' (Kindleberger, 1966: 38–9). The standpoint taken in the present study is that social or cultural factors are normally important in any analysis of contemporary applied problems of economic development in a tropical country, but that they need nowhere form a decisive drag on or permanent impediment to development.

Climate and human comfort and energy.[1] In any discussion of the qualitative aspects of the human resources of the tropical world the suggestion is commonly made that the tropical climate is responsible for much of the present low quality of manpower in low latitudes. Indeed, it has for long been widely accepted that the tropics, particularly the humid tropics, provide far from ideal conditions for man to live in, and that they are associated with ill-health, laziness, inefficiency, and marked physical, mental, and moral degeneration. This viewpoint is remarkable in that primitive man, with his lack of natural protective covering and profuse endowment of sweat glands to enable him to tolerate high levels of warmth with impunity, was originally almost certainly a tropical animal. Moreover, advanced civilizations have existed in the tropics – not only in the tropical highlands, as with the Aztec civilization, but also in the rainy forested lowlands of Ceylon, Cambodia, Java, Guatemala, and Yucatan. On the other hand, most of the world's ancient civilizations were located in subtropical or warm temperate lands, especially in those fertile areas near to the 70° F (21·1° C) annual isotherm; and Huntington (1915) contends that it was in these areas that what might be called 'intrusive' civilizations of the very low latitudes originated. According to this viewpoint, only special advantages of location or soil made it possible for civilizations to flourish in the tropics.

Certainly the tropical climate seems to be far from stimulating. Yet the improvement of life in the tropics must not be obstructed

[1] Much of this section is substantially the same as pp. 91–9 of my *Man in Malaya* (1959).

by an unquestioning acceptance of traditional ideas about the ill-effects of the climate on comfort and energy. Many of these ill-effects have been found to be due to disease, poverty, ignorance, and poor diet. Moreover, it has been found possible by intelligent adaptations to avoid or at least mitigate many of the direct ill-effects of the climate. It is important to try to understand the real nature of the climate–man relationship; to distinguish clearly between fact and fancy; and to adapt one's way of life to the peculiarities of the climate.

In any examination, however brief, of the relationship between climate and mental and physical energy in the tropics, no simple causal relationships can be found. Man's capacity for mental and physical energy and even his physical comfort are affected by a host of variables – nutrition, cultural habits, religion, standards of living, and psychological factors. Though much remains to be learned about this branch of knowledge, and many of the conclusions drawn can only be tentative, the subject has already been given a firm scientific basis. No attempt can be made here to discuss those relationships of a more specious nature: between climate and civilization, climate and suicide, climate and crime, climate and intelligence, or between climate and the number of men of genius. All such relationships involve climatic factors whose role may only be indirect and so strongly neutralized by other non-climatic factors that the influence of the climate becomes almost intangible. Thus the decline of the Mayan civilization in Central America, though attributed by some writers to climatic changes involving the return of a hot, wet climate, was more probably due to a great number of factors, notably soil degradation. Even in skin colour, though it is true that pigmentation is usually heavier in tropical than in temperate skins, the relationship is greatly complicated by ethnic variables: the Malay with his Mongolian origin, for instance, has a much lighter skin than has the African living under similar climatic conditions in Africa.

There is little agreement about the ideal climate. Huntington, basing his conclusions on the statistical analysis of the frequency of deaths in different countries, in different conditions of temperature and relative humidity, tries to express quantitatively what he believes to be the optimal climatic conditions for mental and physical work: these are, for physical work, an outside mean daily temperature of about 64° F (17·8° C) and for mental work a mean daily temperature of 40° F (4·4° C). For both physical and mental work the ideal relative humidity is 75–80 per cent. Seasonal variations in temperature, he says, are desirable, but should not be too great. Brunt (1943), on the other hand, believes that for a healthy and active life the climate should be such that the mean temperature of the hottest month shall never exceed 75° F (23·9° C). Brunt has also specified that the ideal outdoor climate is one in which a man lightly clothed can walk at 3 miles per hour (5 km per hour) in sunshine, without sweating, and rest in bright sunshine or stand in the shade or outdoors doing light work, with light air movement and without body cooling; the optimum for these prescribed conditions is 67° F (19·4° C) for a lightly clothed man, when the relative humidity is near 50 per cent. Another writer states that the temperatures between which a man is at his most efficient are 60° F (15·6° C) and 76° F (24·4° C), according to the relative humidity (ideal 40–70 per cent), the amount of clothing worn, and the amount of body movement; a slight air movement only is assumed (Markham, 1947). Mills (1942) puts the upper limit of comfortable conditions, assuming a low wind speed, at an average temperature of 80° F (26·7° C) with a relative humidity of about 58 per cent; at higher humidities conditions are 'sultry'. The importance of relative humidity in all these concepts of the ideal climate has led to attempts to express comfort in terms of wet bulb temperatures. Taylor (1946) has suggested that wet bulb temperatures between 45°–55° F (7·2°–12·8° C) indicate 'very comfortable' conditions; between 55°–65° F (12·8°–18·3° C) conditions are 'sometimes uncomfortable'; between 65°–75° F (18·3°–23·9° C) they are 'often uncomfortable'; and over 75° F (23·9° C) conditions are 'continuously uncomfortable'.

All writers on the subject, however, imply that the humid tropics have too hot, too humid, and too monotonous a climate for optimal physical and mental energy. Many settled parts of the tropics have average temperatures over 10° F (5·6° C) higher than Huntington's optimal temperature for physical energy and twice that of his optimal temperature for mental energy. And even the coolest months in many parts of the tropics never have an average temperature as low as the maximum prescribed by Brunt. Significance attaches to certain of the tropical highland areas in this respect, for there is some considerable white settlement dependent upon the lowering effect of altitudes on temperature. This is especially so in parts of Central America and in East and Central Africa; but there are also many hill stations elsewhere, as in India where they commonly lie between 6,000 feet (1,830 m) and 7,500 feet (2,286 m).

It is easy to exaggerate the monotony of tropical climates in its effect on human comfort and energy. Thus the wide seasonal humidity contrasts so characteristic of parts of the tropical savanna climate (in which relative humidities may drop to below 10 per cent during the dry season and rise to over 90 per cent in the wet season) are not normally found in the equatorial region. All seasonal climatic changes have their effect on human comfort and energy, though much of this effect is probably psychological. It has been observed of the monsoon in India, for instance, that 'in the rains temperatures are lower, and feel lower than they are. Gratifying as this initial coolness is, however, after a few weeks of eternally cloud-sealed skies the absence of sun has a depressing psychological effect' (Spate, 1967: 55). Something of the same effect may be experienced along the West African coast during the wet season, especially around July. The feeling of monotony in tropical countries can also be relieved by diurnal temperature ranges which can be considerable outside the equatorial region, though even there the diurnal temperature variations may be of real human significance, varying with latitude and distance from the sea. Furthermore, it must be recognized when considering the monotony of the tropical and in particular the equatorial climate that man there is extremely sensitive to climatic changes so small that they would go unnoticed in temperate countries; it is not unusual for newspapers in tropical lands to publish accounts of 'heat waves' when the increase in the average daily air temperature is no more than 2° F (1·2° C).

The tropical climate is indeed far more tolerable than climatic abstractions and traditional notions would suggest. It is necessary to take account, among other things, of automatic and conscious efforts to adapt human activities as completely as possible to the climate in which man has to live and work.

As for *automatic responses*, man in the tropics is almost continuously faced with the problem of how to dissipate heat from the body, and this may be effected chiefly by convection, conduction, radiation, or evaporation. But sweating leading to evaporation is in the tropics perhaps the most important automatic response, for the increased activity of sweat glands is a sign that the cooling of the body by convection and radiation alone is insufficient to maintain an even body temperature, and that evaporative cooling, which takes place when sweat evaporates from the body surface or from clothing in contact with the skin, is also necessary. Indeed, sweating is one of nature's safeguards, though it can lead to a complex of maladies resulting from loss of the salt contained in sweat which commonly contains between 0·2 per cent and 0·5 per cent of salt. But the more moist the air the less easily can moisture be evaporated into it from the body surface. Allowing for a person weighing about 130 lb (59 kgm) and for the specific heat of the human body of 0·8, about 0·22 pints (0·1 litre) of water must be evaporated from the body to reduce the average body temperature by about 2° F (1·2° C). This amount of sweat can easily be produced on the body in the humid tropics by exercising for an hour. The limits of evaporation, however, are passed in still air when the wet bulb temperature exceeds 88°–90° F (31·1°–32·2° C), even when a man is unclothed and doing no work: the surrounding air is then so saturated that no more moisture can be evaporated into it. Though wet-bulb temperatures of this order rarely occur with very high temperatures, the effectiveness of evaporative cooling is widely restricted by the high relative humidities experienced in the tropical wet or equatorial areas, and in the savanna and monsoon tropics during the wet season. The increase in comfort during the dry season in these latter areas is due very largely to the drop in relative humidities, though discomfort from excessively low humidities may then occur.

Partly because of limitations to the effectiveness of evaporative cooling, man's ability to acquire any considerable degree of acclimatization to tropical climates is now generally doubted. The processes of acclimatization, admittedly, include more than the increased activity of sweat glands: acclimatization also consists in a loss of weight with a corresponding increase in conductance and of the ratio of skin area to total weight of body. Yet it is believed that the development and maintenance of true acclimatization to heat is prevented by the lack of stimulating changes of temperature. It has been found, for instance, that Europeans who live in the humid tropics for many months, or even all their lives, do not show those changes in the blood usually associated with true acclimatization to heat. There is little doubt that many tropical peoples withstand poorly not only cooling but also warming. The consensus of opinion is that frequent changes in environmental temperatures in the wet tropics are usually insufficient to allow the processes of true acclimatization to operate satisfactorily.

It may be objected that most of the above remarks, while possibly true of Europeans, are not applicable to indigenous peoples in the tropics. Admittedly, most of the experimental evidence refers to Europeans, but according to most authorities it is unlikely that there is any significant difference in physiological responses between races. The normal temperature of man is the same in all latitudes, and all available evidence suggests that the differences between racial types in physiological response to work at high temperatures which can be attributed to racial factors alone are small. According to the most recent conclusions, 'European workers in hot industry, or Europeans who have lived in, say, Singapore for a hot season or so, Africans in Nigeria . . . Australian aborigines, and Indians and Chinese in Malaya – all these show precisely the same capacity to acclimatize to heat. This, of course, is not really surprising, as on other grounds, genetic and palaeontological, we are aware that modern man is one interfertile species and that the origin of the hominids was certainly in an equatorial region' (Weiner, 1966: 375).

On the other hand, there may be very significant differences between races in psychological response and in their readiness or opportunities to make intelligent adaptations to the climate; indeed, it may well be that the key to the whole problem of comfort and energy in the tropics lies in this direction. Little is known about the psychological aspects of the problem as yet, but tropical fatigue certainly constitutes a serious obstacle to social, economic, and political development. Monotony, boredom, and dissatisfaction undoubtedly affect a man's physical and mental vigour through their effect on his nervous system, and this may be because the climate requires continual loss of moisture from the body so that the nervous system supervising this never or rarely exercises its opposite function – the conservation of heat.

Many of man's *conscious responses* to the climate in the humid tropics are based on the appreciation of two facts: that moving air carries warmth away from the body more effectively than does still air; and that even the slightest air movement acting upon a body damp with sweat will accelerate the rate of body cooling by accelerating the rate of evaporation from the body. Thus if a man sits fully clothed in a room with all windows shut in a tropical climate, he will undoubtedly soon feel warm. If he turns on an electric fan he will feel cooler. If by the time he turns on the fan his body and clothes are damp with sweat, then he may quickly feel uncomfortably cool. The fan, and such more primitive methods as the *punkah*, are based on the principle that movement of air is the great reliever of oppression in the tropics. A breeze can have a similar cooling effect, but only if a house is properly located and designed will maximum benefit be gained from whatever movement of air there is. An open type of house is called for in wet equatorial lowland areas, located where it can be reached by any local breeze. Innumerable subjective observations could be made to support the contention that small differences in siting, aspect, and location of houses can produce appreciable differences in body temperature and comfort. A satisfactorily quantitative statement, however, must await more integrated and comparative research in physiological climatology.

A distinction must be made here, however, between the house type of the lowland equatorial tropics and the house type of the savanna and monsoon tropics. Whereas in the wetter tropics one of the chief ways of promoting coolness in a house is by opening it up to any air movement, in the drier tropics coolness is obtained more by the heavy construction of houses and by the small number and size of windows. In West Africa, for instance, outside the rain forest and mangrove coastal zone, the house type is quite distinctive: walls are thick and made from puddled mud and there are few openings for ventilation. The reason for this kind of contrast is interesting and illustrates human responses and adaptations to differing climatic conditions within the tropics. In the first place, most of West Africa has a distinct dry season, a broad range in relative humidities and sharper diurnal contrasts than are experienced, say, in Malaya. Apart from the availability of materials, which may have some bearing on the question, the house in West Africa must be less open partly to keep out the dust, but primarily to produce more even temperatures: the thick walls protect the house during the day from intense insolation, especially during the dry season, and warm the house during the night. Mud is cheap, easily obtainable, has good insulating properties, and can be remarkably durable.

It is true that wholly suitable house designs and locations must for long be restricted to a very small section of the population. Even new housing in towns is normally of inadequate design and far too congested. On the other hand, present concepts in the design and location of tropical urban housing may become outmoded if the practice of air conditioning becomes widely available to a large section of the population in towns. In a fully air-conditioned house the ideal design is quite different from the design for a house without air conditioning: windows are fewer and smaller, and rooms are smaller and less airy. Air conditioning depends for its success not so much upon moving the air as upon lowering air temperature and relative humidity. As the standard of living rises, air conditioning is becoming more common to the extent that a small but still increasing section of the population sleeps, eats, and works in its artificial climate. However, the European must not too glibly assume that all indigenous peoples would like air conditioning, even if they could have it. There is still a certain amount of prejudice against the practice, though it is difficult to see why if central heating is necessary in England, air conditioning should be considered unnecessary in the tropics.

A further adaptation a man can make to climate is in his clothes. According to their colour, thickness, texture, and tightness of fit, clothes can raise or lower the threshold levels of warmth at which a man begins to sweat or feel uncomfortable. Thus 'in Singapore a lady wearing a thin dress which leaves her legs and arms bare, and light sandals on her feet, may be much more comfortable than her husband in a linen shirt with collar and cuffs and in long trousers and leather shoes' (Glaser, 1955: 1). In this whole question of suitable clothing it is important to appreciate that in the dissipation of heat from man the most important parts of the body are the hands, feet, and ears: that is, those parts of the body where the total surface area is great in relation to the total volume or weight and where the supply of blood to the skin is richest. Clearly, then, the practice of wearing socks and western-type leather shoes in the wet tropics is illogical, for it restricts the feet, especially the toes, as cooling agents. As for colour, it is in accordance with the principle that tropical clothes should have good reflective power and poor absorptive power that they should be white or at least bright in colour. Following on what has been said above, too, it is logical that they should allow good ventilation: clothes should be loose in texture and loose fitting.

Because the highest temperatures are reached in the early after-noon – usually about 2 p.m. – it might be expected, by analogy with certain European countries, that the afternoon siesta would be common. This practice varies with the country, or more pre-cisely with the European power that controls or formerly con-trolled it. Whereas the siesta is fairly common practice in most Latin American tropical countries and in those other parts of the tropics where French, Spanish, or Portuguese control has been exerted, the siesta is not commonly associated with the former British possessions in the tropics. This, of course, affects the distri-bution of work throughout the day.

It is frequently stated that the humid tropics have a climate which is not conducive to mental and physical energy: 'warm, wet climates are inimical to sustained mental work'; or 'labour in the tropics is unlikely to be as efficient as in temperate areas'. There seems to be no evidence to support such statements, however.

Rather must it be insisted that by increasingly intelligent adaptations it will prove possible to negate the ill-effects of the wet tropical climate on human activities. The difficulties of life in the tropics are cultural rather than climatic (Bates, 1952; Simey, 1946). It will be realized that the pattern of living in most tropical countries has been almost slavishly transported from Western European or North American countries. The whole concept of civilized living – in diet, housing, clothing, the distribution of work throughout the day, and recreational habits – must be reassessed against the realities of the natural environment. In relating tropical climate, human comfort, mental and physical energy to economic development, it must be assumed that with continued research in applied physiological climatology, improvements in medical knowe dge and services, and an improved diet and standard of living, there is no reason why anyone should not be as active and efficient in the tropics as elsewhere in the world. The real problem is to find out how to live and work at one's best in any particular tropical country as distinct from anywhere else. It is not enough simply to avoid infections, increase food production, create industries, and improve social services. Tropical peoples must also consider how they can so adapt themselves and their activities to the climate that they can work, think, and live at their best.

Tropical diseases. Many writers have concluded that health is the chief problem in the settlement and development of tropical countries. Yet here again it must be assumed that the tropics can be made as healthy as anywhere in the world, and so to look upon unhealthiness as only a temporary impediment to development. Many of the so-called tropical diseases have at one time or another existed in temperate latitudes, and certain parts of the tropics – notably some of the small island territories – have already been made very healthy.

Disease, nevertheless, is very much a force to be reckoned with. In Nigeria malaria is still a most important problem and one with which surprisingly little progress has yet been made: probably one-third of all Nigerian children die before they reach the age of five, and the bulk of these die from malaria. In Ghana, Hunter

(1966) has shown how rural settlement has advanced and retreated in association with the incidence and spread of river blindness (onchocerciasis). In Malaya, now certainly one of the healthiest countries in the tropics, it is nevertheless reported that there are still areas 'where 50–90 per cent of the population shows signs of malaria, where worm infestations are more or less universal, where yaws is prevalent, leprosy not uncommon and smallpox a constant threat. Tuberculosis, venereal diseases, malnutrition, and a host of lesser ailments, though preventable or curable, are still widespread causes of sickness, disability, and premature death more or less throughout Malaya' (International Bank, 1955: 400). The main diseases now mainly tropical are anklyostomiasis, blackwater fever, cholera, dengue fever, diarrhöeal disorders, guinea-worm, filariasis, dysentery, liver abscess, malaria, sleeping sickness, tetanus, yellow fever, and most skin diseases. There is space here, however, to deal very briefly with only a few of these.

Malaria still plays an important role in restricting economic and social development. It is true that in many tropical countries malaria has lost its menace as the chief killing disease, though official figures of deaths from diagnosed malaria are thought to be very much lower than the true figure. Malaria has in many areas been reduced by control measures and personal prophylaxis to an endemic burden of sickness. In most malarious areas the sickness rate is far higher among children than among adults, and the signs of repeated malaria indicate the hazards of the slow immunizing process whereby adults gain their immunity. Although the number of deaths from malaria has been greatly reduced, the disease is still a serious consideration because of its restricting effects on energy, initiative, and the development of positive good health. Agriculture, for instance, may not receive all the care it needs.

Approaching the study of malaria from the geographical point of view it is easy to find a correlation between the distribution of malaria and the distribution of population. In Malaya, for instance, the well-established, densely populated padi areas on the flat coastal plains, urbanized areas like Singapore, and the western interior foothill belt of rubber and tin-mining settlements are relatively free from malaria. In the sparsely populated interior, on the other hand, the incidence rises rapidly. The incidence of malaria in the peninsula is highest in narrow, isolated, and relatively sparsely populated valleys of the interior. But such remarks do not establish a simple causal relation. It is not true that the pattern of population distribution is in any way determined by the distribution of malaria. The absence of malaria in populated areas is often the effect rather than the cause of settlement, anti-malarial measures being best developed in the more populous districts.

The high moisture and temperature conditions essential for the breeding of anopheline mosquitoes are found almost everywhere in the humid tropics. Attempts have been made to fit annual rainfall curves to the incidence of the disease itself, but so far little success has been had in this direction though rainfall undoubtedly does influence malaria by affecting the height of the water table. More success in establishing climatic correlations has attended attempts to relate malaria incidence and wet-bulb temperatures, though research in this direction is handicapped while climatic data are used from widely spaced stations. The natural conditions immediately surrounding the insect – illumination, humidity, temperature, and air movement – differ from regional averages. The micro-climate has more epidemiological significance than the regional climate, though some general conclusions are possible – for instance that low temperatures inhibit the development of the plasmodium in the fly.

In the application of anti-malarial measures in rural areas of the tropics, the pattern of settlement is an important consideration. Anti-larval measures, used with such success to protect the population in towns, villages, and estates, may be prohibitively expensive in rural areas where the population is widely scattered. Consequently, whereas in Western European countries rural life is popularly associated with healthy living and town life with unhealthy living, in the tropics the converse is generally true: the healthiest spots are the towns where control measures and personal prophylaxis are more easily available and enforceable. The scattered distribution of dwellings also makes it difficult to capture mosquitoes because there is no focal point in settlements towards which they are attracted. Another difficulty in the application of anti-malarial measures is that since the various species of vectors have different environmental requirements, malaria control measures must necessarily differ from place to place. The real key to malaria control in any one area is a knowledge of the vector species and its breeding habits in that particular area; 'the problem is first, last, and always, a local one, success depending upon knowledge of the habits of the particular species of *Anopheles* concerned and the local peculiarities of topography, population, and climate' (Malayan Government, I.M.R., 1950: 173).

The control of malaria, as of other diseases, tends at first to raise the birth rate and lower the death rate, thereby helping to boost the rate of growth of population. On the other hand – and quite apart from humanitarian motives – experience has shown that the control of malaria in the long run reduces the endemic burden of diseases other than malaria, releases energy and initiative, and in general raises the prosperity of the people. This is a feature which, though perhaps not immediately apparent to a visitor to a tropical country, is really more significant to the present study than is the serious and dramatic outbreak of malaria in a country. Continuous contact with tropical peoples emphasizes how insidiously the lack of positive good health can affect attitudes towards work, individual initiative, energy, and capacities for sustained work or thought.

Human sleeping sickness (*trypanosomiasis*) in Africa is caused by *Trypanosoma gambiense* or *T. rhodesiense* and conveyed to man by the bite of the tsetse fly (*Glossina*). Both species finally invade the central nervous system, causing the classical symptoms which have resulted in the disease being called sleeping sickness. *T. gambiense* is widespread, from West Africa through Central Africa to Uganda, western Kenya, and the shores of Lake Tanganyika. *T. rhodesiense* may occur here, but is typically found in the rest of Tanzania, Zimbabwe, Zambia, and Mozambique. The tsetse species of greatest significance are *G. palpalis*, *G. tachinoides*, *G. morsitans*, *G. swynnertoni*, and *G. pallidipes*. Like the various malaria vectors, each species of tsetse has special climatic and other environmental requirements which determine its distribution: thus *G. palpalis* is almost invariably restricted to the humid vicinity of rivers or streams with heavily shaded banks, while *G. morsitans* can survive in arid thorn scrub, provided it can secure shade in thicket.

The detailed distribution of trypanosomiasis is influenced by several factors. During the wet season there is a high density and wide distribution of the fly because conditions are generally suitable; but in the dry season, although their density is low, they tend to concentrate in foci where local climatic conditions are favourable. These foci usually contain pools of water on which man also is dependent, so that close and regular contact is established between the human and fly populations.

The distribution of trypanosomiasis is also influenced by the human population density. According to experimental work in Nigeria, where the population density is below 20 persons to the square mile (8 per km²) sporadic cases may occur, but population densities of 20–100 per square mile (8–38 per km²) have the highest incidence of trypanosomiasis. Over 100 per square mile (38 per km²), fly–man contact decreases because agricultural and other activities disturb the environment and make it unsuitable for the fly. Flies readily follow man, animals, and vehicles for long distances, so that improved communications often result in the carriage of infected flies into uninfected areas. Clearly, then, the reduction of contact between man and *Glossina* must be effected, and this can be achieved by concentrating the human populations or by so altering the environment that the fly departs or dies.

In Nigeria the range of the tsetse fly (*G. palpalis* and *G. tachinoides*) extends from the coast to the open savannas of the north. Only small parts of the extreme north, parts of the Cameroons and the Jos Plateau are fly-free. With the exception of small foci in the south, however, human sleeping sickness is confined to northern Nigeria, and more especially to the Middle Belt, though this relative freedom of the south does not extend to the animal population. The provinces most severely affected are the southern areas of Katsina, Zaria, Plateau, and Benue, which together account for 70 per cent of all cases in northern Nigeria. The problem was attacked by the clearing of vegetation along streams and around settlements with varying degrees of ruthlessness, thereby destroying the pockets of shade and humidity sought by the fly; by the setting up of dispensaries from which mass treatment could be organized; by the prophylactic use of modern drugs in selected populations; and by large-scale resettlement schemes involving the concentration of population, as at Anchau. Originally one-third of the population at Anchau had sleeping sickness and in some villages up to one-half of the population was infected. It was reported that nothing could be done before the population was concentrated; and the Colonial Development and Welfare Fund gave money for a scheme of rural development in which economic development was to form an essential part.

The greater incidence of human sleeping sickness in northern Nigeria has been shown to reflect the greater man–fly contact there. Near Kaduna, for instance, *G. palpalis* survive in the late dry season by concentrating at a few permanent pools in the stream bed. When the pools are utilized by an African village as its sole source of water, man becomes the primary host and is thus heavily exposed to Gambian sleeping sickness. In the humid forested areas of southern Nigeria, however, there is normally a low degree of man–fly contact. Under humid conditions, *G. palpalis* is widespread and barely riverine in habitat. Whereas man in southern Nigeria may be dependent upon stream or other water points, the fly there is not (Page and McDonald, 1959).

Yellow fever is confined to western and central Africa and the northern half of South America. The parent source of this infection is primarily in monkeys, but transmission to man is effected by certain species of culicine mosquitoes, especially the *Aedes aegypti*. This mosquito is common in the whole inter-tropical belt, and usually breeds in the immediate vicinity of human habitations; in small shallow collections of water in old tins, bottles, coconut husks; and, in fact, in almost anything that will hold water. The disease usually arises from the introduction into an area of an infected person. Consequently those areas which have the vector have to guard carefully against the immigration of people from yellow fever countries. Most of the measures are decreed by international conventions, and very strict control is exacted at all airports or seaports in contact with endemic areas.

The incidence and mortality of *tuberculosis* is increasing rapidly in many tropical countries as communications improve and as people congregate in larger communities; it is more of a social than a medical problem, being associated more especially with over-crowding. It has also been introduced in its more malignant forms by European contact, notably in the Congo where the disease spread along lines of transportation and through European settlements into rural areas.

In many of the more advanced tropical countries tuberculosis is now probably the most important single disease in public concern. In Malaya, overcrowding is very common in the types of dwelling known as shophouses, which are believed to constitute the most potent single factor in the production of the high rate of tuberculosis in the country. Over 50 per cent of the urban population of Malaya live in shophouses, the rooms of which are commonly divided into one-family cubicles, leading to very high floor-space densities and producing units of accommodation in which there is often no direct access to light and fresh air. In Sarawak, too, the Dyak longhouse is believed to be an important cause of the high rate of tuberculosis.

Diet and nutrition. The effects of a low dietary on social and economic development are undeniable, though difficult to isolate or measure. Chronic disease in association with malnutrition produce a cumulative effect, since 'it leads to severe debility, which interferes with the individual's capacity to work and hence lowers his production and earnings' (F.A.O., 1966: 12). Poverty and ignorance are probably the chief causes of malnutrition, and in areas where chronic hunger appears to exist, as in parts of tropical Asia, the problem is 'not one of planning for optimum requirements and an optimum diet, but for minimum requirements and minimal diet on a bare subsistence level, and the problem has to be approached from a practical point of view and carefully related to prevailing agricultural standards' (ibid.: 14). Hunger, too, is by some authorities believed to be a direct cause of high crude birth rates; de Castro (1952), for instance, holds the view that hunger, especially when associated with low animal protein consumption, leads not to depopulation but to overpopulation.

The three main energy-producing foods are carbohydrates, proteins, and fats, the last having the highest calorific value; whereas one ounce (28 gm) of dry carbohydrate gives 113 calories in the body, and one ounce (28 gm) of dry protein gives about the same amount, fats are twice as good a fuel, one ounce of fat giving 255 calories in the body. It is believed that the minimum calorific intake per head per day should be about 2,500, though it is held by some authorities that a marked increase in energy and initiative cannot be expected until a minimum level of 3,000 calories per head per day is reached. Davey and Lightbody (1956) recommend 2,500 calories for the average peasant doing a moderate day's work in the tropics, where metabolism is lower than in temperate countries, though in Malaya the recommended allowance for peasants doing manual work has been put as low as 2,100 calories per day. In tropical countries the average figure is usually under 2,500 and in some cases under 2,000. Being average figures, large numbers of the population must exist at even lower figures, and conditions may well be much worse in countries for which data are lacking.

Bearing these facts in mind, it is useful to look at Table 2, which

Table 2. *Net food supplies* per capita *in selected countries* (calories per diem)

Country	Year	Cereals	Pota-toes etc.	Sugar	Pulses and nuts	Meat	Milk	Fats and Oils	Cal. per diem	% animal	Prot. in gm
Brazil	1970	984	464	494	297	208	124	163	2,820	6	63
Colombia	1970	628	314	533	62	198	182	132	2,140	18	50
Venezuela	1970	916	321	385	99	215	143	240	2,430	14	66
Nigeria	1969	988	809	19	37	41	10	230	2,290	3	59
Malagasy	1970	1,372	419	100	78	145	17	39	2,240	8	56
Uganda	1964–6	520	894	183	295	115	47	58	2,160	9	56
Ceylon	1970	1,387	73	239	398	7	40	101	2,340	4	48
India	1969–70	1,354	46	186	187	6	97	83	1,990	6	48
U.S.A.	1970	652	97	542	104	659	384	586	3.300	39	97

Source: United Nations, *Yearbook of Statistics*, 1971; F.A.O., *Yearbook*, 1971.

also shows the contribution of different types of food to the total *per capita* calorific intake in selected countries. Such a table has, of course, many limitations, and it is impossible to draw any definite conclusions from it. Certain ideas, however, are suggested by these figures.

The dominating importance of cereals – commonly rice in much of Asia and millets, wheat or maize elsewhere – is very evident. As a carbohydrate, rice is one of the poorer foods in calorific value, weight for weight, but it has a high yield and so is best adapted to areas of high population density, such as occur in parts of Asia. However, much of the rice is polished before eating, a process which removes some of the nutritive value. Rice may be artificially enriched with vitamins and minerals, and the nutritive value of ordinary rice may be raised by the addition of this enriched rice in appropriate proportions. Two potentially valuable supplements are thiamin and iron, the former to prevent *beri beri*, caused by lack of the vitamin B complex, and the latter to prevent the very common iron-deficiency anaemias. But prejudice against a rice having a different flavour or appearance from that to which people are accustomed is very real and difficult to overcome.

Rice, together with the other cereals, potatoes, and starchy roots such as yams, provide the bulk of the carbohydrates in tropical diets, and Table 2 indicates how high a percentage of calories is provided by such foods. In Pakistan something like 75 per cent of the calories are provided by cereals alone; and cereals, potatoes, and roots commonly provide at least 50 per cent of the calorific intake in tropical countries. Sugar, too, is a source of carbohydrate, though its consumption is strictly limited in most tropical countries outside the Caribbean area.

Taken together, the cereals, potatoes, roots, and sugar are tropical foodstuffs rich in carbohydrates but relatively poor in protein and fats. According to Davey and Lightbody (1956) the average tropical peasant doing a moderate day's work should take 2,500 calories per day which should be made up of 1,650 calories of carbohydrate, 400 calories of protein, and 450 calories of fats. From Table 2 it is clear that, though in many cases even the carbohydrate requirements are inadequate, tropical diets are most strikingly deficient in proteins and fats. This is particularly true of tropical Asian countries which come off badly in almost all dietetic comparisons.

In view of what has already been said, the figures for fats and oils are interesting, even though fat needs may not be identical in tropical and temperate countries. The average person in the United States or the United Kingdom takes over four times the amount of this valuable fuel than does his counterpart in most Asian and African countries, and substantially more even than most tropical

American countries. Even more striking is the set of figures for meat, milk, and eggs. In this connexion, however, it should be pointed out that animals are comparatively wasteful converters of food and are often the first to go when food gets scarce. Furthermore, tropical climatic and vegetative conditions do not in general favour livestock production, and in many parts of the tropics there are religious objections to eating animal flesh so that inferior vegetable protein has to take its place. Yet at least 30 per cent of the recommended 400 calories of protein should be first-class protein of animal origin if certain deficiency diseases such as deoedema or kwashiokor are to be prevented. The ideal minimum animal protein intake per day *per capita* is 1·25 oz (35 gm), but most tropical countries have an average consumption figure well below this.

One important fact that does not come out of the data given in Table 2 is the fluctuation of calorific intake, both in amount and in composition, throughout the year. Much of the dietetic problem in tropical countries, in fact, is of a seasonal or temporary nature. Throughout most of the tropics, and especially in the savanna or monsoon tropics, one frequently encounters references in the literature to the 'hungry season', the 'hunger gap', or 'the hungry months'. Miracle (1958) has argued that this concept may well be an exaggerated one – at least the notion that it occurs regularly. Clark and Haswell (1964) go farther and contend that the whole hunger problem of the tropical underdeveloped world is grossly exaggerated. These authors examine F.A.O. and other data on food requirements and calorific intake, and conclude that there is only a 15–20 per cent and not a 50 per cent deficit as is so often supposed.

Much remains to be learned about many aspects of the health problem in tropical lands. In this field, as in so many others, the chief and urgent need is for more reliable basic data. Continued research in public health, tropical medicine, and entomology is as necessary as it ever was. To some extent, admittedly, any improvement in the general health situation must depend on economic and social development: a decrease in prosperity will affect, for instance, the dietary of the population. But equally, without positive physical and mental health there can be no question of making the fullest possible use of the natural resources and economic opportunities of the tropical world.

. . . . .

While accepting that many tropical peoples possess attitudes and traditions that can militate against their ready absorption into a rapidly developing or industrializing society, neither the available evidence nor common experience suggest that there is any inherent physical or mental incapacity for this kind of change. Rather must it be assumed that the quality of tropical labour is potentially as good as anywhere else in the world. It must also be assumed that tropical labour can be made as efficient as any other kind, given a full understanding of the exact nature of resistance to change in any specific area, and given also that attempts to induce the required change take into account the limits and opportunities set by any particular situation. Sociological, social, anthropological, psychological, medical and educational research, and technical education: it is on such bases that any programme for improving the quality of tropical labour in a rapidly developing society must be built.

CHAPTER 5

Human Resources and the Population Problem

Population data. In perhaps no field of tropical studies are accurate basic data so necessary yet so scarce as in the field of population analysis. This applies not only to the simple totals of population but also to the demographic structure – birth and death rates, age and sex ratios, migration statistics, and the like. According to the available data it seems that rather over one-third of the world's population lives in humid tropical countries today, but tropical countries are not generally densely populated, though many post-war development theories seem to assume that densely populated countries are the prototype of all developing countries. In fact, however, the notion that they are crowded lands is true only of parts of the Caribbean and especially of parts of the Asian tropics. The really high densities of population in the tropics, moreover, commonly occur in one of two main types of area: the small islands associated with plantation economies, such as the West Indies, Mauritius, and Ceylon; and the long-settled, usually large, agricultural countries such as India whose present high density is partly a result of successful development in the past. Countries like India were able to support a high density of population before it started growing in the modern period. In the plantation islands, on the other hand, migrant labour was brought in to add to the indigenous population; high population densities subsequently developed, being helped 'by the relative ease with which diseases such as malaria can be wiped out from the islands' (Myint, 1964: 32).

Beyond presenting Table 3 no attempt is made here to give any detailed regional account of the population distribution. Tropical Asia, it will be seen, alone contains over two-thirds of tropical peoples and a quarter of the world's population. Outside Asia the tropics accommodate only about 8 per cent of the peoples of the

Table 3. *Population numbers and density of tropical countries* (1977 estimates)

	Population in thousands	Density per km²
Tropical America		
Costa Rica	2,071	41
Cuba	8,570	72
Dominican Republic	4,980	102
El Salvador	3,550	158
Guatemala	6,430	59
Haiti	4,770	172
Honduras	2,650	22
Jamaica	2,085	190
Mexico	64,590	33
Nicaragua	2,310	18
Panama	1,770	23
Trinidad and Tobago	1,040	203
Barbados	254	590
Cayman Islands	12	46
Guadeloupe	365	205
Martinique	374	339
Netherlands Antilles	252	262
Puerto Rico	3,303	371
Virgin Islands (U.S.)	66	180
Bolivia	5,950	5
Brazil	112,240	13
Colombia	25,050	22
Ecuador	7,560	27
Peru	16,520	13
Venezuela	12,740	14
Guyana	827	4
French Guiana	64	1
Surinam	448	3
Tropical Africa		
Benin	3,290	29
Burundi	3,966	142
Cameroon	7,663	14
Central African Republic	2,370	4
Chad	4,200	3

Table 3. – *continued*

	Population in thousands	Density per km²
Tropical Africa (continued)		
Congo (P.R.)	1,440	4
Congo Kinshasa (Zaïre)	26,380	11
Gabon	534	2
Gambia	553	49
Ghana	10,480	44
Guinea	4,670	19
Ivory Coast	5,150	16
Kenya	14,340	25
Liberia	1,800	16
Malagasy	8,520	15
Malawi	5,530	47
Mali	5,990	5
Niger	4,860	4
Nigeria	66,628	72
Rwanda	4,460	169
Senegal	5,085	24
Sierra Leone	3,470	48
Togo	2,350	42
Uganda	12,350	52
Tanzania	13,070	17
Upper Volta	6,320	23
Zambia	5,350	7
Angola	5,650	4
Equatorial Guinea	572	11
Mauritius	909	444
Mozambique	9,680	12
Reunion	492	196
Sao Tome and Principe	82	85
Zimbabwe (Rhodesia)	6,740	17
Tropical Asia		
Burma	31,510	47
Cambodia	8,610	48
Ceylon (Sri Lanka)	13,970	213
India	625,018	190
Indonesia	143,282	71

Table 3. – *continued*

	Population in thousands	Density per km²
Laos	3,464	15
Malaysia	12,600	38
Pakistan	72,278	94
Philippines	45,028	150
Singapore	2,308	3,973
Maldives	140	470
Thailand	44,039	86
Viet-Nam (North and South)	47,872	145
Brunei	190	33

Source: U.N. *Demographic Yearbook, 1977*, New York, 1978

world. There are clearly wide contrasts in population density between tropical Asia on the one hand and tropical America and Africa on the other, as well as between different parts of the same sector. There are also wide differences in the pattern of population density: thus the peripheral, coastal distribution of population in tropical South America contrasts with the relatively more even distribution in tropical Africa. Within each country, too, the spatial distribution of population is always an important factor in development: no economic development plan for Venezuela, Nigeria, or Malaya, for instance, could afford to ignore the great range of population densities found within those countries. Finally, in dealing with this question of population distribution, account must be taken of the urban–rural distribution. While it may be true that in tropical countries the role of urban economies in national development is less than in most developed lands, towns in all tropical countries are nevertheless important centres of economic power. The distribution of the larger towns of over 100,000 population reveals a general correlation with the most densely populated areas; there are about three hundred towns with populations over 100,000 in tropical Asia as against two hundred and fifty in tropical America and seventy-five in tropical Africa. Even more striking is the distribution of cities of over one million inhabitants. While the seventeen 'million' cities of Asia are spread over a large area, the fifteen in tropical America are on the extreme outer fringes of the tropical zone. There are still only five 'million' cities in tropical Africa.

In discussing the regional distribution of population, attention must also be directed to the question of population mobility or migration – either rural–urban or rural–rural. And, as Prothero (Steel and Prothero, 1964: 190) points out for Africa, population mobility today is one of the most important factors in African demography and influences the character of the population in many parts of the continent: 'it is of immediate practical concern to governments in the conduct of administration and in promoting economic and social developments'. Whether movements of population should be encouraged and directed by governments in any positive way is very much a matter of opinion. But certainly the present distribution of people in many tropical countries seems to act as a brake on economic development. In particular, it is perhaps difficult to spend long in the tropics without being forced to the conclusion that one of the chief restrictions on development is underpopulation. In very few parts of the tropics does the density of population seem to be too high for successful economic progress. For most areas, in fact, it is perhaps fair to suggest, as Brookfield (1960) has done for New Guinea, that a measure of planned redistribution of population is necessary if the benefits of economic development are to be more widely diffused; in particular, the concentration into urban and rural areas of at present widely scattered populations is perhaps a precondition of development.

Racial and tribal composition. The racial composition of the population is very relevant to any analysis of tropical economic development, for foreigners have in the past played a particularly important role in tropical lands. Apart from the specialized services contributed by Europeans during and since the colonial period, the work of the immigrant Chinese in South-east Asia; of Indians in

Mauritius, the West Indies and East Africa; of Lebanese and Syrians in Brazil; of Lebanese and Chinese in the West Indies; and of Lebanese and other Levantines in West Africa – all have done much to further the growth of the exchange sector of under-developed countries, 'and to promote their economic growth generally. They have accumulated capital, provided skills and aptitudes not present or developed among local people, and have pioneered in the development of trade, transport, and industries. By permeating the economy more extensively than the establishments and activities of the large-scale European mercantile, industrial, mining or plantation concerns, their influence has generally been more widespread and has affected large numbers of local people directly' (Bauer and Yamey, 1957: 107).

The Chinese immigrants and settlers in South-east Asia are especially numerous and have been the subject of several studies. Their contribution to economic development has been striking and they play a particularly important part in the economic life of Malaya. In Sarawak, too, where most of the non-indigenous peoples are Chinese, they occupy the more densely populated coastal and lower valley strips in the relatively well-developed west. As in many parts of South-east Asia, the Chinese provide the chief urban element in the Sarawak population, the capital, Kuching, being 60 per cent Chinese; the Chinese dominate, too, in business, the whole internal trade of the country passing at some stage or another through the hands of Chinese merchants. In most parts of the world, though the numbers of foreign immigrants may now be very small indeed, such immigration, selective as it is nowadays, continues to have an economic significance out of all proportion to its actual volume.

 ˙ Yet while the traditional functions of non-indigenous peoples are still frequently important factors in the economic development of individual countries, the analysis of economic development prospects must now also take account of the far-reaching social and political implications of the resulting plural societies, the problems of minorities, and the European settler problem. While in Africa, especially in East and Central Africa, the problem of the European settler is or has been dominant, in other parts of the tropics more attention is focused on the Chinese, Indian and similar problems: thus in Guyana and Indonesia racial tensions disrupt stability. Yet even within relatively homogeneous racial groups the problem of ethnicity is often an equally serious matter for economic development planning. In Nigeria, for instance, the major human groups – Hausa, Fulani, Yoruba, and Ibo – are, in fact, linguistic and cultural rather than racial groups, but they do, nevertheless, form an important divisive factor in the Nigerian population. The geographical distribution of the ethnic groups emphasizes and perpetuates these differences, being associated with one or other of the three main population nuclei in the north, west, and east respectively. There is also a large number of smaller but still distinct groups, some of which, like the Kanuri, Ibibio, and Tiv, total over half a million each. In Nigeria, as in so many tropical countries, the internal diversity of ethnic groups, languages, and cultures is a fact of fundamental importance for economic development planning.

Population growth. In relating population to economic development in any tropical country the rate of population growth is commonly a more important factor than is the size, density, or distribution of that population. Of the three variables that directly affect change in population numbers – births, deaths, and migration – the first two are nowadays by far the most important. In many countries population growth has in the past been very much a question of migrational surplus: in Malaya, for instance, the population growth up to about 1900 was almost exclusively a function of migration; and until recently Trinidad's population increased for the same reason. Today, however, migration is generally a negligible factor in population growth throughout the tropics, though labour migration – often of a temporary or seasonal nature – is still an important consideration in any analysis of the problem of labour supply, especially in parts of the African tropics.

In spite of the limitations of crude rates, it is worth emphasizing that rates of natural increase in tropical countries are not generally so high as is commonly supposed. Only in a few cases, such as Kenya and some of the Central American countries, is it over 3 per cent (Table 4). On the other hand, the potential for population growth is admittedly very high indeed, for the present figure is kept down – at least in most African and a few Asian countries – chiefly by high crude death rates. As these death rates are brought down, the large potential seems certain to assert itself. Almost all development programmes, indeed, must take account of the fact that the rate of population growth will accelerate as the control of diseases and improvements in maternity, child welfare, and hospital facilities lower death rates. Lewis (1955) distinguishes three sets of factors in the fall of death rates: the effects of better nourishment; better environmental improvements, especially in health; and modern hospitals, clinics, and similar institutions. Lewis calculates that each of these three groups might be responsible for a reduction of 1 per cent over a ten-year period: in other words, taken together, they can bring down the death rate from 4 to 1 per cent in a decade. How dramatically some of these factors can operate may be illustrated from Ceylon where the death rate fell by 34 per cent from 1946 to 1947 as a result of the use of DDT against endemic malaria: from 1945 to 1952 the death rate was reduced from 22 per thousand to 12 per thousand.

This argument varies from one country to another. In Gambia the present relatively low rate of population growth is caused by a high death rate; the infant mortality rate of 110 per thousand is one of the highest in the world; Gambia, consequently, has a large potential for reducing her death rate and so must face the fact that her rate of population growth must rise rapidly. Singapore, on the other hand, can reasonably hope for no significant increase in her relatively low rate of natural increase because this is not a function of a high death rate.

On the basis of available vital statistics, and ignoring for the moment the effects of migration, it can be said that the population of the humid tropics is increasing at an average rate of something between 2 and 3·5 per cent in tropical Asia and Africa, and between 1·5 and 3 per cent in tropical America. In other words, something like 40 million people are being added every year to the population of the humid tropics.

One of the most important demographic implications of this high or potentially high rate of natural increase is a large number of

Table 4. *Crude birth and death rates for selected countries* (1977)

	Crude birth rates/1,000	Crude death rates/1,000	Rate of natural increase/1,000
Tropical America			
Costa Rica	30	5	25
El Salvador	40	8	32
Guatemala	43	10	33
Jamaica	30	7	23
Mexico	42	9	33
Puerto Rico	22	6	18
Trinidad and Tobago	25	7	18
Brazil	37	9	28
Colombia	41	9	32
Surinam	41	7	34
Venezuela	36	7	29
Tropical Africa			
Central African Republic	43	23	20
Congo (Dem. Rep.)	45	21	24
Gambia	43	24	19
Ghana	49	22	27
Kenya	49	16	33
Senegal	48	24	24
Togo	51	23	28
Uganda	45	16	29
Zambia	52	20	32
Tropical Asia			
Brunei	30	4	26
Burma	40	16	24
India	35	16	19
Indonesia	43	17	26
Malaysia (West)	31	6	25
Pakistan	36	12	24
Singapore	17	5	12

Source: U.N. *Demographic Yearbook, 1977,* New York, 1978 (latest estimates)

children in proportion to the population of working ages. Whereas the age median in the United States is twenty-nine, in South-east Asia it is about eighteen. The proportion of the population under fifteen years of age varies from 35 to 45 per cent in several tropical developing countries, and the percentage of the total population thereby excluded, at least in theory, from the effective working population in tropical lands is about 40 per cent, whereas in many developed countries the figure is between 22 and 30 per cent. In practice, however, this theoretical burden of child dependency is lightened by the low age at which children enter the effective working force. For this reason a large family is frequently regarded as an economic asset.

The high proportion of children in the total population limits capital formation: the needs of the whole community have to be satisfied by a small working population so that little is left for the purposes of investment. Moreover, where infant mortality rates are high, an unusually large part of the investment made in the bearing and rearing of children is wasted because so many of them never live long enough to enter the adult labour force. Something like a quarter of the Indian national income is spent in maintaining those who die before they reach the age of fifteen, as compared with a figure of about one-fifteenth in Great Britain. All such figures are useful criteria of the quality and texture of life in a country.

The population problem. In most contemporary discussion on the economic development of tropical countries in America, Africa, and Asia, great emphasis is placed on the 'population problem'. Much is being written of the problems of population pressure and overpopulation, of the 'population explosion', and of the urgent need to limit births (Villard, 1963). Certainly anyone attempting to examine the problems of development in any tropical country cannot fail to see how important to his analysis is the population problem in all its manifestations; yet so diffuse is this whole question that it is difficult always to be precise, either about its meaning or about its implications for development.

Much of the discussion about the relationship between population distribution and density on the one hand and economic development on the other centres around the question of population pressure, and is based on the assumption that some areas are over-populated and that others are underpopulated. To express it another way, it is believed that there are too many or too few people in some areas to allow the fullest economic development. Implicit in any discussion of this kind, too, is the concept of optimal population.

A close examination of almost any particular case study usually reveals important limitations to these ideas. Population pressure is such a relative term – relative to natural resources, the extent of division of labour, the standard of living, techniques of production, and total economic structure – that it is useful only within the framework of a rigid and specific set of variables. Simple density figures are particularly suspect as an indicator of population pressure. Moreover, there is the paradox that 'a country may be over-populated relatively to its agricultural resources, but underpopu-lated relatively to its capacity for industrial development. Some very small countries, like Jamaica or Mauritius, face the problem that their populations are much too large in relation to agricultural development and at the same time much too small to support a wide range of industrial development' (Lewis, 1955: 87).

It can also be suggested that a high density of population is a necessary precondition for economic development in many tropical countries. Without following too closely the hypothesis that moderate physical obstacles to material advance have supplied the main stimulus to the growth of civilizations, there is little doubt that the most striking adaptations of human societies to the limita-tions of their tropical environment have been achieved in areas where population density was so high as to make life impossible without some such adaptations.

Much has been written on this question; but from the point of view of the present study it seems that too much emphasis is commonly placed upon the problem of population pressure in any consideration of economic development in tropical countries. In particular, the term 'population pressure' is too often used loosely as a synonym for high density of population, poverty, or distress. But poverty or distress – relative to conditions in western developed countries – are characteristic features of tropical developing countries almost everywhere, whether heavily populated or not. The use of the term population pressure is generally valid only when the distress or poverty is seen to result directly from there being too many people in an area – too many in the sense that fewer people would result in an improvement in the standard of living. In fact, however, such a relationship can rarely, if ever, be demonstrated; and, in practice, it is to be doubted whether it exists anywhere. Furthermore, it is perhaps not too much to suggest that population pressure in the sense of there being too many people in an area for the available natural resources – whether land or any other kind of natural resource – is a rare phenomenon in tropical under-developed lands. This is so, partly because of the remarks already made about natural resources – that it must be postulated that in no country is the lack of natural resources a limitation to economic development – but also because the whole concept of population pressure rests upon the stability of factors which are essentially dynamic variables. Natural resources (either by trading, applied research, or technological developments); capital supplies; and population numbers and density (by the normal operation of the variables of births, deaths, and migration) – all are continually changing phenomena.

Another idea commonly advanced in any discussion on population pressure in many developing countries of the tropics is the concept of 'disguised unemployment'. This suggests that 'surplus' labour in agriculture (and even in industry) can be extracted from their present occupations without affecting present production and can be put to use in the construction of productive capital goods like roads or irrigation works. In recent years, however, this idea has come in for a good deal of criticism, and the few available case studies suggest that the idea rarely works in practice. Furthermore, the disguised unemployment argument focuses attention, as does so much of the current discussion on population pressure, away from the central problem – how to raise productivity. As Myint (1964) has put it, the exponents of the disguised unemployment idea have tended rather to concentrate on 'how to increase the mere volume of unskilled work by extracting the surplus labour from agriculture, and have made a great point of saying that this can be done without improving the techniques of production' in the agricultural sector (p. 90). But the central problem of how to raise productivity remains.

The whole concept of pressure of population or overpopulation in relation to economic development seems, in fact, to be a vague, ambiguous, and even sterile idea. It is certainly responsible for a great deal of misunderstanding about the nature of development problems in tropical developing countries.

On the other hand, there seem to be firm grounds for asserting that the *rate* of population growth is central to any study of tropical development: in its simplest terms, the chief problem of tropical development is how to increase production at a rate substantially higher than the rate of population growth. The Malthusian position on this is well illustrated in the low-level equilibrium trap (Fig. 1),

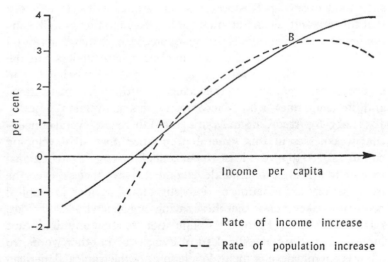

Fig. 1. The low-level equilibrium population trap (after Leibenstein, 1954; Nelson, 1956; and Kindleberger, 1966).

discussed by a number of writers, in which any short-term rise in *per capita* income is quickly exceeded by a more rapid gain in population numbers (A). In this context Leibenstein (1954) emphasizes the need for a critical minimum effort to escape this trap (B).

In terms of capital, as noted earlier, a high rate of population growth is costly. Assuming that about 3 per cent of the national income must be saved to provide capital for a 1 per cent increase in population (U.N., 1955), it follows that in some countries up to 10 per cent or so of the national income must be saved for demographic investment – merely to cope with the additional population without any increase in the average standard of living. In several countries, for instance, the population is growing at the rate of 3–3·5 per cent a year, so that these countries require a net domestic capital formation rate of 9–12 per cent merely to provide the increased population with a *per capita* endowment of capital assets every year. According to many writers, in fact, all developing countries need to save not less than 10 per cent of their national income as a precondition for any kind of development, and without such a rate of savings Rostow (1956) has argued in his stage theory that the 'take-off' as an automatic and self-generating growth cannot occur. In similar vein is the oft-quoted remark that 'the central problem in the theory of economic growth is to understand the process by which a community is converted from being a 5 to a 12 per cent saver – with all the changes in attitudes, in institutions and in techniques which accompany this conversion' (Lewis, 1955: 225–6). According to Myint (1964) there are several conceptual weaknesses in this general proposition that all developing countries need to save at least 10 per cent of their aggregate national income to achieve economic development. Nevertheless, even the most cursory examination of domestic capital savings in tropical countries makes it clear that these savings are generally insufficient, relative to the rate of growth of population, to allow any significant increase in the average standard of living – or in other words, to allow economic development. While some of the tropical American countries – Venezuela, Puerto Rico, Trinidad and Tobago – have annual growth rates in gross domestic product of over 6 per cent, most other countries – notably Honduras and Nicaragua in the Americas; Malawi, Nigeria, and Uganda in Africa; and Malaysia and Pakistan in Asia – are achieving rates of growth of gross domestic product barely sufficient to keep pace with the rise in population.

What measures can be used to meet this problem? There are two main lines of approach – one demographic, the other economic. The demographic approach includes a direct attack on the natural increase by the use of birth-control measures. The value of these in reducing birth rates is very much a matter of opinion. Until very recently, only a minority supported the large-scale artificial restriction of births on the grounds that it was for long unlikely to be effective in tropical developing lands where educational and economic standards are still low, and cultural, particularly religious, prejudices are difficult to overcome. More recently, however, an increasing number of writers have come out in support of propagating birth-control methods as potentially perhaps the most effective means of achieving economic prosperity. The development of the oral contraceptive and the popularization (in some parts of India, for instance) of voluntary sterilization have brought direct birth control much nearer as a practicable proposition.

However, without in any way dismissing the demographic approach to the population problem, it must be pointed out that the more fundamental and difficult task is to make people in the developing countries *want* to use birth-control measures. More important still, the recent upsurge of interest in birth control as a means of inducing economic growth in developing lands was perhaps a rather dangerous trend because birth control seemed to be becoming accepted as the latest and most fashionable of a series of panaceas. In a sense, however, to reduce the rate of population growth, while undoubtedly desirable, is simply to apply a negative solution, for by itself a declining birth rate can do nothing to increase production. An excessive preoccupation with how to reduce the birth rate is thus concentrating attention on the wrong thing. Furthermore, it normally fails to take account of the fact that the rate of natural increase will inevitably tend to stabilize itself when death rates reach the levels already reached in the developed world. Again, by western analogy and by analogy with Japanese experience, birth rates may ultimately fall as economic development – expressed in terms of a rising *per capita* income, urbanization, education, occupational changes, and the weakening of religious ties (Spengler, 1952) – proceeds. Finally, any such reduction of birth rates as envisaged by the supporters of large-scale birth-control programmes would, if successful, have serious long-term repercussions on population age structures. The demographic–economic problem as it has been posed here is very much more than simply a demographic problem. Its solution, therefore, must not lie solely in demographic terms.

As for the economic approach to the demographic–economic problem, this is directed at developing production at a rate greater than the rate of population growth; and under this heading lie two important measures – the increase of agricultural production and the development of industrialization. Both of these will receive more detailed treatment in later chapters of this book. Some of the demographic implications of such development, however, may be briefly noted here.

The increase of agricultural production implies both its areal extension and its intensification. The areal extension of agricultural land, or agricultural colonization, normally has one or more of three aims: to increase the total food production, to relieve population pressure in the area from which colonists come, and to encourage economic development in the area to which colonists go. Thus in Indonesia, official support for agricultural colonization in the islands outside Java is designed to increase the total amount of food produced within Indonesia, to relieve population pressure in Java and, finally, to assist in the development of the more sparsely peopled islands. Although pioneer agricultural settlement may possibly be successful in raising the total amount of food produced within a country, and is sometimes successful in promoting economic development in the new area, there is no evidence that the redistribution of population for agricultural colonization in the tropics has anywhere appreciably lessened population pressure in the country of origin. The numbers involved have never been large enough over a short enough period. In 1953 the Indonesian Government moved some 50,000 colonists from Java to sparsely peopled islands, chiefly Sumatra and Borneo. Such a figure constituted less than one-tenth of the natural increase in Java during that year.

Furthermore, migration may even increase distress in the area of origin because of its effects on the age and sex structure, for migration commonly involves the younger, more active male section of the population. This has been demonstrated in Togo, where it has been shown that far from relieving population pressure, the emigration of Cabrais into central Togo commonly increases distress in the Cabrais country. Of the population present in Cabrais country in 1957, for instance, the female dominance was striking, notably in the fifteen to fifty-nine age group, upon which the bulk of the farm work relies. This disparity, giving a total sex ratio of 120 females to 100 males, is almost wholly the result of emigration.

All schemes for agricultural colonization have to face the dilemma that if the shift of population is large enough and speedy enough to reduce significantly population density in the place of origin, then the rate of immigration into the new area is likely seriously to strain its capacity for absorbing people. And unless it is planned and controlled it can hinder rather than assist development.

As subsequent chapters will attempt to show, the extension and intensification of agricultural production is very much a matter of applied research. Taken together, the extension and intensification of agricultural production constitute important measures to meet the demographic–economic problem in tropical countries. The nature and relative emphasis of these measures must, of course, vary from one country to another, depending on population density and the present pattern and intensity of land use: in densely populated Java the emphasis is on intensification by various means whereas in Sumatra the extension of agricultural land is of first importance. In some countries a combination of these measures is emphasized. Thus in the Philippines the increase of food production from 7·3 million tons in 1955 to 11·3 million tons in 1959 was partly accounted for by the extension of agricultural land – about 5 million acres (2 million ha) of public land was distributed during the five years; production increases, however, also arose from improved farm practices, soil conservation, improvements in irrigation, and the use of fertilizers.

As for industrialization, meaning not only the development of primary and secondary manufacturing industries but also the mechanization of agriculture, one of the commonest arguments for promoting industrialization in underdeveloped countries is that it will be accompanied by urbanization which, by western analogy, brings about a decline in fertility. Certainly the relevant social transformations are more easily effected in towns than in rural areas. But on the other hand, such a decline in fertility must lag well behind the expected decline in death rates previously referred to, so that no immediate reduction in the rate of natural increase of population could be expected. Analogies between western countries and the countries of the tropics are dangerous because the potential for population expansion in tropical countries is in most cases greater than it ever was in western countries at the early stages of their industrialization. Several writers have shown that the increase in population in Western Europe followed, not preceded, the industrial revolution, whereas in the developing countries today the population explosion is preceding the true industrial revolution. The situation in the developing countries today, then, makes any general increase in prosperity more difficult than it was in England around 1780, or in France around 1820.

Urbanization is also held to reduce population pressure on the land, for urbanization is frequently a function of migration from rural to urban areas. Gourou (1966) has advised relieving the rural density in overcrowded tropical Asia by this means. But such an urban drift can lead to increased pressure of rural population because here again there is often a disproportionately large number of young adults in these peasant migrants to the towns, because such migration hastens the decline in rural industries, and because it may lead to a decline in food production in the rural areas. Moreover, urbanization often leads to severe problems of population pressure in the urban centres themselves. As in many parts of the world, the large cities and towns tend to grow more quickly than the medium-sized and small towns. It is chiefly from the large cities that most of the broader benefits of industrialization can be expected to radiate. And although town planning can help to meet the problem of housing in such centres, it can do little to affect the problem of employment arising out of urban population pressure; certainly one of the most distressing features of many large tropical cities is the squalid, congested nature of much of the housing, exemplified in parts of Calcutta, in the slums of Rio de Janeiro, or in the *ranchos* of Caracas.

Industrialization has one important demographic disadvantage compared with agricultural production as a measure to cope with the demographic-economic problem in tropical lands: it is less effective at absorbing labour. The application of those western technological devices aimed at saving labour may appear unsuitable, even illogical, in a tropical context with its problems of under-employment. The high population density in those parts of the tropics most likely to attract and stimulate industrial development must limit the pace of introduction of any labour-saving machinery. This disadvantage applies not only to manufacturing industry but also to the mechanization of agriculture. Consequently, such measures as seed improvement and the scientific use of fertilizers should perhaps play a larger part in schemes for intensifying agricultural production than should the more expensive and labour-saving measures of mechanized agriculture. As subsequent chapters will show, however, the problem is much more complicated than this.

The whole population issue is immensely diffuse and controversial, and it has only been possible here to refer to a few of the major problems relevant to this study. A number of important considerations have been touched upon only very briefly. For instance, little has been said of the absolute size of the population base, although this is important for three reasons. In the first place, a country with a huge population base presents in many ways a more formidable problem than does a country with a small population, even if the latter's population is increasing at a faster rate. The 13 millions being added to India's population every year clearly pose more serious issues than do the 50,000 extra Togolese. Secondly, the varied problems of economic development in those developing countries with large populations today are both more urgent and more difficult than in the developed world where large populations grew up after, and as a consequence of, economic development. Finally, as will become apparent in the following chapters, the lines along which countries attempt to solve their demographic–economic problem are to some extent affected by the size of the total population. While the size of a domestic market is, of course, a function of more than simple population totals, countries like India and Brazil clearly offer more favourable environments for setting up those heavy industries which depend for their success upon economies of scale. On the other hand, countries like Ceylon and Trinidad, with relatively small populations, are believed to be handicapped in their industrial development by the smallness of their domestic markets.

Much remains to be learned about demographic–economic relationships, more especially in the developing lands of the tropics. Much of what has been said above is controversial, and it is always difficult to be quite sure that one is entirely free from cultural prejudices and is not affected by too facile analogies with western experiences. There is no doubt, however, that all tropical countries have a population problem in some form or another, and that this problem must be fully considered in all plans for economic and social development. It has been argued above, however, that the central problem of economic development in all tropical countries is what has been called here a demographic–economic problem – how to ensure that production rates of increase consistently outstrip the rates of increase of population. It has been argued that the solution lies less in attempting directly to control population growth than in a rapid increase of production. The chapters that follow concentrate attention on how to achieve this, beginning with agriculture.

CHAPTER 6
Types of Tropical Agriculture

Of all possible lines of development in tropical developing countries, perhaps the most important and certainly the most widespread relate to the improvement of agricultural production. Any comparative study of agriculture in the tropics, however, reveals striking regional differences in agricultural practices and types of agricultural enterprises; and these differences make it impossible to generalize about tropical agriculture, especially where this concerns problems of and potentialities for development. While some types of tropical agriculture are believed by many writers to be limiting factors to development, other types receive wide support as the rational basis for agricultural development policy. The present chapter makes a brief assessment of a number of the most significant of these agricultural types from the point of view of the part they can play in the general processes of agricultural improvement.

Shifting-field cultivation. Perhaps the most widely condemned of all agricultural types in the tropics is shifting-field cultivation; and attempts to effect a change over from shifting-field to permanent-field cultivation loom large in several agricultural development plans. It is widely assumed that shifting-field cultivation constitutes an important restriction to development, especially in Africa, where it is most common, though it is also widespread in parts of tropical America and to a lesser extent in the more lightly populated parts of tropical Asia.

Much has been written on the question of shifting-field, or 'swidden' cultivation (Pelzer, 1957; Conklin, 1961; Watters, 1960), and a certain amount of controversy has arisen over terminology. As defined by Pelzer (1957) it is an agricultural system which is characterized by a rotation of fields rather than crops, by preliminary clearing by 'slash and burn', and by short periods of cropping alternating with long fallow periods. Only human labour is used – there are usually no draught animals – manuring is not practised, and the chief tool is the hoe. Other writers, however, feel it necessary to distinguish between shifting-field cultivation and rotational bush fallowing, the latter involving no movement of settlement; it is pointed out that rotational bush fallowing has often developed out of shifting-field cultivation as a result of a trend towards fixed settlement. And Brookfield (1960: 237), discussing the case of New Guinea, argues for distinguishing between swidden cultivation, long-fallow cultivation, and semi-permanent cultivation – the latter occurring only when the period of fallow is so short that the actual field boundaries are preserved from one period of cultivation to the next. For the purposes of the present study, however, the term shifting-field cultivation is taken to refer to all types of agriculture that are not strictly permanent-field.

There is irrefutable evidence of the dangers and limitations of this type of agriculture. Clearly the whole system depends on sufficient land being available so that adequate fallowing can take place. Especially where population density is high or where custom restricts the cultivable area, the system can lead to soil exhaustion, loss of fertility (especially by destruction of humus in the upper layers of the soil) and soil erosion. Shifting-field cultivation may also be responsible for the disappearance and degradation of forests. In southern Ivory Coast, for instance, it has been estimated that 12·5 million acres (5 million ha) of forest have been reduced to secondary jungle and bush as a result of shifting-field cultivation methods used by a million or so people living in the forest and needing a farming area ten times larger than that needed by the same number of people using permanent-field methods of cultivation. It will be obvious, too, that shifting-field cultivation is often largely responsible for the very low percentage of land under cultivation in parts of the tropics. Again, this type of cultivation has been held to constitute a major limitation to the spread of permanent tree crops; in Zandeland, de Schlippe (1956) has noted that shifting-field cultivation restricts the development of the oil palm, a crop which, he claims, could become a great asset to the agriculture and nutrition of the Azoroh if, as a crop, it was integrated into a system in which permanency of habitation and protection from bush fires would give it a chance. In many countries, indeed, shifting-field cultivation is now illegal (as in Malaya) or controlled (as in Ceylon).

On the other hand, shifting-field cultivation in some form or another must originally have been the practice of pioneer agriculturalists in most parts of the world and so may be regarded simply as an expression of a civilizational level – a stage through which most agricultural systems have at one time passed. Moreover, the destruction caused by shifting-field cultivation is often exaggerated. The removal of natural vegetation in tropical rain forests containing many large trees is an arduous undertaking, and usually the practice adopted is to remove only the smaller trees and undergrowth and leave the larger trees. These larger trees help in forest regeneration when the land is eventually abandoned, and the ash derived from the burning of the smaller trees and undergrowth helps to provide a soil rich in phosphorus and potash. Then there are a number of local variants, many of which have been empirically evolved to meet some of the limitations of the system. Thus in some forms of the *chitemene* system of Zambia the large trees are lopped and the loppings burnt together with the undergrowth, supplemented with loppings and undergrowth cut from adjoining uncultivated areas. The increase in the amount of ash allows land to be cultivated for longer periods than would otherwise be possible under ordinary methods of shifting-field cultivation.

One important advantage of shifting-field cultivation is that it provides a way of dealing with the very severe weed problem with which tropical cultivators are commonly faced. Burning destroys weeds and controls the growth of weed seeds for some time; and this point has been singled out by some writers as constituting the chief attraction of the whole system for the tropical cultivator. Certainly the imminence of weed invasion is a common indicator used by the farmer to ascertain when it is time to abandon his plot; but nevertheless it has been suggested that one of the best agricultural services which could be rendered in the tropics is to supply peasant cultivators with herbicides to control weed growth (Clark and Haswell, 1964).

Yet another advantage of shifting-field cultivation as an agricultural system is that it requires less labour to produce a specified amount of food than does the system of permanent-field agriculture. This is an important issue, for many writers have assumed the opposite: '*per se* it is no more difficult for an African family to cultivate a piece of land on the lines indicated for permanent cultivation, than to follow its ancient customs of shifting-field agriculture' (Pim, 1946: 21). Yet it is often pointed out that the preference shown by tropical farmers for shifting-field rather than permanent-field cultivation is really one of preference for leisure. Shifting-field techniques of production are more economical from the point of view of labour; 'in spite of the high initial input of labour, overall labour requirements of shifting agriculture are low and discontinuous' (Clark and Haswell, 1964: 71). Present evidence suggests strongly that shifting-field cultivation yields better returns in terms of labour input than does permanent-field cultivation. It is hardly surprising then to find that a tropical peasant may choose the former rather than the latter as long as conditions of population density allow him this choice. There are many examples of the truth of this assertion. Thus the Cabrais farmer of northern Togo, moving southwards to colonize part of the empty 'middle belt', quickly adopts shifting-field cultivation methods instead of perpetuating in his new surroundings the sophisticated system of intensive permanent-field cultivation which has characterized his densely populated homeland for centuries. Again, as Geddes (1954) points out for the Sarawak Land Dyaks, although sedentary swamp rice cultivation gives higher yields of about 1,700 lb per acre (1,903 kg per ha), preference is invariably given to the production of dry/hill rice in the hills where yields are only 1,400 lb per acre (1,578 kg per ha), using shifting-field cultivation methods; for whereas yield per man-hour on the swamp is 0·87 kg (giving a total input of 2,165 hours per ha), in the hill areas yield per man-hour worked is 0·95 kg (giving a total input of 1,663 hours per ha). In areas of low population density absolute yields per unit area are, of course, of very much less importance to the farmer than are yields per unit of labour.

It is possible, then, to defend the system of shifting-field cultivation within limits. The system is by no means to be condemned out of hand. It is not an unsuitable method of agriculture 'where population density is low enough to permit sufficiently long fallow periods so that soil fertility can be maintained by means of a grass ley in those parts of the tropics where shifting-field cultivators work grasslands and by means of a second-growth forest in forest areas' (Pelzer, 1957: 73). On balance it would seem that shifting-field cultivation, or some modification of it, need not necessarily restrict agricultural development and may, in fact, be the best form of land use in the early stages of settlement where population density is low. Pelzer is surely justified in concluding that the least imaginative approach to the problem of shifting-field agriculture in development is that of outlawing the practice, without showing the cultivators an alternative, without showing them how to develop a more intensive type of land use, and without making certain that shifting-field cultivation is not, in fact, sound in the social and natural environmental conditions under which the cultivators live.

The critical factor in any assessment of the unsuitability or otherwise of shifting-field cultivation is the density of population or, to put it in another way, the amount of cultivable land available *per capita*. What exactly the critical density is at which shifting-field cultivation becomes undesirable it is impossible to generalize about, estimates varying from 5 persons to the square mile (2 per km²) in Zambia to over 310 persons to the square mile (120 per km²) in Guatemala. In this connexion specific mention must be made of the work of Allan (1965) who developed in Zambia a method of calculating the carrying capacities, in terms of population, of various indigenous and changing agricultural practices on different types of soil; he also formulated a way of working out for different systems the critical population density beyond which the land would begin to deteriorate. This critical density figure must depend very much on a combination of local circumstances. Within the context of any one specific area, however, there seems to be a strong and natural causal connexion between an increasing density of population and the need to change over from shifting-field to permanent-field cultivation. Once the density of population reaches a point at which adequate fallowing is impossible, then the system of shifting-field cultivation breaks down; it must then be replaced by one in which at least the same amount of food can be produced from a smaller area of land continuously cropped. This relationship between population density and agriculture has been demonstrated by a number of writers, including Grove (1957) for northern Nigeria. In such a change over, however, certain techniques and practices such as manuring and crop rotation are usually essential features. These will be discussed later; but it may be noted here that there are many instances of quite indigenous adaptations or changes along these lines, so that where the need has arisen the shifting-field cultivator has always been able to change over to permanent-field cultivation, with all the refinements of techniques this implies. Apart from the innumerable examples of indigenous intensive permanent-field cultivation in such large areas as the Kano close-settled zone of northern Nigeria and the Boukombe area of north-western Dahomey, there is in almost all parts of the tropics some development of compound-land farming – *kampong* land in South-east Asia – around even the smallest rural settlements.

Presumably, however, large-scale empirical adaptations and changes of this kind occur under natural conditions only very slowly and lag behind the need to change as expressed in a rising density of population and falling levels of living. The central question today is not whether shifting-field cultivation is desirable or undesirable but how to encourage in any specific case a more rapid change over from shifting-field to permanent-field cultivation than that brought about through the stimulus of an increasing density of population. Here is an important though as yet almost untouched field of applied research.

Wet-rice cultivation. Wet-rice cultivation would seem to merit special though necessarily very brief consideration in this study of types of tropical agriculture because it is widely believed to be an ideal towards which many parts of the African and American tropics should aspire. It is often pointed out that wet-rice cultivation is associated with some of the most densely populated and long-settled parts of Asia and with the homes of a number of civilizations. Wet-rice cultivation is also permanent-field cultivation *par excellence*. Rice also has the highest nutritive value per unit area of all the tropical cereals, can grow largely irrespective of the fertility of the soil, and is not normally associated with problems of soil erosion. According to several writers, indeed, the absence of wet-rice cultivation in a tropical country is generally speaking a mark of economic backwardness. And it is certainly true that some of the most remarkable innovations in indigenous agriculture are provided by wet-rice cultivators like the Ifugao people of the Philippines, who cultivate terraces constructed some 4,000 years ago.

The cultivation of wet rice is now being encouraged in many parts of both the equatorial and savanna areas of the American and African tropics. In the Amazon Basin rice is being extended into the tidal and seasonal flood plains; and in the Sokoto region of northern Nigeria the *fadamas* (swamplands) – formerly dry-season grazing grounds for Fulani cattle – are being utilized for wet-rice cultivation on an increasing scale.

The development of land for wet-rice cultivation, however, faces a number of difficulties. Topographical conditions are not always suitable: in tropical Africa, in particular, there are few large flood plains. It is possible to create the necessary topographical conditions by terracing, as is shown so clearly in the Philippines, but unless labour is plentiful such works may be impracticable. As Pelzer has emphasized, 'land that can be kept inundated for all or part of the year is more valuable than high land from the cultivation point of view. This reflects the amount of labour that has to be invested in order to alter the topography, so that water can be held at a desired level and drained off when necessary' (Pelzer, 1957: 12). Climatically, too, the Asian sector of the tropics is favoured by the monsoonal conditions which give sufficient water but also guarantee substantial periods of dry, sunny conditions: truly equatorial conditions are by no means ideal for rice growing in that the cloud cover is too sustained and rain is always likely. The tropical savanna climate is also not ideal in that the total amount of rainfall is usually inadequate by itself.

Perhaps the greatest limitation to the extension of wet-rice cultivation in the tropical sectors of America and Africa, however, is cultural. It is difficult, for instance, to see the Yoruba of West Africa changing over quickly or easily from a yam-cassava to a rice culture. To most Africans, indeed, yams, cassava, maize, millets, sorghums, and plantains are their traditional basic foodstuffs; and most agricultural efforts to increase food production will probably continue to be directed chiefly at the production of these crops. Only in certain specially restricted areas are there real hopes for extending the production of rice. It is certainly misleading and un-realistic to suggest that rice, any more than any other single crop, should form the keystone of tropical agricultural development policy.

Subsistence and cash agriculture. Only rarely is it possible to make a clear distinction between subsistence and cash agriculture. To some extent this is a semantic problem. Some writers refer to 'sub-sistence crops', meaning thereby cereals and roots, and others talk of 'subsistence crop farming' to mean shifting-field cultivation or equivalent 'primitive' forms of agriculture. Yet another use of the term subsistence is to refer to 'subsistence economies' which clearly include the consideration of manufacturing as well as agri-cultural activities.

More important, however, the difficulty of distinguishing clearly between subsistence and cash farming is due to the fact that pure subsistence agriculture, in which no crops are produced for cash exchange at all, is now a very rare phenomenon indeed. In practice, a clear distinction can only be made between subsistence farming and cash or commercial farming at the extreme ends of the range – between a farmer who grows nothing at all for cash at one end and the farmer who grows everything for cash and nothing for local consumption at the other end. More commonly, tropical farmers practise a system which may involve a considerable degree of sub-sistence agriculture, varying perhaps from year to year and from season to season, yet always involving too an element – sometimes a substantial element – of cash cropping (McMaster, 1962). Sub-sistence agriculture today may perhaps most usefully be defined as an agricultural type which is devoted mainly to the production of food for local consumption but includes also a varying proportion of cash cropping. The very imprecision of this definition, how-ever, is significant. One of the critical factors, clearly, is the in-tention of the farmer. If the farmer merely sells his surplus or sells some of it when he needs a bit of extra cash, then he is still a sub-sistence farmer; whereas if he cultivates with the intention of sell-ing most of it he is a cash or commercial farmer. Yet this intention is itself a highly variable factor. Whether a Yoruba farmer, for in-stance, keeps all his yams, sells some of them or sells all of them, depends on his own particular food requirements in that year, the price of yams, his assessment of future price changes, and a host of other variables, many of them non-economic. Finally, it is not always clear whether to participate in local as distinct from more distant or external exchange for the disposal of agricultural pro-duce implies a departure from subsistence agriculture.

Almost any tropical country is full of examples of how this difficulty of distinguishing between subsistence and cash agri-culture operates in practice. For Malaya it has been shown how a Malay will, 'with the help of his wife, cultivate enough rice for himself and family, grow vegetables after the rice harvest to supplement the family diet and sell in the local market, and have a small area of rubber trees which he taps to sell the produce to a Chinese dealer for export. This mingling of activities has its advantages, by spreading the risks .... His subsistence agriculture, then, serves as a kind of backlog for his economic system, and con-centration on the export crop alone would result in an unbalanced system of production' (Firth, 1946: 22). This kind of situation is nowadays very much the rule rather than the exception.

It is clear, then, that the whole concept of subsistence agriculture is essentially a dynamic one, and is perhaps best thought of as being but part of a continuum or succession of stages. Thus for Africa, indigenous agricultural resources have been divided in United Nations reports into crops mainly for local consumption; crops partly for consumption and partly for export; and crops

mainly for export. Another classification refers to different economies – 'commercial', 'commercial-subsistence', and 'subsistence
with some commercial' – using the criterion of reducing propensity
to exchange. Winter (1956) has outlined the stages of agricultural
development from the point of view of an administrator imposing
taxation (Clark and Haswell, 1964):

(i) pure subsistence (no cash crops, no taxes, no import or
export of labour);

(ii) subsistence with taxes (some cash crops, labour going to
seek employment primarily to pay taxes);

(iii) subsistence and cash crops (cash crops grown primarily
for own cash needs, not primarily for taxes. No labour export);

(iv) subsistence and cash (cash crops grown primarily for own
cash needs, not primarily for taxes. Labour export important);

(v) agricultural plantations (most agricultural labour working
for wages);

(vi) industrial economy.

Winter's scheme is of particular value here in that it sketches the
normal trend of subsistence farming through commercial agriculture towards 'industrialized agriculture' and an industrially
oriented economy. In spite of its limitations, this scheme does
provide a conceptual framework within which to examine the
highly variable and discrete data about tropical cultivators and
their place in the general processes of economic development.

The importance to tropical development studies of this notion
of a continuum between purely subsistence farming at one end
and commercial farming at the other is emphasized by the common
assumption that successful economic development involves a decrease in the proportion of subsistence farming and an increase in
cash cropping. Some economists, indeed, do not regard subsistence
agriculture as an economic activity at all. Yet while most tropical
countries are rightly concerned to extend their non-subsistence
sector, the fact remains that still the larger proportion of food consumed by many, probably most tropical peoples, is still grown on a
subsistence basis. Consequently, far from trying to push subsistence farming farther into the background in development planning,

an immediate need is to try by all possible means to improve the efficiency of the subsistence sector. One of the limitations of subsistence farming is that little attention has been paid to scientific research into the staple food crops with which subsistence farmers are most closely concerned. Agricultural research in the tropics has concentrated upon the commercial crops which are exported to industrial countries (sugar, rubber, tea, and cocoa) and has almost entirely neglected what is produced for home consumption (yams, cassava, and sorghums). Only over the last decade or so has the picture begun to change. This is an important issue. It is not a question of trying artificially to bolster up subsistence farming with the intention of delaying any natural transition to commercial farming on the part of tropical cultivators; for apart from any other considerations, the crops involved are not exclusively 'subsistence crops' at all but crops which play an important part in cash farming as well. The transition from subsistence to cash farming does not imply a complete change of crops on the farm.

Without here questioning the need for a transition from subsistence to cash farming on the part of many tropical cultivators, a few of the implications of this transition may usefully be pointed out (Upton, 1966). One of the economic implications of the introduction of cash cropping is that land requirements per man tend to increase. There are two reasons for this: each man is willing to devote an increasing proportion of his working year to agriculture, assuming the effectiveness of the incentives for him to do so; and technical improvements increase the area which a man can handle (Clark and Haswell, 1964). There are difficulties, then, to be encountered in trying to encourage a greater proportion of cash farming in densely populated rural areas, although as a subsistence economy develops it is able to direct a gradually increasing proportion of its labour force to non-agricultural tasks. Furthermore, while in the normal course of events we should expect agricultural growth beyond the subsistence level to be in livestock products or crops other than staple food crops such as cereals and roots, in practice a country may continue to expand its production of these crops beyond its own requirements and export some of them. Another consideration to bear in mind is that as a subsistence farming community becomes more of a commercial farming community it tends at first to consume more of its own food: in other words, with the increase in cash farming the demands on subsistence crop farming increase. Here is further support for the view that subsistence farming must not be viewed simply as an anachronistic if picturesque survival from the past.

In spite of these reservations, however, there can be little doubt that the development of cash farming is a vital element in economic development and is a necessary prerequisite for and concomitant of industrialization and urbanization. But this accepted, the question arises – how is this development to be brought about? To a very large extent the effective extension of political, social, and economic control within the boundaries of most countries in the tropics has introduced taxation and so, inevitably, at least some element of cash farming; indeed, European administrations in colonial times frequently introduced taxes with the deliberate objective of promoting a transition from a purely subsistence agriculture to a cash economy. But as Winter points out, the tax incentive is generally left behind in subsequent stages in the trend towards purely commercial farming.

Once a community has discovered the opportunity of earning and spending cash, it does not automatically seek to work longer hours in order to earn more money. Numerous instances of this point have been described and the reasons for it discussed. One reason why the purely economic incentive does not always work is related to differing attitudes to work and material rewards on the part of the tropical cultivator. Thus in Indonesia it has been noted that 'preference for periods of idleness among Indonesians is to some extent derived from a philosophical outlook, backed up by bitter experience, which has taught that a life of ceaseless toil is hardly human, because it allows little opportunity for development of the spirit' (Indonesian Govt., 1951). In their non-agricultural hours, too, tropical peasants may have to make clothes, build and repair houses, or perform religious and similar duties. To some extent it is true that the opportunity to earn more may itself bring about the desired change in attitudes on the part of the tropical cultivator. But, again as Clark and Haswell (1964) have pointed out, an examination of the economics of subsistence agriculture commonly reveals a falling off of marginal returns to further labour inputs in any given area.

This whole question of incentives is clearly crucial in any consideration of specific measures to encourage cash farming. Much emphasis is often given to technological developments of one kind or another, but to the farmer concerned with the problem of whether or not to increase his cash crop participation perhaps the most critical factor is market opportunity. Most immediately the peasant is concerned with his own local market opportunities and organization for handling his cash crops, though on a wider scale this may be a matter of world markets. As one writer has noted, 'production for the world market has been an essential element in providing a large part of the peasant's cash income and raising his standard of living. But until a system has been evolved of effectively controlling the prices of raw materials (or food) on world markets so as to ensure a reasonable long-term security for the producer, the peasant has a serious problem in deciding what time and energy he should put into export production as against subsistence production' (Firth, 1946: 2). Another most important and closely related factor is transport. Both these factors will be examined in more detail in later chapters.

Smallholdings and plantations. Though the development of the production of cash crops may be accepted as a necessary element in economic development, there is some controversy over the relative merits of the two main methods of achieving such development – by the plantation or by the smallholding system. Historically, it is true, the production of cash crops for export on a large scale has been most closely associated with the plantation, especially for bananas, cocoa, coconut products, coffee, oil-palm products, rubber, sugar and tea, though the relative share of plantation and smallholding cultivation has always been subject to violent changes. Yet in West Africa, for instance, the cocoa industry has been built up almost entirely by native smallholders; and in Malaya smallholders are responsible for some two-thirds of the rubber production. The importance of the smallholder in tropical agricultural production is widely underestimated, especially in such exporting countries as Burma and Thailand (for rice), Colombia, Ivory Coast, and Togo (for coffee), Bangladesh (for rice and jute), Ghana and Nigeria (for cocoa), and Uganda (for cotton). Small-holdings – using the term in its widest sense to cover small shifting-field cultivators as well as the most sophisticated forms of peasant permanent-field cultivation – have always been responsible for the bulk of agricultural production, if not of large-scale export pro-duction, in the tropics. There are, in fact, few if any exclusively plantation crops; cocoa and oil palm, for instance, are peasant smallholding products in West Africa, but are plantation products in Brazil, Indonesia, and Malaya.

The plantation usually refers to a large-scale combined agri-cultural and industrial enterprise that is both labour-intensive and capital-intensive; it also raises, and usually processes industrially, agricultural commodities for the world market. Size and processing equipment are often important criteria. But the definition varies from country to country and from crop to crop: in Malaya, for in-stance, the rubber plantation is defined simply in terms of size, 100 acres (40 ha) or more constituting a plantation. In general the size of plantations tends to increase, except where they are indi-genous, as in parts of West Africa, or sold to indigenous peoples. On the other hand, recent studies on the smallholder in tropical agriculture indicate that the smallholder percentage in total pro-duction is increasing.

Most cash crops affected by plantation activities are tree crops, and in this fact lies much of the significance to tropical develop-ment of the relative advantages of the smallholding and plantation systems. For as many writers have pointed out, the development of tree crops is one of the keystones of tropical agricultural develop-ment. Pelzer (1957) notes that after the forest is cleared the soil may produce one good annual crop, but a second crop is greatly reduced in yield after the wood ash has been used up; thereafter it hardly pays to continue cultivation for the production of annuals. On the other hand, it may well pay to plant less demanding tree crops, such as rubber, on relatively infertile soil, especially where the woody matter is not burned but is broken down more gradually by the micro-fauna and micro-flora inhabiting the soil. Again, from the ecological point of view the cultivation of deep-rooting perennials, such as trees, is a highly desirable form of land use in the tropics, especially where land cannot be brought under ley-field cultivation or when soils are of medium or low fertility and therefore not suited to continuous cropping with shallow-rooting annuals.

There is little agreement about the relative long-term prospects of plantations and smallholdings in plans for economic development. Wickizer (1960) thinks that plantations can assume risks better, are better informed – they are certainly much more likely to apply the results of modern research than are smallholders – and are better able to judge future requirements. Bauer (1957), on the other hand, says that rises in wages and salaries have substantially weakened the competitive position of estates against smallholdings, and may well weaken the world's demands for tropical plantation products and stimulate the production of synthetics; he regards as a weakness of plantations their heavy overhead costs and the reliance of plantations on large numbers of hired workers, many of whom may leave when prices are higher elsewhere. Pelzer (1957) agrees that peasant holdings can certainly compete with plantations in the labour market. Reference is also commonly made to the arguments advanced against the establishment of the plantation system in West Africa, where the British authorities supported peasant smallholding agriculture as having in the West African context the advantages of firmer roots, lower costs, and greater adaptability to rapid expansion or change. As McPhee (1926) has noted, the value of the peasant method in West Africa was that it could be easily grafted on to the traditional economy.

A further argument against the plantation system rests upon the historical association of plantations with monocultural economies. Early European pioneers saw potential profit in developing the almost unlimited virgin lands of the tropics. Towards this end they imposed agricultural methods which were based on the practices of peoples of the temperate regions. Not infrequently these practices resulted in the establishment of monocultural systems of production, with consequent ill-effects on fertility. Moreover, monocultural systems of agriculture may leave a country wide open to world price fluctuations and crop failure. Thus Brazilian economic development has been held to be restricted, not by want of land or natural wealth but by want of labour and capital, 'and the fact that for 400 years the economy of the country was dominated by a series of monocultures': sugar-cane, cacao, tobacco, cotton, rubber, and coffee (Humphreys, 1946: 112–13). Again, the monocultural system is particularly susceptible to the onslaught of diseases. This holds true in temperate climates to some extent, but under tropical conditions infestations can easily become widespread epidemics; blights which have affected the cotton, cocoa, rubber, and banana industries in the past may face the monocultures of the future.

It seems that in certain circumstances and for certain crops – notably tea – the plantation may well be the best system for tropical countries, and in many countries plantations are now being introduced or reintroduced. Many new political leaders in the developing countries, however, still view the plantation with suspicion as an institution created by and for colonialism, though they recognize that in certain circumstances the plantation system has important advantages over the peasant smallholding system of cultivation. On the other hand, it is equally clear that smallholdings have a number of advantages over plantations in that they are usually more diversified in their crop structure and may include an element, perhaps an important element, of subsistence food agriculture; in this sense the smallholding system can provide greater security. Most of the available data suggest the invalidity of many of the comparisons commonly made between the two systems. To some extent they are not comparable because the criteria of judgement are different: to the smallholder interest focuses around maximum production per man-hour and per unit area, whereas in plantations maximum yield per tree and per tapper are normally the more important criteria. Furthermore, the smallholder's interests are more diffuse, for he often has other crops – including subsistence crops – which take some of his interest. This is clearly an important point in development planning, since policies aimed at improving smallholder cultivation are not necessarily relevant to the improvement of plantations.

In one of the most important analyses of the role of the smallholder in tropical export-crop production, Wickizer (1960) examines the relative significance of the smallholding and plantation systems for specific tropical crops. He comes to a conclusion that fits in with trends in tropical export-crop production since his work was published: the role of the smallholder in commercial agriculture in the tropics is quite clearly increasing, but without completely displacing the plantation system or its equivalents.

Livestock farming. The need for introducing livestock into the agricultural systems of many parts of the tropics has already been indicated on a number of occasions. Apart from dietetic considerations – in particular the provision of animal protein elements in diet – there are many agricultural and industrial products associated with livestock rearing, notably hides, skins, wool, and dairy produce. It is especially desirable where there is a short rainy season and farming operations have to be concentrated into very short time periods. Finally, and perhaps most important, by providing manure, livestock farming constitutes an important element in attempts to effect that change over from shifting-field to permanent-field systems of cultivation discussed earlier in this chapter.

The generally small amount and poor quality of tropical livestock farming is due to a number of factors. In the first place, the average quality of the indigenous livestock – buffaloes, zebu cattle, swine, goats, sheep, and poultry – is low. As Tempany and Grist (1958) have noted, the chief methods of improving animals in the tropics are by selection within the native type, by grading up with improved types or breeds from other countries, and by the development of new types from animals that are partly graded towards the improved type. Increasing attention is being paid to the reaction of animals to climatic factors, a subject of particular importance because the upbreeding of indigenous tropical livestock frequently entails introducing animals from temperate regions. Disease is also responsible for the absence or poor quality of livestock in many parts of the tropics. Especially in tsetse-infected areas, the extension of livestock management must depend either upon controlling the fly distribution or upon the successful rearing of further disease-resistant strains.

At least of equal importance to the quality of the stock, however, is the quality of the pasture. Fodder grass is more abundant than good pasture grass in most tropical countries. Elephant grass (*Pennisetum purpurem*) has been found to be one of the most satisfactory fodder grasses, though it is unsuitable for pasture – except in its early stages – because it grows up to as high as 15 feet (4·6 m). Guinea grass (*Panicum maximum*) is another good fodder grass, though again it does not seem to be a satisfactory pasture grass. Generally speaking, tropical grasses are lacking in nutritive value, even where they are abundant, and result in a slow growth of animals and in the need to allow large areas of grazing per animal. At present, research on tropical grassland agronomy is only in its infancy and the potentialities of the tropics in this respect are not fully known. Sufficient experiments have not yet been made on the extent to which efficient grassland management and improved animal husbandry can influence the production of different plant associations under the wide range of conditions of soil and climate which occur in tropical latitudes. Nevertheless, it does seem that the grass resources of the tropics have not yet been tapped to any extent and that substantial increases in yield can be obtained from certain natural grass associations or cultivated grasses by the use of such simple measures as improved grazing management or the application of fertilizers. In parts of Central America experiments seem to have been generally successful in the growing of *Pangola* grass (*Digitaria decumbens*), used as paddocked, fertilized, and irrigated pasture. In conditions of good soil (or with fertilizers) and with adequate rainfall (or irrigation water), production levels have been as high as one ton of beef (live weight) per hectare per annum. This is twice the current yield from the best meadows in France (Dumont, 1966: 73).

The need to control and improve grazing management is strikingly illustrated by the damage which has already been done to tropical grasslands by overgrazing. The ecological balance on rolling tropical grasslands is sensitive: once disturbed its restoration may be impossibly expensive. As already noted in Chapter 3, overstocking and overgrazing have been responsible for serious soil erosion and soil exhaustion, notably in eastern and southern Africa.

in Malagasy and in India. Not only is damage done by the stripping of the vegetation and by the hooves of animals, but burning is also an essential part of a pastoral economy in many parts of the tropics. It is believed that in some areas this has been a much more important cause of soil exhaustion and soil erosion than has agriculture or hunting: 'the cultivators' clearings and the desire to track down game easily when it has been frightened by fire or to get honey and wax are far less effective causes of the burning. They must burn to destroy the old hard grasses and encourage the new young grass' (ibid.: 291). However, burning for livestock rearing is probably inevitable in a tropical country with long grass and a well-marked dry season, though the whole question has aroused some controversy. But burning is desirable, under certain conditions, in removing old dried vegetation of little or no nutritive value and in facilitating the growth of new grass at the onset of the rains. It is also claimed that burning helps to keep bush encroachment in check. However, to the peasant cultivator the labour and time involved in cutting down the bush during the dry season is so great that it is safe to say that he would not cultivate or graze the area he does without burning. From the point of view of pasture improvement the effect of burning varies very much with the pasture. Certainly in Brazil, controlled burning is practised with the object of improving the composition and quality of herbage. And in Africa the dominance of certain desirable species of red cat grass (*Themeda triunda*) is favoured by burning, while certain undesirable species are suppressed.

Finally, the humid tropical climate tends to limit livestock and dairying industries because of the difficulty and expense of processing, storing, and preserving the products – especially milk, butter, meat, and cheese. Yet all these problems are clearly capable of solution, given time, continued applied research, and – particularly in the processing, storing, and preserving stages – large-scale injections of capital.

Mixed farming. By analogy with developed agricultural systems in temperate countries and indeed by the example of a number of indigenous economies within the tropics, it seems true to say that the ideal system of husbandry is one in which crop and animal production are combined to form systems of mixed farming and alternate husbandry, producing both crops and livestock simultaneously or alternately from the same land (Stamp, 1964). Such systems of mixed farming, however, are little developed in tropical countries except, perhaps, in India. In most parts of the tropics there is little connexion between pastoralists and cultivators, though in certain parts of West Africa nomadic tribes may for short periods pasture their herds on the resting lands of the cultivators – a practice which helps to maintain fertility and may assist the cultivators to shorten the fallow period.

Mixed farming, however, should go far beyond a system in which animals simply supply manure, energy for pulling farm implements, and milk or meat. True mixed farming implies the integration of crop and animal farming in which the mutual benefits of the system are maximized; in particular, cultivation must provide the livestock with feed that is both regular and of a quality able to raise substantially the productivity of the livestock. It is possible to argue, however, that full integration of livestock and crop farming should be reached only in the middle and later stages of an animal's life. Dumont (ibid.: 108) has referred to the practice in which young animals are reared and brought up in non-cultivated areas – nursery grounds – from which they are sent eventually to the cultivated zones to provide draught labour, manure, milk, and meat. Upon reaching maturity the animals are fattened and moved on towards the chief exporting or consuming areas. Dumont cites the case of Brazil, where the land around San Salvador de Bahia is laid out so that the inner belt around the city is reserved for horticultural and dairy produce; the second belt beyond consists of rich fattening pastures; while the third belt provides livestock-rearing grounds for the first three years of an animal's life. The most distant areas – the *sertao* – thus produce the young calves and constitute the nursery country (ibid.: 108).

It is sometimes suggested that in the tropics better results are to be obtained from the use of artificial manures than from attempts to develop animal husbandry. One must also recognise the possibilities of a transition from hand to mechanical power taking place without the intervening stage of animal traction. But from the point of view of nutrition and diversification of agriculture, advantages attend the successful incorporation of animals into existing farming systems.

Several writers, however, emphasize the difficulties of extending mixed farming to the tropics. Some authorities find such a system more suited to drier areas where inherent fertility of the soil is greater and pasturage is richer. And it is suggested that mixed farming is perhaps 'more readily organized in countries that experience sub-humid or semi-arid conditions than in super-humid and humid regions' (Tempany and Grist, 1958: 52–3). Yet another authority is cautious about applying the system to the tropics, though finding it the best answer in the world as a whole. He concludes, however, that in due course and suitably modified through research and experimentation it may be extended to the tropics (Stamp, 1964).

The problems of mixed farming include peasant resistance to the introduction of draught animals into a hand hoe economy. This has been well illustrated by Haswell (1963) who discusses unsuccessful attempts to introduce draught oxen into Gambia. The peasant cultivators there objected that they could not feed both themselves and their oxen; and measurements of agricultural output and human and animal consumption showed this to be true. In milled rice equivalents the level of agricultural productivity did not exceed 438 kg per person per year, and averaged only 270 kg; whereas the ration recommended for draught oxen included 365 kg per beast per year. The local oxen there are a mixture of Ndama and Zebu and are fairly resistant to trypanosomiases except when underfed or overworked. This appears to be a common finding, and it is unlikely that draught animals will easily be introduced into areas where productivity is still too low to make their use economically feasible. There is, as Clark and Haswell show (1964: 48–68), an economic equilibrium between the ox plough and the hand hoe; and not until production reaches an average figure of 500 units kg grain equivalent per year is it worthwhile employing animal rather than human labour. In Indonesia, De Vries (1954) shows that the cost of keeping a buffalo only doubtfully balances the additional output obtained through its labour, and that the use of draught animals leads to further substantial increases in production only if sufficient land is available for the extra cultivation: Grove (1957: 11) makes the same point for parts of Katsina Province in northern Nigeria. On the other hand, it must be noted that there are certain parts of the monsoon tropics with a short but very wet season where the use of draught animals is a necessary condition without which agriculture would hardly be possible at all.

However, there are grounds for some optimism regarding the future of mixed farming in tropical countries. There are, after all, examples of indigenous developments of this type of farming. Among the Cabrais of northern Togo, for instance, a careful and intensive terraced agriculture is carried on, incorporating not only crop rotation but also the application of human and animal manure, the use of leys and the keeping of animals. Among the Chagga of Mt Kilimanjaro and the Ukara of Lake Victoria, too, similar developments may be seen where cattle are fed on cultivated fodder, kept in sheds, and the manure composted and spread on the fields. While it is true, therefore, that mixed farming calls for more knowledge and skill on the part of the farmer, he has, where necessity has demanded, been able to develop the necessary experience and skills. With indigenous mixed farming, as with other indigenous systems of tropical agriculture, no attempt at improvement can afford to ignore the ready fund of empirical knowledge already enshrined within the existing systems and types of agriculture.

CHAPTER 7

The Increase of Agricultural Production

Some remarks about the relevance of agriculture to economic development have already been made. That it constitutes an important means – in some countries the most promising single means – of dealing with the demographic–economic problem and so of raising the level of real income per head, cannot be doubted. But there are a number of difficulties about increasing agricultural production in tropical countries, many of which arise out of two features of tropical agriculture: low agricultural productivity *per capita* and per unit of land; and a low percentage of land under cultivation. The present chapter concentrates attention on these two characteristics and examines some of the related problems of development.

1. Intensification of agricultural production
Low agricultural productivity *per capita* and per unit area is one of the characteristic features of tropical developing countries. Whereas in North America the average annual agricultural output per person is 2·5 tons, in Asia it is less than 0·25 tons and in Africa less than 0·125 tons. Crop yields in tropical countries are almost invariably very low indeed. In Pakistan the average yield of rice is 828 lb per acre (930 kg per ha), compared with 2,334 lb in the United States, 3,360 in Japan, 4,582 in Italy, and 4,450 in Spain. As one report on African agriculture puts it, 'the increase in agricultural production has fallen behind the growth of population, and earnings from agricultural exports have steadily declined. On a *per caput* basis, production was lower in 1962–3 than five years before . . . and food production *per caput* was estimated to have declined by about 4 per cent . . . and may in fact have gone below the pre-war level' (F.A.O., 1966: 5–7).

115

Much has been written on the whole question of the intensification of agricultural production in the tropics, and success is clearly to be related to the entire field of agricultural improvement, including those issues already discussed in previous chapters – water supply and irrigation, soils, human resources, and the change from shifting-field to some forms of mixed farming and permanent-field cultivation. Similarly, issues to be discussed later – mechanization, technological improvements, marketing, and trade – are equally relevant to this question of how to intensify agricultural production in the tropics. It seems convenient, however, to concentrate here on five issues: land tenure; crop improvement; fertilizers and manuring; crop protection (pests, diseases, and weed control); and crop succession, plant populations, and plant spacing.

Land tenure. A great deal of discussion has centred around problems of land tenure in tropical lands, and it is now generally recognized that agricultural productivity may be dependent as much on the evolution of sound systems of land tenure as upon the development of improved agricultural practices. The relevance of the land tenure problem to the intensification of agricultural production is made explicit in most current economic development plans. In Pakistan's Second Five-Year Plan, for instance, particular attention is drawn to the small and uneconomic size of land holdings and to the excessive fragmentation of holdings as being among the chief causes of low crop yields; plans to increase crop yields, therefore, include the consolidation of holdings and the elimination of excessive fragmentation. Similar policies are to be found in the Fourth Five-Year Plan for India, where considerable progress has already been made in the Punjab, Uttar Pradesh, Maharashtra Gujarat, Madhya Pradesh; but elsewhere in India much remains to be done, especially in the Travancore-Cochin (Kerala) area where 95 per cent of all holdings are still under 5 acres (2 ha) in size. The splitting up of land into small, often widely separated fragments is commonly the result of laws of inheritance. But however it comes about it is undesirable for a number of reasons: it wastes time in the need to supervise; it makes capital duplication necessary; the small plots are difficult to work with ploughs;

weed and pest control is made difficult; and it limits experimentation.

Another common element of the land-tenure problem is the form of land ownership. Communal land ownership tends to give way to individual tenure as agriculture develops; but in many contemporary communities, especially in Africa, there is still a general absence of the concept of land as a negotiable possession. Such a system may conceivably operate satisfactorily as long as land is plentiful and as long as annual crops and nomadic grazing constitute the agricultural system; but difficulties arise where there is much demand for land. Even more important, the capital needs associated with the intensification of agricultural production have emphasized the need for a system of land tenure based on titles which can be sustained in law and so used as security for loans for development. Without such provision, many of the measures for increased production noted later on cannot be applied, and farmers are not so likely to take a long-term interest in their lands. In Trinidad and Tobago this problem was recognized in the 1961 Agricultural Smallholdings' Tenure Ordinance which provides for better security of farmers' holdings and allows farmers to obtain loans to develop their smallholdings; this measure is believed to be already affecting productivity and performance. Moreover, soil erosion difficulties are likely to be reduced, 'for farmers will know that to ensure a continuous stream of income from the soil he will have to take measures to care for it' (Trin. and Tob. Govt., 1963: 72). In Tanganyika, the oft-quoted report of the Royal Commission stated the need for new local land-tenure legislation and set out a number of basic requirements, the most important being to 'establish grounds for confidence that existing property rights will not be arbitrarily disturbed' (International Bank, 1961: 72). Without such confidence, it was argued, farmers could not be expected to show adequate interest in their lands.

Systems of land tenure in tropical countries are so varied and often so little understood that they cannot easily be subjected to general description or analysis. According to Meek (1948), however, the importance of land tenure cannot be exaggerated in former colonial countries where land is, for the most part, the only form of capital and its exploitation the only means of livelihood a farmer has. A number of writers argue that land reform can release energy for increased production in agriculture and can stimulate education, road construction, labour organization, entrepreneurial initiative, and industrialization (Kindleberger, 1966: 220). In Latin America, Carroll has called land reform a 'catalyst of a large chain of complex socio-economic movements' (1961: 175); and for India Krishna (1959) has demonstrated the great importance of land-reform measures. According to these viewpoints, no successful attempt at social and economic change can be made without appropriate land-reform measures; and this applies not only to indigenous small-scale land units but also to those large European alienated lands still to be found in parts of eastern and southern Africa (Floyd, 1962). The 1965 famine in Kenya, for instance, seems to have been due in part to a too rapid, perhaps too politically motivated change over from former large European farms – usually over 3,500 acres each in size – to small African smallholdings, most of which are under 24 acres in extent. Furthermore, this land reform measure was accompanied by little success in bringing the African out of a subsistence into a market-oriented economy. The result was a dramatic and catastrophic fall in maize production.

A contrary opinion about the significance of land-tenure systems is expressed by Lewis (1955) who contends that it is easy to place too much emphasis on such institutional matters as land tenure and too little upon other means of increasing agricultural efficiency, especially through improving water supplies, seed farms for improved seeds, fertilizers, and agricultural extension services. The present institutional framework, Lewis argues, is in most developing countries quite adequate for an important advance in productivity by means of the introduction of improved technology. Land reform is certainly by no means the only or even the most important precondition of improved agricultural efficiency. Bauer and Yamey (1957) note that such means as the transfer of land to small-scale tenant cultivators or the scaling down of rents or debt charges are unlikely to bring about any significant improvement in agricultural productivity. Moreover, while legal arrangements preventing a holding below a certain size from being divided up can admittedly prevent further fragmentation of holdings, they can do nothing to improve the ratio of land to population. Similarly the measures taken in India to consolidate (by exchange among small-holders) holdings formerly divided into several tiny plots, often widely separated from one another, are a needed reform, but cannot solve the fundamental problem of too little land (Lewis, 1955).

Crop improvement. The increase of agricultural productivity by crop improvements is very much a matter of applied research and covers a very wide range of adaptations to environment or to something which results in more being harvested. The primary aim of the plant breeder is to produce more uniform high-yielding populations. But he may also breed for disease-resistant or pest-resistant strains; attempt to improve the look or quality of a product; increase its oil content or fibre strength; or improve a crop's storage properties. The plant breeder may also attempt to produce more convenient sizes or shapes of plants: in Congo Kinshasa, West Africa, and Malaya, for instance, some attention has been given to the breeding of oil-palm varieties which do not grow to great heights and so save expense and energy in the reaping of the crop.

Perhaps the most striking point to make about crop improvement in the tropics is that until recently attention was directed at improving a few of the more important commercial export crops, such as cotton, rubber, oil palm, and coffee. Relatively little so far has been done about detailed research into methods and problems of improving many of the basic food crops – maize, millets, and sorghums, dry or wet rice, yams, sweet potatoes, bananas, or plantains. But as a perusal of journals like the *Empire Journal of Experimental Agriculture* or *Agronomie Tropicale* reveals, this picture has been changing rapidly over the last decade or so. Research into the improvement of tropical staple food crops is now being energetically pursued.

Most economic development plans already have a good deal to say about the needs and possibilities of applied research into plant improvement. In India, seed farms are being established in all development blocks to meet the requirements of foundation seed of improved varieties, the aim being for every village to produce its own requirements of improved seed. Apart from rice, on which a good deal has now been done, much work has also gone into evolving high-yielding hybrids of maize, and it has been found that with moderate amounts of nitrogenous fertilizers the yield of maize hybrids increases to over twice that of local varieties: 25 per cent of the maize area is now being sown under hybrid varieties. Similar work is also going on in evolving hybrid jowar seeds. In Costa Rica good results have been obtained with work into the black bean and coffee, while in Trinidad sugar research has already led to significant increases in yields through improved varieties. In Trinidad, too, cocoa planters have been able to draw on the results of applied research which has developed very high-yielding and disease-resistant varieties: clonal and hybrid seedlings are now available for distribution to planters.

But in spite of the obvious value of developing new crop varieties for particular purposes – all aimed fundamentally at increasing production – the limitations to crop improvements along these lines cannot be ignored. Potentially high-yielding varieties of crops can prove successful only if their cultivation requirements are adequately met. Higher crop yields also mean increased demands on soil fertility which must be satisfied by manuring, fertilizing, and more careful cultivation. Improved varieties of crops also usually require good soil structure, adequate water supply, and disease and pest protection.

Some of the difficulties of introducing improved crop varieties into an existing farming system have been well illustrated in the Abakaliki district of eastern Nigeria (Blanckenburg, 1962). Here the variety of rice recommended by the extension service is BG 79, a variety developed at the rice station at Badeggi. The bulk of the Abakaliki farmers, however, still use a mixture of this variety with inferior indigenous strains. These different strains have a number of different characteristics so that the material is very unequal, especially with respect to maturity date and the size and quality of grain. This makes harvesting and processing difficult. Another problem here is that many farmers do not use fully developed seeds at all, but use winnowings with yields of something less than the yields to be obtained from the BG 79. The reason for this practice is simply that the winnowings are very cheap, whereas the BG 79 seeds are expensive. Although the returns from the improved seeds are better, lack of initial capital forces the farmer to plant inferior seeds.

Again, in India, hopes of increasing food production are now resting very largely on greatly extending the use of high-yielding varieties of cereals. Under the 'new strategy' in India, 35·5 million acres (13·2 million ha) of the best existing land – that is, about 8 per cent of the total arable land in India – was said to be under new varieties of wheat, maize and rice by 1970–1. Research stations and farmers have already shown that when properly used the new varieties can increase yields by between 50 and 200 per cent. But these new varieties demand different techniques precisely applied; they need good water control; and their vulnerability to pests and diseases is high. Moreover, these new varieties demand the application of large amounts of the appropriate fertilizer – 200 lb per acre (222 kg per ha) – compared with 40 lb per acre (45 kg per ha) – for the old breeds.

Fertilizers. In discussing fertilizers in tropical agriculture it must be emphasized that much still remains to be done in utilizing natural manures, and to point out once again that many indigenous developments of permanent-field cultivation have been accompanied by the careful use of human and animal manures. In some areas animal manure is wasted on a dramatic scale, notably in India where nearly 400 million tons of cowdung (wet weight) – equivalent to 60 million tons of firewood – are burnt every year instead of being put on the land as manure. Some authorities question the role of natural manures in tropical agriculture, and this controversy is really part of the wider question of the function and importance of organic matter in tropical soils already referred to (p. 35). As the rate of disappearance of organic matter in the tropics is so rapid that it is doubtful whether humus (as it is defined in temperate countries) is ever formed, it has been questioned whether organic manuring really has any beneficial effects on tropical soils. The bulk of the available evidence, however, suggests that in some cases organic manure is generally effective and is occasionally even better at maintaining fertility than is inorganic manure or fertilizers: 'apart from any possible effect on direct fixation of nitrogen, organic matter is needed to supply energy for the processes of the nitrogen cycle and for the production of carbon dioxide which assists liberation of mineral plant food. An appropriate balance between carbon and nitrogen seems to be essential, and as the rate of disappearance of organic matter in tropical soils is more rapid than under temperate conditions, the aim must be to maintain this balance' (Tempany and Grist, 1958: 3).

The need for fertilizers – either by manuring or by artificial fertilizers – is now widely accepted, and some authorities give this much prominence in their analyses of how to increase agricultural production in the tropics. The F.A.O. suggests that if modest levels of nutrition are to be attained by 1980 the less-developed regions of the world must increase fertilizer consumption to about 30 million tons of plant nutrients by that date. Certainly as far as artificial fertilizers are concerned, tropical soils are now thought to be much more amenable to improvement than many earlier writers believed possible. The critical factor is structure; for if a soil has adequate structure then the use of fertilizers is likely to be practicable, as long as the right kind of fertilizer is known for any particular soil and the appropriate amounts of application have been determined for any particular crop.

Only three types of fertilizer can be mentioned here: nitrogenous fertilizers, phosphates, and lime. In the tropics, where losses and gains of nitrogen take place rapidly, adequate supplies of nitrogen in forms capable of assimilation when the crop needs it are of great importance. The most popular form is sulphate of ammonia, which is highly nitrogenous, relatively cheap, easy to apply, and easy to transport. Examples of its use are for sugar-cane (in the West Indies, Mauritius, and Hawaii), tea (in Ceylon and India), cotton (in the Sudan), rice (in a great many countries), and rubber (in Malaya). Another, though generally less satisfactory inorganic nitrogenous fertilizer, is nitrite of soda. As for phosphorus deficiency, this occurs extensively throughout the tropics, especially in tropical Africa, where it frequently forms a major limiting factor to plant growth. It is important in connexion with root growth, fruiting, and seeding of tropical plants. In Nigeria. field trials on the fertilizer requirements of groundnuts have shown that soil deficiencies of phosphates or sulphur are limiting factors, and nitrogen as a fertilizer confers no benefit because provided that sulphur is not limiting, then the groundnuts appear to be capable of fixing all the nitrogen they require. In these conditions, superphosphates have been found to produce the best results. Finally, the approach to liming under tropical conditions is quite different from what it is in temperate latitudes. In the tropics, where many crops tolerate or prefer acid soils and where lime is expensive, it should be looked upon more as a fertilizer than as a soil amendment or conditioner.

Largely as the result of experimental work, knowledge about the response of tropical crops to fertilizers has increased immeasurably over the last century. For obvious economic reasons the application of artificial fertilizers was first and most vigorously directed at plantation crops – notably to sugar-cane in the West Indies, Mauritius, Java, and Hawaii in the latter half of the nineteenth century. In more recent years, however, the use of fertilizers in smallholdings for staple food crops has also been studied, and an extensive literature now exists on, for instance, the effect of fertilizers on rice crops in Asia, groundnuts in West Africa, and maize and millets in East Africa. Nevertheless, a great deal remains to be done; and differences in climate and soil conditions have in some cases resulted in widely divergent conclusions.

As with crop improvement, however, there is some danger of exaggerating the importance of fertilizers in increasing agricultural production in the tropics. Hardy (1951) has emphasized that unless the three prime factors of crop production – water, air, and root room – are present in satisfactory quantities, any attempt to augment nutrient supply by the use of fertilizers will be ineffective and wasteful. Furthermore, whether or not it is economic to use fertilizers must depend on the cost of fertilizers, the resulting increase in yield, and the cash value of the crop. Lack of capital or credit facilities may also inhibit the use of fertilizers. Certainly there can be no question of looking upon fertilizers as the panacea for tropical agriculture. Yet they can clearly make very real contributions to increasing agricultural production, levels of nutrition, and standards of living.

The consensus of opinion in F.A.O., indeed, is that the use of fertilizers should be looked upon as the spearhead of agricultural development (U.N., 1963). The Freedom From Hunger Campaign (F.F.H.C.) Fertilizer Programme, begun in 1961, has been working in a number of countries, especially in West Africa (Hauck, 1966) and northern Latin America, and has shown convincingly that fertilizers can be used successfully by small peasant farmers using their traditional methods. Small peasant farmers can increase their crop yields by an average of over 50 per cent by using fertilizers alone; and it is difficult to set a limit to the possibilities when fertilizers are combined with other improved methods of farming. The Fertilizer Programme has shown the governments of the participating countries how to persuade small farmers to use fertilizers, and how to organize fertilizer distribution and credit systems where necessary. The need is primarily for advice and instructions about what fertilizers to use and how to use them in any particular area. Once the farmers have convinced themselves of the value of fertilizers, they will be all the more willing to try other modern methods of farming – better varieties, crop protection, improved cultivation, and mechanization.

Pests, plant diseases and weed control. Pests and plant diseases are perhaps especially serious problems in tropical agriculture because of the favourable climatic conditions of continuous high temperatures and high humidities; another factor has been the introduction of crops into different environments, a procedure which frequently encourages pests and diseases of plants. The history of tropical agriculture abounds with examples of destruction or damage by pests and diseases: the 1727 Trinidad cocoa 'blast', the stem-root disease in sugar-cane in the West Indies in 1890, the swollen-shoot disease of cocoa in West Africa, the 'sudden death' disease among Zanzibar cloves, and the 'wither tip' disease of Dominican limes. More recently the virus disease of groundnuts (rosette disease) caused havoc in the early years of the East African Groundnut Scheme, and in West Africa there was a serious development of maize rust from 1949–53. This was introduced from America into the ideal conditions for spore germination and infection along the Guinea coastlands and resulted in a loss of maize yields of up to 40 per cent.

The importance of plant protection is now fully recognized and receives explicit mention in most development plans. In India an area of 50 million acres (20·23 million ha) is now under protection against damage to crops from insects, rodent and other animal pests, diseases, weeds and parasitic flowering plants. While it is difficult to assess the precise extent of damage caused by such pests and diseases, 'there can be no doubt of its serious dimensions . . . big losses are (also) caused by deterioration of food grains and other agricultural commodities through insects, rats, mice' (Indian Government, 1961: 39).

Crop protection clearly embraces some of the points already made in connexion with crop improvement, especially as regards the breeding of disease-resistant strains. During the 1953–6 period the maize-rust disease in Africa was largely controlled by breeding disease-resistant varieties, most of which were developed by utilizing varieties of Central American and South American origin. Considerable natural selection, however, also took place during this period. As for insect pests, methods of controlling these include mechanized devices, trapping, the use of insecticides, close seasons, the control of alternative hosts, and the protection of stored produce. In some cases, too, biological control is appropriate, as with the control of the leafhopper by the introduction into Africa of a capsid bug from Australia and Fiji.

Other ways in which crop protection can be achieved include environmental selection in which crops are grown only under the climatic conditions most suited to them. Outside of these conditions crops are likely to be very much more susceptible to diseases. The classic example of this is the Hemileia leaf disease of arabica coffee. As Masefield (1962) has shown, below 5,000 feet (1,520 m) in East Africa the coffee becomes heavily infected with Hemileia and other diseases and pests, and must be replaced by robusta coffee. Furthermore, a great deal can be done by the very act of cultivation. Since over 90 per cent of insects spend at least part of their lives in the soil, cultivation is itself an important method of control, killing some insects by crushing, some by burying, and some by exposing them to the sun, birds, and other enemies. A good deal can also be done by appropriate methods of cultivation. Thus in West Africa the maize-rust disease can be reduced by early planting. And in Zambia it has been found that early planting gives maximum yields of high-quality groundnuts and minimizes the effects of rosette and leaf-spot disease.

Finally, the control of weeds – which tend to grow very rapidly in the tropics during the wet seasons – is an important factor in plant protection and in the intensification of agricultural production. Many of these weeds can be controlled or removed simply by hand-weeding or hoeing. But many areas also have their own special weed problems arising from a combination of climatic and cultural practices. For instance 'couch grass' (*Digitaria scalarum*) is the most serious weed in cotton, coffee, tea, sisal, and plantain crops in East Africa and in Congo Kinshasa. This particular weed has roots which run laterally beneath the surface, and repeated cultivations are necessary to eliminate it. In Malayan rubber estates 'lalang' (*Imperator cylindrica*) is a similar menace. Elsewhere *Eleusine africana* is an annual grass which rapidly colonizes maize fields and seriously affects the nitrogen supply to the crop. Some grasses or sedges have underground storage organs and a rapid rate of regrowth; and these characteristics make control particularly difficult.

There is no doubt that weeds seriously reduce crop yields in many tropical countries. Ashby and Pfeiffer (1956) estimate that such losses are two to three times as great as in temperate zones; a loss of 50 per cent in cotton yield due to *Digitaria*, with a greater loss of the bean crop, has been quoted; and several writers stress the crucial nature of weed control in the early stages of the East African Groundnut Scheme.

The reason why weeds are generally restrictive on agricultural production, especially in attaining high yields, is that weeds compete with crop plants for oxygen and plant food, moisture and light; some weeds are also alternative hosts for fungus diseases and insect pests; while other weeds are parasitic on crops. Another

argument against weeds is that they limit the area of land cultivated by a farmer. According to some authorities one of the reasons
for the relatively small dimensions of many tropical farms is the
battle the farmers anticipate they will have to wage against weeds.

It is no doubt true that probably the most important means of
weed control is cultivation: weeding, in fact, is often considered to
be the most important function of cultivation. This is perhaps
especially true in the tropics where selective weed killers are not
only expensive and often difficult to apply, but where they also
have one important limitation: whereas the selective weed killers
so far available are most effective against broad-leaved weeds
among cereal crops, some of the worst tropical weeds are grass
weeds in broad-leaved crops. Chemical weed control is both rare
and difficult in the tropics, for not only are grass weeds there more
important than broad-leaved weeds, but most smallholder crops
have a relatively low value, the plots are capable of being hand-
weeded, and widely differing responses to existing chemical weed
killers have so far been noted for different crops.

Weeding is clearly an important factor in the intensification of
agricultural production in the tropics. It has been recognized,
however, that indiscriminate weeding can create more problems
than it solves. It is now known, for instance, that the *Oxalis* weed
in the tea estates of Ceylon has no detrimental effect on tea production but in fact helps to guard the soil against erosion and is a
useful indicator that the soil *ph* is sufficiently low. In Malaya it was
soon found that clean weeding in rubber estates encourages soil
erosion and that it can lead to loss of soil moisture, although this
depends very much upon local climatic and edaphic conditions.
In West Africa the very low atmospheric humidities during the dry
harmattan wind season favour evaporation from the soil surface;
but this evaporation is believed to be less than losses occurring
from weed growth. Under such conditions, therefore, and in spite
of the dangers of soil erosion, clean weeding of fallow land is often
adopted to conserve moisture, while mulching is practised with the
same object in view. Similarly, certain crops like maize are particularly susceptible to damage by weeds owing to the fact that they
are slow starters and planted in widely spaced rows. While under

wet tropical conditions clean weeding does obviously entail a serious risk of erosion, weeding is nevertheless advocated, at least while the plants are young. Wet rice, too, is adversely affected by weed growth, largely because of the effect weeds have on reducing light. But in areas where draught power is lacking, adequate weed control in wet rice fields is very difficult indeed to achieve.

Crop succession, plant populations and spacing. If land is cleared and continuously cultivated with annual crops, ultimate failure almost invariably results. This occurred in Malaya as the result of the continuous cultivation of cassava and pineapples on upland soils without manuring and without adequate protection against soil erosion; the situation there was made worse by the invasion of the cleared land by *lalang* (*Imperator cylindrica*) which, by reason of its rank growth and liability to catch fire during the dry weather, prevents re-establishment of normal vegetational succession and so hinders regeneration. A similar situation arose in parts of Sierra Leone where continuous peasant food production of one crop – upland rice – led to the abandonment of large tracts of land.

A well-chosen succession of crops is clearly of great importance in maintaining fertility, for different crops have varying food requirements. Furthermore, depth of rooting varies, and a deep-rooting crop will utilize food which cannot be reached by those with shallow-rooting systems. A resting period, too, is desirable, so that fallow of one kind or another is often advantageously included in the succession. Examples of successful successions are, in northern Nigeria, guinea corn, cotton, groundnuts, and bush fallow; and, in eastern Java, rice, beans, and sugar-cane.

Frequently included in the rotation are leguminous plants, the value of which as a means of enriching soil has been recognized since ancient times. Today they enter into many successions in tropical countries: 'when their roots and stubbles are turned into the land, and . . . consumed on the land by livestock, they greatly increase nitrogen in the soil. Moreover, because they are deep-rooting, they help to bring mineral plant food from the sub-soil to the surface of the soil' (Tempany and Grist, 1958: 105–6). However, the use of crop successions is often limited by lack of labour;

and unless it produces unmistakable improvements in subsequent crops and includes only crops which are needed, either by the farmer or by some accessible market, a new, unfamiliar crop succession is unlikely to be accepted by peasant cultivators.

As for plant populations and spacing, not a great deal of information exists on this aspect of tropical crop production; but the work already completed indicates that yields can be very substantially increased in this way. Fayemi (1963) has shown that plant populations and spacing can have striking effects on the yield of maize in the tropics, finding in Nigeria a progressive increase in grain yield for populations up to an optimal figure of 14,500 plants per acre (36,000 per ha), above which a decline sets in, though drill planting methods can raise the optimal figure to as much as 19,630 plants to the acre (48,000 per ha).

· · · · ·

A final point emphasizes perhaps the most important practical issue in attempts to intensify agricultural production by any of the means discussed above: how to propagate the knowledge and techniques and to ensure their acceptance by tropical cultivators. Here is an almost untouched field of research; and it is to be hoped that some of the existing concepts and techniques of studying and directing the diffusion of innovations will be applied to tropical field studies by geographers. There are numerous attempts – some more successful than others – to bring about required types of agricultural change. The experimental case study at Uboma in eastern Nigeria (Upton, 1966: 7) is one of the more promising attempts. This is sponsored and managed by the Shell Company of Nigeria in collaboration with the Eastern Nigeria Ministry of Agriculture and was begun with a careful local socio-economic survey, followed by measures to induce the kind of technological and attitudinal changes required. There seem to be few grounds for the kind of pessimism about the transformation and improvement of tropical agriculture such as is revealed, for instance, in the writings of Dumont (1962; 1966). Various forms of agricultural extension work, however, are essential features of any attempt to encourage farmers to learn how to use the more successful disease-resistant strains or higher yielding varieties of crops, or if the farmers are to be reached by those capable of performing bud-grafting and similar specialist services. It is not enough simply to provide the results of applied agricultural research in the form of new technologies – fertilizers, improved seeds, insecticides, irrigation, or machines; nor is it enough simply to tell the farmer what these techniques are, to demonstrate them and exhort him to change. It is equally important that the farmer be provided with the social, psychological, and economic environment in which his land tenure system, co-operative farming, credit facilities, and access to markets provide him with the necessary inducements to change. There is a close connexion between agricultural development on the one hand and, on the other, the general processes of social and economic development. Community development, education, schools, dispensaries: all are really part of the attack on low agricultural productivity in tropical lands.

2. The extension of agricultural land

The generally low proportion of land under cultivation has led a number of writers to see the extension of the cultivated area as an important means of increasing agricultural production in the tropics. The proportion of land area actively under cultivation is certainly very small. Many tropical countries still have the bulk of their surface covered with forest, woodland, and wasteland (Table 5), even a relatively well-developed country like Malaya still having some 70 per cent of its surface classed as tropical rain forest. In Brazil only 2 per cent and in Congo Kinshasa only 1 per cent of the total land area is cultivated (excluding fallow); and in Sarawak only 11 per cent of the total area is cultivated, even including fallow. In spite of the many limitations to such data, the low proportion of land said to be used for agricultural purposes in most tropical countries indicates that land resources in the purely quantitative sense are ample. This is, of course, less true of the densely populated countries of parts of tropical Asia: in India, for instance, the percentage of total land area under cultivation is as high as 30 per cent.

But in practice the extension of cultivation is rarely an easy or practicable proposition. It is certainly misleading to suggest that there are vast open spaces – in Borneo, Africa, and in Brazil, for instance – just waiting for colonists. Apart from the demographic objections to large-scale migration and colonization already noted (pp. 89–90), the extent of the use of land is never a measure of economic efficiency in the use of land resources. Moreover, the qualita-

Table 5. *Land use in selected countries* (Percentage of total land area, 1970)

	Arable and permanent crops	Permanent meadow and pasture	Forest and woodland	Others
Guyana	4	13	73	10
Brazil	3	13	61	23
Brit. Honduras	2	1	46	51
Uganda	25	25	47	3
Nigeria	24	28	34	24
Burma	28	—	68	4
India	50	4	19	27
Malaysia (West)	22	—	78	—

Source: F.A.O., *Yearbook of Agriculture*, 1971.

tive aspects of land resources are in this context at least as important as the amount of land available and still unexploited. Uninhabited is not the same thing as habitable. For the Dry Zone of Ceylon, it has been shown that 'an examination of rainfall and water-supply problems drives home the fact that the "empty lands" of the Dry Zone most certainly do not provide unlimited opportunities for settlement' (Farmer, 1957: 39); and this conclusion, significantly, conflicts with the view of Ceylon's Dry Zone as 'the granary for the future and as a home for the rapidly growing population of the island' (International Bank, 1962: 72). Soil conditions and a whole complex of economic and social considerations – communications, capital availability, essential skills, markets: these are but a few of the factors that may inhibit successful colonization in an area. Others include the difficulty of clearing operations in many tropical countries, while land tenure and health hazards in the receiving areas, too, are frequently discouraging to prospective migrants. Colonists today demand high standards of economic and social security from the moment they arrive in the area to be opened up. Almost any instance of modern standards in agricultural colonization includes model labour contracts conforming to governmental requirements and often also to the requirements of the International Labour Organization. Furthermore it is often very difficult to find sufficient numbers of colonists, for in few areas is population pressure on land already so critically severe as to make people want to move away from their traditional homes. In many countries, too – notably in Africa and tropical America – the human resources are so limited in size that intensification of production by increasing yields and by fighting pests and diseases is clearly the only possible agricultural policy, even though the country may contain large uninhabited and apparently cultivable lands.

It will be recognized that the extension of cultivation must normally involve an expansion into areas of often unproven quality, lying beyond the present settled limits, and farther from or less accessible to markets. The unknown variables and so the risks are therefore greater. As Farmer (1964) has emphasized, the decision about the relative value of extending the cultivated area and intensifying production in areas already cultivated requires difficult benefit – cost analyses, and in any case the whole problem is frequently crucially affected by non-economic considerations. Indeed, it is perhaps legitimate to question two assumptions: that these two complementary means of increasing agricultural production – by extension and by intensification – are normally available in most developing countries of the tropics; and that an extension of the cultivated area must necessarily be useful so long as cultivable land remains uncultivated.

On the other hand, it would be misleading to dismiss altogether the extension of cultivated land as a means of increasing total agricultural production within a country. Some writers give this point a great deal of attention. Lord (1963) argues that however much industrialization and intensification of agriculture are preferred as measures to meet the expanding needs and demands of

Africa's populations, the next decade or so will undoubtedly see an extension of agriculture into the largely empty lands. As will be shown later, a large number of schemes for extending agricultural land have already been undertaken. But in relating such schemes to the central demographic–economic problem as it has been posed in these pages and, more specifically, in relating these schemes to the need to increase total agricultural production, it will be realized that in fact the motivation of many of these schemes has often been highly complex. The extension of agricultural settlement may take place largely for political reasons, or in an attempt simply to relieve so-called population pressure elsewhere. If this is so, then the scheme has fairly to be judged by criteria other than the total agricultural production within a country.

3. The large-scale scheme

The large-scale scheme has played an important, sometimes dominant role in recent attempts to extend agricultural land; only rarely has it been applied to existing agricultural land. Yet while the difficulty of obtaining colonists has commonly made this the only practicable means of extending the agricultural land, a good deal of controversy nevertheless surrounds the whole concept of the large-scale scheme for agricultural development. On a number of economic and social grounds some writers prefer the small-scale peasant farm as an instrument for agricultural change. Lewis (1955) argues that peasant farms encourage more intensive, less wasteful cultivation; that a peasant farmer works harder and more carefully than the hired estate worker; that a family-size farm makes few demands upon supervisory staff; and that peasant farms have less serious repercussions upon the social life of indigenous communities. Certainly the assumption that the large-scale operation must necessarily be more efficient than the small-scale peasant farm has been shown to be untrue in many tropical countries. Not only is the large-scale scheme costly in terms of management and capital outlay, but it also often makes the maintenance of soil fertility and the avoidance of soil erosion very difficult to achieve, especially where the local physical environmental conditions are but little understood.

In most tropical countries today, indeed, increasing emphasis seems to be being placed upon the peasant farm or some rationalization of it rather than upon the large-scale scheme for agricultural development. The reasons for this change of emphasis include the dramatic failure of so many post-war attempts to increase agricultural production through large-scale schemes.

The East African Groundnut Scheme at Kongwa is perhaps the classic instance of how a large-scale scheme for agricultural development can run into all kinds of difficult and often unforeseen problems. This scheme was heralded as 'a kind of crusade for the betterment of African and Briton alike; the vision of swords being turned into ploughshares was to become a reality, and at a cost equivalent to that of only 2–3 days fighting' (Kimble, 1960: 271). Yet it failed for a number of reasons. In the first place, the main purpose of the scheme was to increase the supply of oils and fats for consumption in western markets – in other words, the motive was basically exploitative. Secondly, before work was begun no time was spared for 'satisfactory and sustained primary reconnaissance and survey, for preliminary photographic work, for topographic soil conservation and soil maps, or for adequate investigation of meteorological information bearing on rainfall' (Frankel, 1953: 146). Rainfall and soil data that did exist were sometimes interpreted as if Tanganyika were a temperate country, ignoring the fact that such data as the intensity and effectiveness of rainfall, and the relative functions of rainfall, soil, and temperature in agriculture are not only different but require different interpretation in a tropical context. There was also a tendency to assume a much greater uniformity in the natural environment and resources than does in fact exist: the amount and reliability of rainfall and the details of soil–crop relationships were found in practice to differ widely over surprisingly short distances. Thirdly, there were serious miscalculations about the cost and so the economic feasibility of the whole project. Soils were found to be especially difficult and costly to work for part of the year; the wear and tear on machines and equipment was much greater than had been expected; and the cost of keeping the machines maintained by European technicians proved to be prohibitive. Finally there were several serious problems relating to road and railway construction and the adequacy of port facilities at Dar-es-Salaam.

Another scheme – the Mokwa Scheme (Niger Agricultural Project) in Nigeria – failed for a number of somewhat similar reasons. Here again the motivation for the scheme and the whole general approach have been criticized. Great efforts were made to ensure that it bore no resemblance to a European-type enterprise at any stage. Large-scale initial planning, in particular, was virtually eliminated, and little information was available on the choice of crops, varieties of crops, planting dates, the use of fertilizers, weed control, practicable sizes of holdings, suitable types of tractors, the cost of mechanized operations, the marketing of produce, and the supply of labour. This lack of prior knowledge is particularly difficult to understand in the case of Mokwa because there was already some agricultural settlement there. Very little if any of the local knowledge was utilized, the African farmer's fund of empirical knowledge being largely ignored. For political reasons only immigrants from Bida and Kontagora emirates were accepted as settlers at Mokwa; yet these were the very people who could in no way be said to be suffering from population pressure on land resources in their own homelands. Furthermore, the new villages and facilities provided for the immigrants were not adapted to local customs (Baldwin, 1957).

Both the Kongwa and Mokwa experiments point to three main lessons. First, any successful agricultural extension scheme based on large-scale, highly capitalized methods, depends initially on adequate knowledge about the characteristics and significance of tropical conditions, about the theory of this kind of development, and about the complex of conditions existing in the actual area in which the development is contemplated. Secondly, any kind of agricultural innovation should proceed slowly and carefully, for the object of rural development should be simply to graft on to indigenous life the things that it lacks. Finally, these two schemer have emphasized the common fallacy that agricultural operations easily lend themselves to economies of scale. In fact, this idea runs counter to the accepted principle that 'agriculture is the least likely form of economic enterprise to yield considerable large-scale economies: its factors of production cannot be readily centred or supervised, nor in general are they sufficiently homogeneous to allow easily organized repetitive processes of production' (Frankel, 1953: 149).

With the large-scale scheme, as with the small peasant farm, many of the applied problems of agricultural development are essentially local ones. Research findings must be tested under operational conditions in experimental and pilot projects before committing them to larger-scale undertakings.

4. Mechanization

Over the last two decades or so a considerable amount of experience has been built up on the value of mechanization as a means of increasing agricultural production in tropical lands. This applies not only to the extension of agriculture but also to the intensification of production in existing areas of agricultural land. The chief advantages of mechanization are believed to be (i) the saving of labour; (ii) the gaining of time – in particular, land that could not otherwise be cultivated (as in areas where the soil is too heavy or where weather conditions allow too little time for hand methods to cope) can be brought under cultivation; and (iii) mechanization economizes because it releases for human use land which has otherwise to be used only for feeding draught animals, as in India.

Yet while the potential contribution of mechanization to tropical agriculture cannot be doubted, a number of difficulties have been shown to exist. In the first place, it will already be apparent from what has been said that tropical countries do not in general have any need to save either labour or time. As far as the saving of labour is concerned, the problem can most simply be stated as one of output per worker versus output per acre; while mechanized production is usually more productive per worker, it is usually less productive per acre, hand labour usually being carried out with more care and the land utilized more intensively. In a heavily populated country like India the objective of agricultural policy might be to maximize output per acre, not output per worker; and in such a situation, clearly, mechanization is not necessarily logical. In areas of much lower population densities, as in much of tropical Africa or tropical South America, however, the chief aim of agricultural policy is perhaps more commonly aimed at maximizing production per unit of labour; and in such circumstances mechanization of agricultural production is clearly desirable. As far as the saving of time is concerned, it has already been shown that this is not normally a problem in tropical developing countries where, indeed, underemployment is a characteristic, even endemic, feature. Only in areas where there is a short rainy season – as in parts of India – is the saving of time an important factor.

Secondly, the feasibility or desirability of mechanical cultivation depends upon a number of conditions related to land. Mechanization is clearly best suited to areas where land is relatively flat, where the size of farms is not too small, and where holdings are not too fragmented or scattered. Then the difficulties of using wheeled machines in soft, sticky clay are well known; simple manual methods may often be the only feasible ones. In the Mokwa Scheme, too, it was found possible only to make use of machines for ploughing and ridging the land, for no machines capable of doing the other necessary operations could be found. The Mokwa Scheme also showed that while mechanization may speed the clearance between rows, it cannot help with weeding in between plants in the same row. In the early days of the scheme, land was cleared rapidly, but the rapid restoration of the undergrowth and small trees showed that the clearing, which was almost entirely by hand, had to be more thorough and therefore slower. Even then the prolific root system just below the surface of the ground caused severe losses from breakages of agricultural implements; the costs of repairing and replacing were very high. The desirability of mechanization also depends to a large extent on the crop. A low annual crop, such as groundnuts, is very much more suited to mechanical cultivation than are the taller perennial crops. Other problems are the poor quality of tractor drivers and the spreading of the working season of the tractors. This last point was again well illustrated in the Mokwa Scheme.

Thirdly, there is a whole group of problems related to the economic feasibility of mechanization; and many of these are related to initial capital availability, the cost and quality of supervisory and technical labour, and the seasonal flow of demand for mechanized processes in farming. As Clayton (1963) has shown in Kenya, this is one of the main reasons why mechanization is not always an effective capital substitute for labour in a physical sense. The use of tractors in the farms Clayton studied economizes labour only during the seed-bed preparation periods of the long and short rainy seasons; if restricting seasonal labour peaks do not coincide with these periods, then mechanization is unlikely to be effective or economic. This gives rise to the apparent contradiction of situations where labour, though underemployed, is nevertheless restricting but which cannot be ameliorated by factor substitution, that is by mechanization. Clayton finds that increased production on family farms is limited by labour and not by land, but that mechanization brings substantial gains (20 per cent or more) only on farms which can grow a high-value cash crop, such as pyrethrum, and which have land–labour ratios of not less than 2·9 acres (1·17 ha) to one man on farms with two cash crops and not less than 2·5 acres (1·01 ha) to one man on farms with only one cash crop (ibid.).

Mechanization of agriculture, in fact, is likely to be effective and fully economic only if applied simultaneously with all other appropriate measures to increase crop yields and farm returns. Initially, too, it is perhaps best applied to the 'bottle-necks' of farming operations rather than indiscriminately to all activities on the farms. Moreover, 'it is of the utmost importance that efforts to introduce mechanization of peasant farming in the tropics should not be attempted until its implications on the social habits of the people have been completely appraised, and not before practical trials of machines and organizations have been made on a sufficiently large scale to provide the necessary technical and economic and social experience' (Tempany and Grist, 1958: 136).

CHAPTER 8

Agriculture or Industry?

Three points of view. One of the central issues confronting tropical countries is sectoral balance, and in particular concerns the relative significance of agriculture and industry in development planning. While decisions on this issue sometimes reflect differences in natural, human, and financial resources between countries, they perhaps more commonly reflect an adherence to one of three widely divergent viewpoints. First, there is the view that increased agricultural production is the only sure foundation for successful industrialization at a subsequent stage in the development of an economy. A second point of view is that only a rapid increase in industrialization can ever enable a developing country's economy to break out into something approaching that of a developed country. Finally, and somewhere in between the two other standpoints, is the view that agricultural and industrial development planning cannot usefully be considered separately, and that in development planning they are equally important. It seems necessary at this stage in the discussion to look a little more closely at these three very different points of view.

The view that agricultural development must be given greatest weight in economic development planning in tropical countries usually finds more support in actual development plans than in the theoretical literature. The International Bank Mission Reports to Uganda and Malaya discussed in the previous chapter, for instance, recommended emphasizing agricultural development for the very simple reason that these countries are still very largely agricultural. This pragmatic argument varies in its applicability from country to country, and the case of Trinidad, also discussed earlier, is just one example of a tropical country whose present level of prosperity is largely dependent on non-agricultural production. However, it is generally true that rather over 50 per cent of the national income of tropical countries comes from agricultural sources, and in few tropical countries is less than 70 per cent of the working population in the agricultural sector: in these two senses, certainly, agriculture is easily the most important economic activity in the tropical world, and economic development there must largely imply rural development (Balogh, 1966).

Another argument in favour of emphasizing agriculture rather than industry is that while in the past a great deal of attention has been given to export cash crops, relatively little research, capital, or expenditure has gone into improving the domestic food situation in the tropics. Yet in terms of diet and health the need to increase domestic food production is very urgent and should perhaps be given priority over any other form of economic development planning. The potential domestic market for increased food supplies is clearly immense, and the redistribution of surplus rice, maize, or other food production between the various countries of the tropical world could also form a useful basis for the growth of inter-tropical trade.

Again, it can be argued that an agricultural revolution should perhaps always precede an industrial revolution, and in particular that the advantages of technological change in the first instance are most appropriately channelled into agriculture – notably by the mechanization of agriculture – and not into manufacturing industry; for large-scale modern industrialization, with its emphasis on labour-saving devices, is illogical in tropical countries where underemployment is a widespread, even endemic feature of economic life. Furthermore, industrialization is usually capital-intensive and so, again, is not wholly appropriate in those parts of the world where supplies of capital and domestic savings are so short. Then the demands on an educated and more particularly on a technologically educated élite are very great in industrialization, and it seems unwise to encourage industrialization on any scale before the basic needs in terms of human resources have been provided. Finally, social changes of many kinds are rapidly helping to bring about increased urbanization; and this implies a need for greater efficiency in the production of surplus food for the growing non-agriculturally productive sections of the community. For several of these reasons, Benham and Holley (1960) have advised Latin American countries to choose agricultural and mineral development rather than industrialization.

A contrary viewpoint is expressed by the school of development economics that assigns to agriculture a relatively minor role and argues that pride of place should be given to industrialization, together with all associated lines of development except agriculture (Rosenstein-Rodan, 1961). According to this viewpoint, only industrialization can break the vicious cycle of underdevelopment and create the necessary preconditions for economic 'take-off'. Some economists go farther than this and regard economic development and industrialization as roughly synonymous terms.

Of the many arguments put forward by the proponents of this school, the first is to suggest that industrialization is demonstrably responsible for the higher material standards of living in the developed countries. It is pointed out that the value of output per man is greater and is growing more rapidly in industry than in agriculture, and that the proportion of the population engaged in industry is normally higher in wealthy countries than in poor countries. The success of Russia and Japan as rapidly developing industrial states is often quoted to support this viewpoint.

Secondly, it is argued that industrialization is the best way of bringing about greater economic diversification and stability – something which all tropical countries are seen to need. At present they depend in their external trade upon the export of a comparatively restricted range of agricultural and mineral raw materials. In this sense most tropical economies are non-diversified and so liable to instability, making development planning difficult. Industrialization can also add value to existing raw material exports by processing before export and can further help the balance of payments situation by the final processing or assembly of imports. Furthermore, industrial growth is cumulative and can stimulate progress in other sectors of the economy, particularly in ventures which meet its requirements for engineering, repairing, transport, fuel, electricity, finance, and distributive services.

Thirdly, industrialization may be advocated as a more important need than agricultural development in tropical countries in that it can absorb workers who are at present 'underemployed' in agriculture or petty trading; the value of their work to the community and so their own incomes will thereby be increased, the marginal value product of labour being in these circumstances higher in industry than in agriculture. The advantages of specialization of labour are also much more easily achieved in industrialization.

In the fourth place, it is possible to question the view, implicit in the argument of those who give priority to agricultural development, that the agricultural sector in a tropical country is sufficiently commercialized to respond to the usual economic incentives. The view that agriculture is more important than industrialization depends entirely on this initial assumption, which is perhaps not valid where subsistence agriculture is dominant. In most tropical countries the key to development 'is provided by an increase in industrial productivity . . . Policies aimed at lifting production in the agricultural sector are in this setting unlikely to foster self-sustaining growth and may even frustrate it' (Gutman, 1957: 291). A requirement for economic take-off is a class of farmers willing and able to respond to the possibilities opened up for them by new techniques, land-holding arrangements, transport facilities, and forms of market and credit organizations. Without such a class of farmers no substantial leap forward in economic development is possible through agriculture.

Again, in supporting the 'industrial' school a number of writers point to the greater flexibility and adaptability of industrialization. The demand for agricultural products is relatively inelastic. Furthermore, the proportion of fixed to operating costs is much smaller in industry than in agriculture, so that industrial activity can be more easily cut down or expanded than can agricultural production. Industrial production can more easily be controlled in relation to costs, prices, and demand. Control and flexibility are also easier in a situation where production is so little dependent upon the vagaries of nature. The fundamental disadvantage under which agriculture labours, in fact, is that the farmer has little control over the natural forces of his environment, and any kind of change in crops or techniques is commonly inhibited by the way in which the agricultural way of life is so clearly woven into the fabric of tropical society.

It is also pointed out that industrialization has a powerful, indeed irresistible, psychological attraction. Most tropical countries equate civilization and power with industrialization and are determined upon the rapid development of the industrial sectors of their economies. Whatever theorists may say, industrialization, at a pace and to an extent which many would call too ambitious, is certain to take place; and if this is so, then it is only practical policy to try to facilitate and direct the processes of industrial development.

A final argument for emphasizing industrialization is related to the demographic–economic problem referred to earlier (pp. 89–93). According to available comparative data, industrialization seems to lead inevitably to urbanization. Particularly in its early stages, manufacturing industry is related to the urban centres where markets, labour, and a range of public utilities are available; and it can be argued that this urbanization, resulting from industrialization, will eventually help to reduce the rate of population growth.

The third school of thought includes a wide spectrum of viewpoints, but in general embraces all those who recognize the essential interdependence of agriculture and industry. Lewis (1953) and Nurkse (1959) are perhaps the best-known exponents of this school, but over the last few years it has received a good deal of theoretical expression, especially by Jorgensen (1961), Ranis and Fei (1961), and by Johnston and Mellor (1961). All argue that agriculture and industry are equally necessary to economic development. Either explicitly or implicitly, most geographical writings support this third school of thought.

According to this viewpoint there are no inherent advantages of manufacturing industry over agriculture or for that matter of agriculture over industry (Viner, 1953). Spate has illustrated this for India where 'without a great increase – and a better distribution – of rural income, industry cannot develop to the full, since agrarian poverty severely restricts the effective demand of the numerically huge internal market, and continually maintain, or at least augment, the immense pool of landless or underemployed rural labour and thus keeps the worker's wages low, his living conditions often unspeakably bad, and his efficiency as a natural consequence poor. Conversely, the vital significance of the industrialization contribution to agricultural reconstruction is patent: fertilizers, cheap machinery, and a market. Field and factory, then, are symbiotes' (Spate and Learmonth, 1967: 257). India, indeed, provides a good example of the need for the 'feedback' of industry into agriculture, not only in mechanization but perhaps even more immediately important in the field of fertilizer and pesticide manufacture. In extending the use of the new varieties of wheat, maize and rice in India, one of the chief difficulties has been the supply of fertilizers and pesticides upon which the successful cultivation of these new varieties depends. In 1966 the domestic production of fertilizer was only about 40 per cent of requirements at that time, the remainder, together with most pesticides, being imported at high cost in foreign exchange. Present strategy demands a great increase in fertilizer and pesticide production, which can be achieved only if foreign capital can be induced to invest heavily and quickly.

Again, a need has been noted for the mutual self-support between agriculture and industry, whereby the surplus agricultural population is siphoned off into industry as agriculture, under the stimulus of greater demand, becomes more efficient and as industry in turn raises the market for agricultural produce (Mountjoy, 1963: 85). As another writer has summed it up 'industrialization is dependent upon agricultural improvement: it is not profitable to produce a growing volume of manufactures unless agricultural production is growing simultaneously. This is also why industrial and agricultural revolutions always go together, and why economies in which agriculture is stagnant do not show industrial development' (Lewis, 1955: 433). According to a number of well-known historical analogies, too, the connexion between agricultural improvement and industrial development is very close. In Britain, for instance, the Industrial Revolution was made possible by the mid-eighteenth-century introduction of scientific farming, better crops, the stall-feeding of animals and a new rotation of crops which included the turnip, as well as by subsequent improvements in drainage techniques and ploughing (Ernle, 1937).

The need to try to achieve a balance between the two forms of development – agricultural and industrial – can be argued on three further grounds. In the first place, the diversion of labour from rural to urban occupations implicit in industrialization requires that the depleted ranks of rural labour should provide the rapidly expanding urban food demands. If agriculture fails to provide food for the growing industrial and urban populations, then much-needed capital will have to be spent on importing foodstuffs and development will be retarded (Mountjoy, 1963: 79). This is a particularly important issue because of the high elasticities of demand in food in the early stages of economic development. There is always a real danger that increased incomes will be spent chiefly on food to the extent that 'demand for food will expand more than the supply, while the supply of industrial products increases more than the demand' (Kindleberger, 1966: 215). Important data on this whole question have been presented by Kaneda and Johnston (1961) in their study of urban food expenditure patterns in tropical Africa. According to their findings, normally between 50 and 68 per cent of total household expenditures are devoted to food, and urban income elasticities of demand for food are normally very high (0·6–0·9) compared with relatively low figures (0·2–0·3) in developed countries. Total expenditure on food in African urban areas, then, tends to rise very substantially as income rises.

Secondly, the movement of resources from agriculture to industry is advantageous to the total economy only if the resources left in agriculture are employed so as to produce, at reasonably low costs, certain of the raw material requirements of industry. And finally, an enlarged and diversified agricultural sector may be necessary to produce exports with which to obtain the foreign exchange needed for industrial development.

The validity of the hypothesis that sustained industrial growth is closely linked with the expansion and improvement of agriculture must vary considerably from country to country. In Ceylon, export agriculture still earns good net returns whereas in Burma and Thailand the chief agricultural export – rice – is now highly depressed. By and large, however, the market situation as well as psychological and political needs seem already to demand a moderate and selective development of industries in most tropical countries.

Agriculture must still be expanded wherever it has better scope; but this expansion will itself necessitate and permit industrialization. Higher agricultural productivity will provide capital and markets for new industries, while the industries will absorb the surplus labour which agriculture must release in its process of improvement. Thus industrial and agricultural development are complementary.

. . . . .

Any review of the existing empirical evidence seems at first sight to give general support to the third 'balanced growth' viewpoint. Industrialization must be accompanied by increased efficiency in food production; but this increased efficiency in food production cannot be brought about without a feedback from industry into agriculture, making it possible to apply to agriculture what has been called 'the tricks of manufacture'. Two important qualifications, however, need to be made. In the first place, the examination of specific case studies can lead one to diametrically opposed conclusions about the relative roles of industry and agriculture in the economic development of different countries. While some theoretical or conceptual framework is necessary to any informed analysis of a specific case study, the details of the local situation make any indiscriminate blanket model or theory quite impossible; as Martin (1961) has noted, for instance, Lewis's prescriptions for Ghana and the West Indies are quite different as far as emphasizing agriculture or industry is concerned. Secondly, the viewpoint that agriculture and industry should be given equal weight in development planning must clearly accept the fact that in terms of employment, agriculture should become relatively less and less important, while secondary and especially tertiary production should become relatively more important. Rising income levels have to be accompanied by a corresponding change in employment structure involving a relative shrinkage of the agricultural sector (A. Fisher, 1935; 1939; Clark, 1957). If a 70:30 ratio of agricultural to non-agricultural labour is typical of developing countries, then something like a 30:70 ratio is typical of countries at a high level of economic development. A convenient assumption

for an economy in a fairly rapid process of economic development
is that the agricultural population will remain constant in absolute
numbers and that changes in structure will be brought about by a
concentration of the natural increase of population in the non-
agricultural sector (Singer, 1964: 385; and Fig. 2). The aim is thus
to increase agricultural production with the constant numbers of
people employed in agriculture, yet to provide sufficient food for the
increased population in the non-agricultural sector, and to provide
for such increases in consumption as are part of the development
programme.

The development continuum. It seems appropriate here to point out
that the dichotomy between agriculture and industry implied in
much of the discussion outlined above is to some extent false. It is
always difficult and sometimes quite impossible to make a clear
distinction between them, except in the earliest stages of economic
development; and it is only quite arbitrarily, in fact, that the
line dividing the two forms of economic activity can be drawn.
Quite a large part of the industrial sector in tropical developing
countries both depends upon agriculture for its raw materials and
is itself aimed at feeding back into agriculture the products and
techniques of industry. After a certain critical stage in the development of agricultural systems, the feedback of technology from
industry into agriculture is crucial.

Fig. 2 indicates in broad terms this line of thought about the
agricultural–industrial continuum and relates it to different stages
or systems of agriculture as well as to population density. The two
extremities of the continuum are represented by shifting-field
cultivation and what has been termed 'industrial agriculture'
respectively. Somewhere in between lies the stage of permanent-
field cultivation, the spontaneous or indigenous development of
which was earlier shown to be related to critical population densities
(p. 97). In the first half of the continuum the chief agent of change
in agricultural systems is a rising population density; but in the
second half of the continuum the technological feedback from
industry (whether in the same country or originating from outside)
is the main agent of change and results in a relative decrease in the

agricultural population as population density and urbanization increase. The actual timing of the indigenous permanent-field cultivation stage depends on a great number of unknown variables, making precise generalizations impossible; and the exact shape of the population growth curve will similarly vary. But it is contended

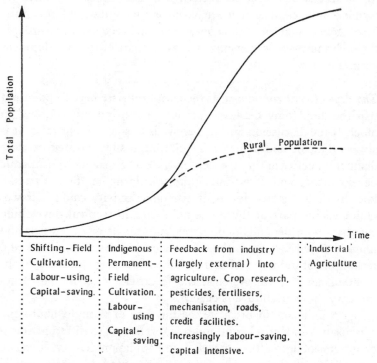

Fig. 2. The development continuum from agriculture to industry.

that one of the overriding aims of economic development planning in tropical developing countries should be to proceed along this continuum as quickly as possible – though without attempting to jump any of the intervening stages – and that the feedback from industry into agriculture cannot usefully be attempted until at least the stage of indigenous, simple permanent-field cultivation has been reached. In this sense, there are obvious weaknesses in trying to apply to most African agricultural economies the kind of measures to improve agricultural production that appear to be appropriate in, for instance, the heavily populated, wet-rice cultivated areas of the Asian tropics.

This notion, if valid, has a number of practical implications for agricultural development planning, one of which is that in those areas where shifting-field cultivation is still a dominant form of land use any attempts to effect a change over to permanent-field cultivation must be concentrated at those points where population densities are already so high as to make an early changeover inevitable. Another is to suggest that attempts to induce greater efficiency among shifting-field cultivators by the application of any of the methods indicated for the second two stages of the continuum are likely to be productive only of failure. And thirdly, it suggests that once permanent-field cultivation has evolved or been induced, then a rapid feedback from industry into agriculture should be encouraged, emphasizing from the start labour-saving, capital-intensive technology and making economic efficiency the sole criterion of judgement.

There is, of course, a great deal of controversy over this latter stage. Some writers, while accepting the general notion of stages in the transformation of an agricultural economy, suggest that capital-intensive, labour-saving technology should be reserved only for the very latest stages of development. Johnston and Mellor (1961), for instance, distinguish three stages of transformation – the preconditions for agricultural development, involving particular emphasis on land reform; the stage of emphasis on labour-using techniques in agriculture, together with education, agricultural research, roads, credit, irrigation, and community development; and finally, the stage of labour-saving technology in agriculture, emphasizing mechanization and capital-intensive methods generally. In this work the authors are in effect suggesting a compromise between capital-intensive and labour-intensive technology, reserving the former until a fairly high level of productivity has been achieved. As will be noted later, however, this argument seems to be restrictive on development in that it helps to perpetuate existing land–labour ratios and so encourages stagnation and inhibits self-generating change. But the emphasis in the earlier stages of permanent-field cultivation on such measures as agricultural research, education, transport facilities, and the provision of credit facilities seems entirely logical.

While this idea, expressed diagrammatically in Fig. 2, is necessarily very tentative and generalized, it does suggest a framework for thinking about the whole very complicated and diffuse issue of the transition from primitive to advanced forms of agricultural activity. It also summarizes, however crudely, many of the points made in these pages; it supports the belief that all economies, whether tropical or non-tropical, are at some stage along some kind of development continuum; and it rejects any rigid concept of 'developed' and 'developing' economies as mutually exclusive categories (see Appendix).

CHAPTER 9

Industrialization

Labour-intensive or capital-intensive technology? Some of the remarks made in the previous chapter imply a point of view about the relative importance to tropical developing countries of labour-intensive and capital-intensive technology, either in agriculture or in industry.

The main conflicting viewpoints on this matter can be put very briefly. Those writers, like Hayek (1955), who support concentrating on labour-intensive technology, are concerned with the implications of existing factor proportions, especially capital/labour ratios. Where labour is abundant and capital is scarce the only appropriate technology, so it is argued, is one that is labour-intensive; in much of India, therefore, labour-intensive technology is always to be preferred. Against this point of view it can be argued that the labour-intensive approach is essentially static, negative, and, in the long run, inhibiting to economic advance. Furthermore, much of the argument for emphasizing labour-intensive technology rests on strictly non-economic grounds – on, for instance, the need to maximize employment rather than output (Eckaus, 1966). As Kindleberger (1966) argues, however, the decision whether to maximize employment or output is not a matter for an economist to decide upon. It is also important to point out that many, perhaps most, tropical countries do not have abundant labour and that densities are not nearly so high as is commonly believed; the 'endemic underemployment' characteristic, in fact, is often exaggerated.

The case for emphasizing capital-intensive technology wherever possible rests not only upon theoretical arguments but also upon empirical and historical evidence. Leibenstein (1960) argues that capital-intensive techniques should be preferred to labour-intensive techniques both because of their immediate productivity and because of their greater contribution to savings and hence future growth. He suggests, furthermore, that in most developing countries capital can be substituted for labour in capital-intensive production methods, but not in labour-intensive methods. Gerschenkron (1962) uses historical analogies to support similar conclusions. The introduction of capital-intensive technologies into developing societies seems to him essential for economic development, for historically 'borrowed technology was one of the primary factors assuring a high speed of development in a backward country entering the stage of industrialization' (Gerschenkron, 1962: 8).

It must be admitted that any emphasis on capital-intensive technological change may have some unfortunate social, psychological, political, and even economic implications – such as those associated with what is sometimes called the dual economy, well analysed for Indonesia (Furnivall, 1948; Boeke, 1942; and Higgins, 1959). Moreover, it is once again unwise to generalize about the merits or demerits of particular lines of policy without specifying the actual country under consideration. Some tropical countries, like Malaya or Venezuela, are already well along the development line, while others, like many of the African countries, have hardly started; some have high population densities while others are very sparsely populated and suffer from a shortage rather than from a surplus of labour.

Yet the general arguments in favour of emphasizing capital-intensive technology – either in agriculture or in industry – seem convincing. Not only do these arguments fit in with the available empirical evidence but the emphasis on capital-intensive techniques gives further support to the development continuum expressed in Fig. 2. As long as the capital-intensive, up-to-date techniques are able to operate in situations where capital can earn sufficiently high returns, and as long as such technology is diffused throughout the economy through training and labour stimulation, then the transfer of modern technological innovations from the developed to the developing countries is not only to be encouraged: it is critical to the kind of rapid economic advance required.

The obstacles to industrialization. Three obstacles to the industrialization of tropical countries are given particular prominence in the literature. The first is the poor quality of industrial labour. Some reference to this point has already been made in discussing the qualitative aspects of human resources, and it was concluded that given time and proper training there is no reason to suppose that tropical peoples have any less innate capacity for industrial activity. This is not to suggest that difficult social, psychological, and economic problems do not arise in trying to create an industrial labour force in tropical countries. Some of these problems have been well described for growing industrial areas by a number of writers. But none of this work necessarily implies any basic incapacity for industrial operations on the part of indigenous workers. From a study of industrial operations in Nigeria it has been concluded that the African there does not possess any inherent incapacities or attitudes which are detrimental to efficient production in modern industry: 'in fact it can be argued that regarding continuous labour and repetitive operations he is peculiarly well-suited to modern production. Second, the African's willingness to work considerably exceeds that of labourers in developed economies. Third, with regard to machine technology, there are certain aspects of machine operation and maintenance to which the African, because of his environmental background, does not naturally adapt. Training, however, will rectify these shortcomings. Investment in human skills, the training of competent craftsmen and technicians, is of recent origin. Careful selection, training, marketing incentives, and surveillance from higher management will reduce supervisory weaknesses to negligible proportions. Thus one may say that the quality of African labour is adequate to meet the needs of developing economies' (Kilby, 1955: 22).

The problem of manpower for industrialization in tropical countries clearly resolves itself into a question of training and experience, not only for semi-skilled and skilled labour but also at the organizing and managerial levels. This may well form the most important single brake on the pace of industrial development; for investment in human resources is never a very speedy process, and some of the related problems of social change may involve opposition to the introduction of industrial processes. The reasons

for and the nature of such opposition vary from place to place –
often over very small distances – and may reflect the intensely
practical but parochial interests of small individual social groups. In
West Africa one writer has described the opposition to oil mills
among the Mba-Ise people of Iboland. The reasons for this opposition include the fears that women would lose their rightful profit
from the kernels, that oil mills would put out of business the small
middlemen and middlewomen, and that widespread idleness would
result. These reasons for opposing the mills show an intelligent
self-interest on the part of the Mba-Ise people (Ardener, 1953).

A related aspect of the qualitative manpower problem is the
entrepreneurial shortage. Little attention has been given to this in
the literature on economic development, though it seems to be no
less serious a handicap (Harbison and Myers, 1964). Capital cannot
by itself produce anything – it must be harnessed for producing
capital goods and the capital goods in turn harnessed for producing
consumer goods; and this investment process requires the services
of some agent or intermediary who initiates, organizes, makes
decisions, takes risks, innovates, and sometimes also manages.
According to Hirschman (1958), decision-making of this kind is
'the scarcest talent' in developing countries. In the developing
economies of the tropics the necessary sponsors or entrepreneurs
are very few in number, and this is probably an important reason
why industrial development is slow to take place. On the other
hand, some writers have argued that the entrepreneurial ability of
many tropical societies is already very great, as in parts of India
and in Guatemala.

A second major obstacle to industrialization in tropical countries
is lack of capital. According to some writers, capital accumulation
and industrialization are in practice virtually identical processes;
and though some increase in industrial production is possible by
improving industrial organization, methods, the quality of labour
and factory management, the scope of such measures is limited.
For a large advance in industrial production, particularly if it is to
exceed the increase in population, capital formation on a large scale
is indispensable. Yet the amount of capital required per worker in
modern manufacturing industry is high, and this is one of the main

reasons why the 'take-off' into self-sustained growth is such a difficult operation. Furthermore, capital requirements for industry are commonly higher in tropical than in non-tropical countries: in West Africa, for instance, the initial amounts of working capital and fixed capital required per worker in 1957 were said to be £13,150 for a cement factory, £3,000 for a vehicle assembly plant, and £2,800 for a plastics factory: the equivalent figures for about three-quarters of British industry all lay between £1,000 and £3,000 (U.A.C., 1957).

A third obstacle – the narrowness of market opportunities – is a distinctive feature of most tropical countries. The nature and causes of this condition vary from one country to another, but in general they can be said to include a lack of capital for storage, inadequate and costly transport, and, above all, the low purchasing power of the population. Market opportunities and economic prosperity are clearly closely linked and it is perhaps only an analytical convenience to distinguish between the supply and demand sides of the problem of increasing production.

Home market opportunities for industrial products, though automatically widening as economic development and population growth take place, can be widened still further by various means. As will be shown in a later chapter, one of the arguments for improving internal lines of communication is that they will help to increase the extent and intensity of market contacts within a territory. It is possible to advocate the enlargement of the home market by the simultaneous expansion of a large number of industries which buy one another's products; this kind of group advance will automatically create its own market and will also, if localized, increase the external economies enjoyed by each firm and so reduce costs (Nurkse, 1953). Then there have been attempts to widen and diversify the domestic market by creating regional groupings of one kind or another, like the East African Common Market, the South-east Asian Common Market, or the Caribbean Economic Community. According to Prebisch's thesis, indeed, many nation states in the developing world are too small for effective industrialization. Where countries have only small populations, industrial costs are higher, so that highly protective tariffs are forced upon them and small uneconomic plants develop. Large-scale industrialization cannot be built upon fragmentation of this kind; and the need for regional groupings for industrial development among developing countries is therefore urgent (U.N., 1964). It has also been suggested that the home market may be enlarged for home products by capturing what is at present supplied by foreign producers – that is by creating import-substitution industries – and to this end the development plans of many countries include such incentives as duty drawbacks, investment allowances, and tax concessions. However, in relating the home market to industrial expansion, where market limitations are especially cramping, the pattern of spending among tropical peasants must not be ignored.

The narrowness of foreign markets is no less inhibiting to industrial development in tropical countries. More will be said on this point in a later chapter, but it can hardly be overemphasized. In the absence of adequate domestic market opportunities, industrialization in tropical countries must look for market opportunities in the developed world; yet it is difficult to envisage a situation in which the peoples of the developed world would be prepared to buy manufactured products from the developing countries when they can buy the same, probably better and cheaper, products from each other.

These three obstacles to industrialization – lack of skilled labour and any substantial managerial or entrepreneurial class, lack of capital, and the narrowness of domestic and foreign markets – are met with in varying degrees in all tropical countries and must deeply affect the extent and nature of economic planning.

Cottage and small-scale industry. There is a substantial body of opinion which holds that the main objective of industrial development policy in tropical countries should be the encouragement of a variety of cottage, small-scale industrial enterprises; it is argued that the concept of industrialization as necessarily involving large-scale, heavy industrial enterprises, is not relevant to the needs of countries in the tropical world.

An important reason for arguing in this way is that small-scale cottage industry can deal most effectively with the three obstacles to industrialization already discussed. Cottage industry is the kind of venture which depends upon traditional skills and so can help to build up the supply of manufacturing, managerial, and entrepreneurial experience which in turn can form the basis of a subsequent, more impressive, industrial expansion; it economizes with the scarce factor of capital and makes a fuller use of manpower, being labour-intensive rather than capital-intensive; and it is aimed at producing the kinds of consumer goods with which the domestic market is already acquainted and which it is more likely to be able to afford. Both from the population and employment angles, indeed, small-scale cottage technology would seem to be logical in tropical countries.

Another argument sometimes produced in support of small-scale or cottage industrial activity is that developing countries, especially tropical developing countries, are not well endowed with the natural resources essential for the development of heavy industries such as those of iron, steel, and motor vehicles. Yet if the remarks made in Chapter 1 – that the natural resource base must be assumed to be potentially as adequate in the tropics as anywhere else in the world – are indeed valid, then this argument seems to have little validity.

Nevertheless there does seem to be particular scope for the encouragement of small-scale or cottage industry in the tropical world, especially in the production of such goods as textiles, footwear, domestic hardware, glassware, ceramics, umbrellas, soap, and biscuits. Japan has gone a long way in converting family industries into decentralized light industries, and her example may profitably be followed by the countries of the tropics. Where cotton is grown locally it should not be difficult to get the co-operation of overseas capital and expertise to make it up – as at the Kaduna Textiles factory – a joint venture between Northern Nigeria and Lancashire enterprises. In India some notable successes in small-scale industrialization have already been achieved, especially in the state of Punjab at Ludhiana.

On the other hand, it is only too easy to exaggerate the potential role of small-scale or cottage industrial enterprise in the industrial development of the tropics. It should perhaps be pointed out that the present differential in industrial activity between the developed and developing world is to some extent the result of European nineteenth-century colonialism which tended to inhibit industrialization in the tropical world. During the nineteenth century the western countries looked upon the tropical developing world largely as a source of raw materials; later on, 'as the internal market in Europe began to show signs of satiety, the western powers began to look overseas for markets as well. One consequence was to flood the Orient with cheap manufactures and ruin the handicraft industries of India and China which might otherwise have been growing points for industrialization' (B. Ward, 1964: 52). There are numerous examples of local cottage industrial activities being unable to compete with imported Western products; and the result has been that indigenous cottage industries in many areas are now stagnant or derelict and can hardly be expected to form the basis of any substantial increase in industrial production. Furthermore, whatever the theoretical or indeed the practical advantages of the small-scale or cottage industrial enterprise may be, there is no doubt that it is already irrevocably supplanted in the minds of most tropical peoples by the large industrial enterprise. The powerful psychological attraction and mystique of large-scale modern industry can only confirm the trend towards the large-scale industrial unit in development planning. And the United Nations Committee for Industrial Development (U.N., 1966) has supported the view that small-scale industry should only be developed within the total framework of industrialization programmes, and not instead of, or in preference to, large-scale or medium-sized industry.

Intermediate technology. Many of the arguments presented above for cottage and small-scale industry lie behind the movement towards medium or 'intermediate' technology which applies throughout the whole range of development activity, including agriculture. Intermediate technology, as understood by the Intermediate Technology Group (ITG), has been defined as intermediate between the hoe and the tractor; it is also a technology which is, or can be brought, within reach of the poor, by which they can become self-reliant. As Schumacher (1964) puts it, the twin evils of mass unemployment and mass migration into cities – both normally characteristic of large-scale industrialization in poor countries – can only be combated by fulfilling four requirements. First, work-places have to be created in areas where people are already living. Secondly, these workplaces must be, on average, cheap enough so that they can be created in large numbers. Thirdly, the production methods must be relatively simple, so that the demands for high skills are minimized. Finally, production should be largely from local materials for local use (Schumacher, 1964: 87).

The Intermediate Technology Group, set up in 1965, has stimulated, in Britain at least, a new emphasis and direction in development thinking which is likely to play an increasingly significant role in development planning. The rapidly growing literature on intermediate technology has already documented many successful case-studies in intermediate technology, perhaps more particularly where applied to the bottlenecks of production, organization, raw-material supply and marketing (Schumacher, 1964; Schumacher and McRobie, 1969).

'Appropriate technology', as it is now commonly called, has in recent years come in for a good deal of criticism, expressed succinctly in the dictum 'small is stupid' (Beckerman, 1979). Nevertheless, in 1980 the 'small is beautiful' approach of Schumacher (1973) still enjoys wide popularity with its recognition of the unsuitability of modern technology for developing countries; its belief that the wrong sort of industrialization is being pursued; and with its warnings that large-scale industrialization is creating new and dangerous forms of dualism.

CHAPTER 10

Transport

The role of transport. The urgent and now widely recognized need to improve and extend transport facilities in tropical countries is clear from the fact that transport and communications commonly take over 40 per cent of the total public outlay in development planning. Many aid funds have been selectively applied to this particular field of development; and the principle is now generally accepted that the improvement of transport forms perhaps the most valuable single contribution towards economic, social and political development. Certainly in the early stages of economic advance in communities where subsistence agriculture is still important, transport is probably the key to development: 'fertilizers, improved strains of seed, education and other objects are all of the greatest importance. But the need for transport is prior to all these' (Clark and Haswell, 1964: 216).

There are two major reasons for emphasizing the role of transport in economic development, more especially in tropical developing countries. First, transportation is seen as the *sine qua non* of colonization and so vital in the extension of settlement in a region. Humphreys (1946) has shown how important transport facilities are to the opening up of tropical South America. The eastern valleys of Bolivia and parts of Peru and Ecuador are potentially good areas for settlement, but they are inaccessible and too distant from markets and ports. Then there are great areas bordering the Amazon Basin now empty of people but which will prove suitable for settlement when such highways as the Lima–Tonjo Main Pacific Highway have been constructed. The Matto Grosso is hindered in its development by lack of communications, as is the open plain country at the foot of Bolivia near Santa Cruz de la Sierra. According to Humphreys, if transport were improved sufficiently Brazil could support a population of some 400 million people – well over four times the present population. The building of the new capital of Brasilia is one example of attempts to direct attention away from the coast towards Brazil's vast but thinly populated interior. Brasilia is located at the nodal point of a new and extensive road network from Brasilia to Rio de Janeiro, to the Pacific coast, and to Belem on the Amazon River.

Secondly, and more important, improved and extended transport facilities are necessary to the widening and fusion of the market in areas already settled, and in stimulating further production for internal or external trade in a country and so in encouraging the growth of a modern exchange economy: 'cheapening transport fuses markets, bringing additional buyers and sellers into contact with one another, increasing elasticities of demand and supply' (Kindleberger, 1966: 167). Furthermore, transport allows the free exchange of goods between rural areas and urban centres, 'whereby it becomes possible for the economic position of the cultivator to rise above subsistence level, consuming locally grown food and simple handicrafts produced in his own village, and practically nothing else; while in the absence of transport towns could not exist at all' (Clark and Haswell, 1964: 167). Transportation facilities also encourage and facilitate the geographical specialization of agricultural production. Finally, improved transport facilities may make possible the intensification of agricultural production, with all the improvements in techniques this implies: it is useless, for instance, to try to encourage the use of manures or cultivated fodder on fields far distant from the farmstead where 'the farmer or his wife has no means of transporting it other than by head porterage. Intensification calls first of all for continuing efforts aimed at reducing the costs of all the operations involved, starting with the production and transport costs of cultivated fodder and manure' (Dumont, 1966: 71).

Forms of transport. Over the larger part of the tropical world most transport services are still performed by the individual, often in the form of head, shoulder or back porterage, and without any capital equipment at all; and it has been suggested that the extent of human porterage – if it could be measured – might well provide one of the more illuminating indices of levels of economic development (Bauer and Yamey, 1957). Simple carts, wagons, or beasts of burden may also be used, and the bicycle is playing an increasingly significant role in the movement of goods where topographical conditions make this possible. All such elementary forms of moving goods must for long provide the bulk of transport services, even where they become merely tributary to major modern lines of transport.

The individually small-scale nature of all these simple, often primitive means of transport in tropical countries is not to be condemned and discouraged out of hand. In the majority of cases, indeed, the present means of transport may be said to be adequate in the prevailing physical, social, and economic conditions. Nevertheless, there are many areas where they can already be said to present a barrier to economic development. Certainly in economic terms the apparently 'cheap' method of transport – human porterage – is commonly prohibitively expensive. Human porterage has been said to be some nine or ten times as expensive as transport by water, motor vehicle, or rail; forms of transport at present available to the bulk of tropical peoples, in fact, are so costly that produce often 'only has to be carried a limited distance before most of its value, from the point of view of net returns from the sale, has gone' (Clark and Haswell, 1964: 156). This is partly because of the frequent repetition of transport movements demanded in a situation where only very limited amounts can be carried by the individual in each operation; but it is also partly due to the fact that distances covered by human porterage are necessarily severely limited. According to Gourou (1966) the average figure is 30 miles (50 km) a day at an average load of 88 lb (40 kg). The implications of this point for economic development are obvious, but include the important one that the choice of crop is often determined at least partly by reference to the costs of available transport facilities. In East Africa, for instance, it has been shown that Africans have chosen coffee because the value of the crop makes it one of the few crops which can support the existing burden of transport costs (Clark and Haswell, 1964: 156). Again, high transport cost have been shown to affect the price of land in Mindanao

(Philippines) where land prices drop markedly with distance from markets.

The other simplest form of transport – by water – is in economic terms perhaps the least costly of all forms of transport. The role of water transport in tropical countries is commonly underestimated and has received remarkably little treatment in the literature, perhaps because it commonly applies to areas with relatively low population densities and often with only primitive forms of economic development. Yet water transport has played an important role in the early penetration and development of large parts of the tropics; and in many countries the river is still the real focus of economic life and commonly provides the only means of transport. This is particularly true of the lowland equatorial tropics: in Congo Kinshasa, Sarawak, and northern Brazil, for instance. But in many other areas throughout the tropics the potential for water transport and development is considerable. This is illustrated by the detailed report of NEDECO (1960) on the improvement of navigation on the Rivers Niger and Benue in Nigeria.

The present poverty of rail transport in most tropical countries is very striking and, especially where the final stages of the movement of export crops and minerals are concerned, this may certainly be restrictive on development. The economic history of most countries in the tropics abounds with examples of how crop and mineral production had to await the building of railways: cocoa in Ghana was stimulated by the Accra–Kumasi railway; the production of cotton in Uganda was made feasible by the construction of the Kenya–Uganda railway; and the mining of tin on the Jos Plateau of Nigeria and of copper in Katanga also had to await the arrival of the railway before any great development could take place. In particular, as the case of Nigeria shows, the correlation between export crops and railway building has sometimes been remarkably close. Groundnuts did not figure significantly in Lagos exports until after the completion of the Lagos–Kano railway in 1912; and the same is true of cotton and hides and skins, all of which originated in the northern savanna lands.

In recent years, however, the emphasis has shifted away from the role of the railway to the role of the road in economic development, though the traditional role of the railway in development has by no means been destroyed. Controversy over the relative merits of railways and roads in stimulating economic advance is still common, and striking instances of this have occurred over the last decade or so. In Nigeria the International Bank Report of 1954 considered proposals to build a railway reaching into the north-eastern corner of the country and, on reviewing the evidence, rejected them; but it supported alternative proposals to extend the road network into the same area. Subsequent work and political considerations, however, led to a reversal of this decision, and the Bornu Extension Railway, as it is now called, was finally constructed between 1960 and 1964. The avowed purpose of this line was to bring to north-eastern Nigeria the same opportunities of agricultural expansion and cash crop production, based on cheap transport, that are already being enjoyed in Kano Province; and it was hoped and expected that as purchasing stations for groundnuts and cotton were established along the line in Bauchi and Bornu Provinces, the population would migrate towards the line and turn to the cultivation of substantial surpluses for sale through the apparatus of the Marketing Boards. This, it was hoped, would succeed because the region is thinly populated, so that land for commercial agriculture is readily available. The railway had turned the Kano close-settled zone into a major producing area of groundnuts for export, and it could do the same for Bornu, where rainfall and soils were no less favourable (Emerson, 1959). Already, however, it is becoming clear that the build-up of traffic on this line is unlikely to be fast enough to enable the railway to be run at a profit; certainly it will not enable Nigerian railways to undercut substantially the rates charged by lorry operators for carrying agricultural produce to the coast (Barbour, 1966).

There seems little doubt that the road will continue to capture an increasing share of internal traffic in most tropical countries. In Uganda, O'Connor (1966) has shown that road transport has continued to remain more important that the newly constructed railways, and that the latter have had remarkably little impact on local or regional trade. Not only is the road a much more flexible instrument for inducing economic development – it can proliferate more easily and can be tapped at any point for the purposes of distribution – but the road is also a much less capital-intensive method of providing transport facilities. It is not only that construction and maintenance costs are higher for railways than for roads, but also that railways are indivisible investments. These are normally built and owned by governments, simply because railways represent heavy investment based on future demand patterns. In a few cases, as in Costa Rica, private companies have built the main railways; but in general it is true that private enterprise could not be expected to be interested in such risky investments. Roads, however, represent divisible investments, and road transportation can be developed in relatively small divisible units. Government participation is required only in the construction of the basic road network itself, while the rest of the investment is commonly provided by private enterprise. As a number of writers have pointed out, indeed, this divisibility of investment in road transport, compared with investment in railways, may be crucial in the early stages of a country's economic development, when domestic markets are narrow and the volume of traffic is small. Furthermore, as another authority has emphasized, although the adverse effects of tropical climates upon surface structures make it costly to build roads and railways, the latter 'require to be kept in a much better state of repair in order to maintain services' (Hawkins, 1962: 29); and experience in Costa Rica has demonstrated very clearly the difficult and costly problem of railway maintenance in a tropical, mountainous environment. Yet there may be a danger that the wholesale and indiscriminate building of roads will become accepted as automatically beneficial – almost as the latest of a series of panaceas for the problems of developing countries.

The economics of transport. A great deal, certainly, needs to be known about the economics of transport, and the available evidence in almost any field of transportation studies in tropical countries is both scanty and fragmentary. Hawkins (1958) has suggested that when traffic reaches 300 vehicles a day on a road then bitumenization becomes economically worthwhile in Nigeria. Sargent (1960) estimates that each kilometre of road built has the effect of opening some 60 hectares of new agricultural land in Sabah. In West African countries Pedler (1955) puts the savings from bitumenization at 18 per cent. But all such data can as yet do little more than enable us to ask our questions rather more precisely than before: the answers to most of the urgent practical problems of transport economics in developing countries of the tropics have still to be found and must await the kind of thorough descriptive analysis presented for the movement of export crops in Nigeria by White (1959).

Some of the difficulties in building roads in tropical countries are well illustrated in Sarawak where new roads are a costly undertaking, not only because of the difficult terrain but also because the climate and general unsuitability of local building materials make a high and expensive standard of construction essential if the road is to give reasonable service. Moreover, the sharp contrasts in population distribution, and the low average density of population in the country means that roads have to pass for long stretches through uninhabited country and so face large initial operating deficits. Again, in Nigeria, as in most countries of the tropics with a substantial and definite dry season, earth roads are likely to be usable only during the dry season. Nevertheless, so expensive are bitumenized roads that even today still only 4,000 miles (6,440 km) out of 37,000 miles (59,500 km) are bitumenized, the balance consisting of gravel and earth roads.

. . . . .

Attention in this very brief summary has been concentrated on transport in relation to economic development in a tropical country as seen from inside that country. But equally, of course, transport facilities in relation to economic development must be considered at an international level: in fact, it is rather arbitrary to make any clear distinction between internal and external transport facilities in discussing economic development. Air transport improvements have their repercussions upon many sides of the complex process of economic development, as is well shown in West Africa and Latin America; and the importance of creating, maintaining, and improving port facilities is particularly obvious in countries whose prosperity continues to be so closely linked to the export of basic raw materials or commodities and whose economies depend so heavily upon imported manufactured goods (White, 1959). Both internally and externally, it is probably impossible to exaggerate the importance of transport to economic development in the developing countries of the tropical world. The theoretical and practical arguments for giving priority to such issues in the early stages of a country's economic planning are familiar and convincing. Whether at the national or at the individual level, increased production is always likely to be frustrated unless two requirements – good cheap transport and good market opportunities – are fulfilled. The next chapter concentrates on the second of these two requirements.

CHAPTER 11

Markets and Trade

Most of the literature on economic development and, indeed, perhaps the larger part of the present volume, is concerned with the problems of increasing production as seen from the supply point of view. The utilization and improvement of natural, human, and capital resources is viewed primarily in relation to the aim of increasing production. Both at the local level and at the level of national economic development, preoccupation seems commonly to be with the supply side of production in all its various manifestations. Quite clearly, however, this is a somewhat arbitrary and misleading emphasis, for it is little more than an analytical convenience to distinguish rigidly between the supply and demand sides of the problem of increasing production. The present chapter concentrates attention on the demand side as expressed by internal and external markets and trade.

Internal markets and trade. It has already been necessary on a number of occasions to refer to the narrowness of the home market in tropical developing countries. This narrowness is a characteristic of underdevelopment and is frequently held to constitute a formidable obstacle to agricultural and industrial development. The nature and causes of this condition vary from one country to another, but in general may be said to arise from the low purchasing power and restricted spending habits of consumers; from lack of capital for storage; and from inadequate and costly transport. Market opportunities and economic prosperity are here closely interdependent.

Home market opportunities, though automatically widening as economic development and population growth proceeds, can be widened still further by various means. As was shown in the previous chapter, indeed, one of the arguments for improving internal lines of transport is that they will help to increase the extent and intensity of market contacts within a territory and so lead to economies of scale. Another way in which the domestic market can be widened is by providing capital for storage and credit facilities to farmers. Again, Nurkse (1953) advocates the enlargement of the home market by the simultaneous expansion of a large number of industries which buy one another's products; this, he argues, will automatically create a market and will also, if localized, increase the external economies enjoyed by each firm and so reduce costs – which is one reason why industries tend to be gregarious. It has also been suggested that the home market may be enlarged for home products by capturing what is at present supplied for foreign producers. This may be possible in a few fields, particularly in small-scale industries. But in relating the home market to industrial expansion, where market limitations are especially limiting, the pattern of spending among tropical peasants cannot be ignored. In Ceylon, for instance, the average consumer spends 60 per cent of his total expenditure on food and only 2·5 per cent on clothing and 0·1 per cent on shoes. The level of income is so low that these percentages would not be likely to alter much even if incomes rose moderately. In many tropical countries, especially those that are heavily populated, the income elasticity of demand for food is close to unity: in other words, people would still continue to spend the bulk of their income on food until their income reaches a certain critical figure above which Engel's law applies and the consumption of food decreases as a percentage of income. Data for Greater Delhi seem to support this general principle (Table 6). In this situation, clearly, a producer will be reluctant to launch into any ambitious schemes for the production of manufactured goods. There are important differences in elasticities, both of demand and supply, between developing and developed countries; and some economists argue that in developing countries the price system is therefore ineffective and that the normal marginal analysis associated with the price system of advanced societies is inappropriate in the context of developing societies.

However it is accomplished, there can be little doubt that to widen the home market opportunities and to improve opportunities for trading and marketing are crucial in any attempt at inducing economic development. Some writers give this point pride of place in their analyses and prescriptions, arguing that unless the producer's incentives to change or increase his production are affected, then no technical or institutional improvements are likely to have

Table 6. *Household expenditure patterns in Greater Delhi*
(*Average monthly figures*)

Expenditure Range (Rupees)	Total (Rupees)	Percentage of Total				
		Food	Cloth	Fuel	Rent	Other
<100	62·4	61	10	7	7	15
100–249	138·4	58	10	6	8	18
250–499	285·7	53	10	5	8	24
500–999	513·3	47	10	4	9	43
>1000	1169·5	38	8	3	8	43

Source: Rao and Desai (1965), p. 239

much success. And it is undoubtedly true that a tropical farmer is unlikely to increase his production unless an increased demand is there, is seen to be there, and is easily accessible. Improved seed, fertilizers, and better irrigation facilities: a tropical cultivator is unlikely to use these to increase his total production unless the market for his increased production is first seen to exist and is accessible. It is probably always true to say that there is no point in a farmer having a new crop variety or fertilizers, which will enable him to increase his food production very substantially and immediately, if at the same time his form of transport is so costly or the demand for the extra produce is so uncertain or so distant as to make such an increase worthless. From the point of view of the individual farmer who makes the increase, increased production implies increased sales. And increased sales implies an increased demand which the farmer is aware of, responds to in terms of his spending habits, and which he can easily and economically reach (Krishna, 1959). Only when these conditions are fulfilled is it logical to attempt to improve crop production by the application of scientific methods and research or to attempt any of the more complex agricultural or infrastructural changes increased agricultural production implies.

Unfortunately, however, our knowledge of the forms, mechanisms, and institutions of indigenous trading and marketing in most tropical countries is very scanty and uneven (Galbraith and Holton, 1955), and has to depend very much upon the attempt to draw analogies with early market institutions in Western Europe or upon contemporary work in non-tropical countries, notably in China (Skinner, 1964-5), where it is argued that the phenomena described are really characteristic of all 'peasant' or 'traditional' agrarian societies. As pointed out elsewhere (Hodder, 1961), the geographical analysis of the economies of tropical countries commonly concentrates either on the productive sector or on large-scale internal and external exchange sectors. Remarkably little attention has been paid to the local exchange sectors or to the functions and characteristics of local market institutions like the rural periodic markets of Africa or the water markets of parts of South-east Asia. Yet for the bulk of the population, both in rural and in urban areas, it is through some form of local market that most agricultural and cottage industrial products enter the exchange economy; and it is through these same market institutions that goods from abroad and elsewhere are absorbed. Clearly, then, it is at the level of local exchange that we must look in any attempt directly to affect the production and consumption of the majority of tropical peoples.

To take the case with which the writer is personally most familiar – West Africa – the lively system of local trade there has been shown to be of considerable economic significance. The general characteristics of some of the market institutions of West Africa have now been presented in a number of studies (Bohannan and Dalton, 1962; Hodder, 1961, 1965a, 1965b; Hill, 1966a, 1966b), and some of the facts about the periodic markets – their cyclical or periodic nature, their organization into market rings or circuits, their commodity structure and economic functions, for instance – and about the daily markets, especially their relevance to 'central-place' theory, are now beginning to be understood, though a great deal remains to be known about markets in the region. It is still impossible to generalize confidently about the processes and socio-economic significance of all West African market institutions.

The origins of traditional, pre-European, indigenous markets in West Africa have been examined elsewhere (Hodder, 1965b; Ukwu, 1965), it being suggested that political control of a kind able to guarantee the market peace, a sufficiently high density of population, and location on or near long-distance trade routes were necessary elements in the rise of indigenous market institutions in West Africa. This point about market origins is important to the present study, not so much because it helps to explain why West Africa has such a highly developed system of market institutions – the region having a number of powerful early political states, being threaded by long-distance trade routes of great antiquity, and having by African standards a high density of population – but because it may be relevant to contemporary attempts to induce self-generating change to a market economy among those peoples of the tropics who as yet lie largely outside modern economic influences. If this notion has any validity, it means in modern terms that only where there is an effective political administration, a sufficiently high density of population – probably not less than 50 persons to the square mile (20 per km²) – and long-distance lines of transportation, especially good trunk roads, are efforts to induce rapid economic change likely to be effective. And where these conditions are not fulfilled, then their provision must be a precondition for any significant economic development.

How far local trade and its associated institutional mechanism of the market place is increasing or decreasing relative to other forms of trade is a controversial issue. As far as West Africa is concerned, it has been suggested by some writers that market institutions are declining in importance, for as economies become more sophisticated these institutions become less necessary: 'the more pervasive the market principle the less the economic importance of the market place' (Bohannan and Dalton, 1962: 25). Yet there are strong practical reasons, such as increased urbanization, improved transport, higher purchasing power, increased occupational specialization, for presuming that the total quantity of goods sold in West African markets is in fact increasing proportionately far more quickly than the size of the population (Hill, 1963). This is not the place to discuss the relative merits of these two opposing viewpoints, except perhaps to point out that the evidence from the few studies so far made is conflicting and that much more serious study of specific communities is indicated (Ukwu, 1965). What is beyond doubt, however, is the fact that the character of most West African markets is beginning to show signs of radical changes. Two of these changes are the shift from periodic to continuous trading and the shift to specialized wholesale markets. Though markets in West Africa today still largely take the place of shops in Western Europe, the tendency is for the balance to change – for indigenous shops to increase in number and importance, especially around the periphery of the larger daily markets in the main towns; and for periodic markets to take over most of the largely wholesale functions in distribution. This is a process quite independent of the existence and growth of introduced European retail and wholesale shopping nuclei which are still the dominant form of shops in almost all the larger towns of West Africa.

This point about the development of indigenous shops and the changing relative significance and functions of periodic and daily markets can be related to an hypothesis which sees all types and operations of markets in West Africa as intermediate stages on a single, albeit many-stranded continuum from the most primitive to the most complicated economies. Simply stated the argument can be expressed as follows:

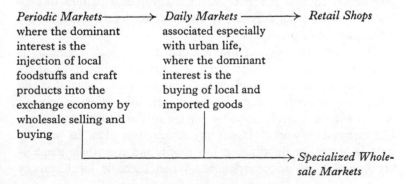

Periodic Markets———→ *Daily Markets* ————→ *Retail Shops*
where the dominant associated especially
interest is the with urban life,
injection of local where the dominant
foodstuffs and craft interest is the
products into the buying of local and
exchange economy by imported goods
wholesale selling and
buying

————————————————————→ *Specialized Whole-*
sale Markets

This hypothesis, tracing the development of markets from the simplest periodic markets through to the retail shops and large specialized wholesale markets in the largest towns, appears to fit in with the facts so far available; and this notion is further strengthened by a number of analogies drawn between markets in West Africa and those of Europe from medieval times to the present day. Any attempt to widen this hypothesis to other regions of the tropics must await similar work elsewhere. But the immediate and practical importance of such considerations for urban and rural planning and for the processes of economic development needs taking into account in all such research.

As for internal market opportunities and trade within a country, material in this field is even more scarce than in the field of local markets and trade. Once again, West Africa is rather better served in this connexion than are most other parts of the tropics. For Dahomey, Tardits (1962) has described how the agricultural products of the south are exchanged between the different geographical units – plateau and valley, coasts and inland areas – and how goods are sent from the rural areas into the urban markets of Cotonou, Porto Novo, Ouidah, and Abomey; for Ghana, White (1956) has demonstrated the internal exchange of movements of staple food crops; and Tricart (1956) has described the nature and characteristics of internal trade in Togo. In East Africa, Ford (1956) has described the trade of Lake Victoria. In the context of a nation's economic development planning, clearly, internal trade of this kind is of great importance and is of particular interest to the geographer in that it expresses the geographical pattern of ecological regions with different agricultural and craft products and specialization of production.

This whole question of internal distribution and marketing is perhaps of particular importance in large countries like India where food-surplus areas and food-deficit areas are widely separated and where an ancient, unorganized but normally effective system carries surplus cereals from the village to the consumer centres. But this system works without any direction or plan. Its purpose here is not really distribution but profit, and the whole machinery operates on price variations. When there is local scarcity prices rise, bringing more food on to the local markets but reducing consumption: when prices go up sharply the poorest in the villages may begin to starve. The system works in the same way on the national level, cereals going from the food-surplus states (Andhra Pradesh, Madhya Pradesh, Maharashtra, Orissa, Punjab, and Madras) to those states which do not produce enough food for themselves. But at this level political interference begins. In times of relative or expected scarcity the governments of the food-surplus states may resist, openly or furtively, the export of food to the usual markets.

External markets and trade. It is widely held that the economic development of many tropical countries has been restricted by their existing patterns of foreign trade. This has a number of important implications for development, one of which is that apart from South-east Asia, where there is some considerable movement of rice from the surplus countries to deficit countries, trade between the various countries of the tropics is only very small. The reasons for this are well known, and include the important one that the range of raw materials available for export is generally so small and frequently so similar that tropical countries have very little to offer each other. A further implication is that most of the efforts to improve production within tropical countries have been controlled and financed by the metropolitan powers and have been directed almost exclusively at those crops and other raw materials most needed by the manufacturing nations of the developed world. As noted earlier in the present chapter, this concentration on foreign trade items and on foreign trade as a process has usually been at the expense of other exchange sectors. The resulting 'économie de traite' is vividly illustrated in the pattern of internal communications in tropical countries. Only in a few cases, such as the palm-oil export industry in West Africa, in Bombay or in Minas Geraes, did this kind of economic development lead to any rapid advance in local modernized farming or local industrialization.

Independent tropical countries have also been left with a legacy of external trading organization which many believe to restrict rapid economic advance. In particular, the association in the minds of tropical peoples between colonialism and export economies is emphasized by the concentration of the large-scale export and import trade in the hands of a few large, mostly European, concerns. This has been illustrated for West Africa where the external trade is still largely in non-African hands: in 1949 about 85 per cent of the import trade in Nigeria was handled by European firms, about 10 per cent by Levantine and Indian firms, and only about 5 per cent by African firms. It is true that attempts are now being made to reduce this concentration in the import–export trade of West Africa, more especially since independence. But so far there has been little success in this direction. The reasons why these firms continue to be few and large include the fact that capital requirements are very substantial in the export of such primary commodities as palm oil, groundnuts or cocoa. Storage and transit difficulties in the prevailing conditions of poor transportation, scattered populations and immense distances, too, favour large organizing units. And all these facts call for the kind of sophisticated supervisory and technical management only likely to be encountered in the large European, or at least European-type, firm.

But probably the central problem in this context of external markets and trade is the perpetuation of the nineteenth-century pattern of external trade whereby tropical territories export certain raw materials, in which they have a comparative advantage, to the developed countries, and import manufactured goods from the same sources. Primary, mainly agricultural products and some minerals, dominate in exports; and finished consumer goods – textiles, vehicles, bicycles, cement, building materials, and machinery – account for most of the imports (Table 7). Furthermore, in many tropical countries exports comprise only a very few items: Senegal and Gambia both have over 80 per cent of the value of their exports accounted for by groundnuts; Sierra Leone has over 80 per cent of her export earnings provided by mining; 95 per cent of Columbia's foreign earnings come from coffee, petroleum, and bananas; and 88 per cent of Ceylon's earnings come from tea, rubber, and coconut products.

Much has been written about this tendency to depend on a small number of export raw materials in tropical countries. Some of the problems it raises are related to the repercussions such a pattern of exports has upon the production side of the economy, on labour market policy, on soil fertility and conservation, on crop pests and diseases, and on the improvement of dietary standards among tropical peoples. Some writers contend that the relation of productivity to prices in tropical lands is such that the exchange by them of primary products for the manufactures of developed

Table 7. *Import–export structures in selected countries*

	Major Imports as % of total imports by value, 1969		Major Exports as % of total exports by value, 1969	
Venezuela	Machinery and transport materials	44	Crude petroleum	69
	Manufactured goods	18	Petroleum products	27
			Iron ore	4
Ghana	Manufactured goods	27	Cocoa	51
	Machinery and transport materials	24		
India	Machinery and transport materials	25	Textile yarn	26
			Tea	9
	Manufactured goods	17	Jute fabrics	12
	Food products	21		

Source: U.N., *Yearbook of International Trade Statistics,* 1969.

countries, while especially profitable for the latter, is almost inevitably injurious to the former (Viner, 1953). Other authorities, for example Myrdal (1956), do not accept this view. But it is on the economic instability caused by overdependence on one or two raw material export products that attention is normally concentrated. Certainly the purchasing power of exports may fluctuate quite dramatically. Between 1959 and 1961, for instance, the average price of Ghanaian cocoa dropped by 32·4 per cent; and such fluctuations are always likely to occur in a situation where the manufacture of synthetics or substitutes – notably fibres, resins, detergents, dyestuffs, and nitrites – is common and where demand patterns are continually changing. Then, too, many other technological developments are likely to work against the developing countries simply because they reduce the possibility of advance towards industrialization by transforming exhaustible natural assets into valuable man-made wealth; for the whole tendency of technological advance, as was pointed out in Chapter 1, is to make natural resources more homogeneous, both in quality and in their distribution, and to reduce the actual or potential value of high-quality natural resources that were once essential for industry (Barnett and Morse, 1963).

Again, increased agricultural productivity in the developed, industrial countries has usually been accompanied by measures to protect these producers from adverse price effects arising from competition from low-income tropical countries. Similarly, the protection of other domestic producers, such as oil and mineral producers in the United States, denies low-cost producers in the developing countries any ready access to existing industrial markets.

In whatever way and from whatever cause these fluctuations in world market prices and so in the value of exports arise, these fluctuations affect not only export earnings and so the balance of payments situations in developing countries but result also in changes in revenues to the governments in the form of customs duties. This is an important point in countries where export–import duties still make up over half the total government revenues.

The problem, then, is that the low-income countries of the tropics are today faced with a fluctuating and often generally declining world market for their traditional raw materials. It may be true that fluctuations in export earnings are really no greater in tropical developing countries than for advanced countries. Yet tropical countries have few alternative opportunities for international trading in other agricultural or industrial products. Present trends in the pattern of international trading would seem to favour increasingly the industrial countries at the expense of the low-income countries of the tropical developing world. It is now commonly argued, moreover, that the widening gap between rich and poor countries is caused by the fact that the consumption of primary commodities by the rich nations does not increase at the same rate as their economic expansion; new processes and new materials tend to reduce the consumption of industrial raw materials in relation to output; and with food products, higher incomes do not lead to a parallel increase in consumption in the rich countries (*The Times*, 1964: 27 October). The terms of trade seem in the long run to favour developed countries and turn against developing countries, illustrating the Prebisch effect – that primary production tends to increase beyond what is required by the relatively slow increase of demand. And it was partly the great interest in this fact that led to the setting up in 1964 of the United Nations Conference on Trade and Development (UNCTAD).

One way of dealing with this broad problem of external trade in tropical countries is to encourage diversification. This can be pursued in export crop production by introducing new export crops: in West Africa, for instance, ginger in Sierra Leone, beniseed in Nigeria, and karite seeds in Upper Volta are being expanded. In this sense, changing land-use patterns are both caused by and are the cause of changing patterns in international trade. Then diversification of production for the home market is sometimes prescribed as the solution to the problem of economic instability arising from the dependence of export economies on a fluctuating market, though there is some controversy over this policy. It is true that diversified production for the home market as a substitute for specialized production for the export market might well involve loss of productivity and a deterioration in living standards; and it will be appreciated that a country like Malaya has been able to achieve a relatively high level of *per capita* income largely because of her specialization in the production of exports for the world markets. And some writers, indeed, argue strongly against diversification and point to the fact that a country like Malagasy, which has a wide spread of crops and products, has a weaker economy than many of its 'one-product' neighbours. But on the other hand – and quite apart from considerations of economic nationalism and the revolt against the 'colonial pattern of foreign trade legacy' – the tendency to change the emphasis from export industries in favour of diversified production for the home market has to varying extents been forced upon tropical countries by the changing nature of world markets. As already noted, the demand for primary commodities in which tropical countries have traditionally specialized is becoming weak and uncertain where new sources of production, natural and synthetic, are being tapped; and the export outlook for manufactured goods is even less promising because of severe competition from highly industrialized countries and restrictive trade policies in most importing countries.

Industrialization represents yet another way of trying to deal with the problem of overdependence on a few raw materials in world markets. In this context industrialization has among its aims not only the desire to earn more foreign exchange by the further processing and therefore the increase in value of raw material exports, but also the desire to save foreign currency by substituting domestically produced items for manufactured goods at present imported from abroad. In West Africa some success has been achieved in this direction with the rapid increase over the past few years of such import-substitution industries as flour-milling, beer, tile, ceramic, and cheap textile industries; meat and fish canning; and car assembly plants, especially in Nigeria, Ghana, and Ivory Coast. On the whole, however, the effects of import-replacing industrialization on the foreign trade of West Africa has so far shown little sign of changing the traditional pattern of trade by reducing the imports of manufactured items. In Ghana, and in spite of such industrialization, agricultural raw materials continue to dominate Ghana's exports, and manufactures her imports. What has changed is the composition of imports from manufactured consumer goods to manufactured capital goods. Here again, perhaps the crucial issue is market opportunity. Industrialization, as we have seen earlier, is severely limited by the very characteristics of developing societies that it is intended to remedy. Yet it would be misleading to overemphasize this as a continuing problem. There are already clear examples of tropical countries diversifying their exports by industrialization and by finding the necessary markets within other countries of the tropics. One example is Kenya, where every effort is being made to widen the base of the exports to include a greater quantity of manufactured goods. Kenya is fast becoming a major supplier of neighbouring countries in Africa and the Indian Ocean. Including exports to

Uganda and Tanzania, over 43 per cent of Kenya's total exports by value are sold within Africa, for, in addition to manufactured goods, many African countries have to import the temperate climate's agricultural and dairy produce which Kenya is ideally suited to supply. During 1966 there was a sharp increase in exports to other African countries outside East Africa. This increase was in part due to the temporary problems facing Zambia, but more significant was the substantial increase in exports to Congo Kinshasa, Rwanda, Burundi, and the Sudan (*The Times*, 1966: 20 October).

Another means of lessening the ill-effects of existing trading patterns upon the economic development potential of many tropical countries has been the establishment of a number of centralized marketing institutions. These have been particularly important in West Africa, more especially for specific export crops. Known as Marketing Boards or, in some of the French-speaking territories, as *Caisses de Stabilisation*, they have monopoly powers for the purchase and sale of the principal export products. Attempts have also been made in a number of cases to eliminate or at least to reduce the problem of market competition between individual countries, as with the International Coffee Organization.

The arguments lying behind the formation of these boards and other organizations concern matters of efficiency, standardization, and stability. Certainly these marketing boards and their equivalents have had some effect in stabilizing incomes, if not prices, from year to year. On the other hand, their effect on forecasting and controlling surpluses has not been remarkable for, as several authorities have shown, the export surpluses of a number of West African countries were relatively about the same before the war as during the post-war period of statutory marketing schemes. A number of writers, indeed, have come out strongly against all such monopolistic and centralized schemes. Bauer (1963b), in particular, has attacked the whole concept of these boards, partly on the grounds that they choke normal competitive instincts and so limit individual experience in marketing.

A fourth way of dealing with the external trading problems of tropical countries is to encourage regional economic co-operation between groups of states in an area (Urquidi, 1962; Allen, 1961). A number of attempts at establishing preferential trade agreements between groups of countries can be cited: the Latin American Free Trade Association (LAFTA), Gran Colombia, the Caribbean Free Trade Area, the Benin–Sahel Entente, the Customs Union for Equatorial and Central Africa, the East African Common Services Organisation (EACSO), and the Southeast Asian Free Trade Association. The international framework within which all these attempts have operated or continue to operate is the General Agreement on Tariffs and Trade (GATT), the successor of the International Trade Association (ITA). This agreement has laid down the two exceptions to the general rule prohibiting trade discrimination: that countries forming a customs union can eliminate tariffs between them and adopt a common tariff against the outside world; and the granting of 100 per cent mutual preference in specified commodities by developing countries. As Kindleberger (1966) has pointed out, all these customs unions, free-trade areas and 100 per cent preferences in specified commodities would appear to be a useful means of co-operation between developing countries. By widening their domestic markets the member countries are able to achieve the economies of scale necessary to any rapid industrialization programme; and if the developing countries are in foreign exchange difficulties, mutual exchanges even of high-cost products are a means of getting goods which they might otherwise have to do without.

In fact, however, there has not been to date any really successful attempt at this kind of regional economic co-operation in trade. The difficulties are many. As pointed out earlier in this chapter, tropical countries trade very little with each other. Furthermore, in new goods which might be produced in the region, it is difficult to arrange who produces what. Tariff reductions are also difficult for countries with a weak balance of payments. Again, there is the problem of the gains and losses among the various countries: the richest of the member countries might believe itself to be suffering from having to make larger contributions than its neighbours while the poorest members might suffer from having to open their markets to the industries of the more prosperous states. Yet again, differences in language, in currencies and in existing trading ties can so easily frustrate successful co-operation. Finally, political difficulties of many other kinds commonly arise; and it is possible to argue that the basic obstacle to regional co-operation for economic development is political rather than economic.

The interdependence and significance of markets and trade. Geographical, economic, and anthropological research in the tropics has tended to ignore the many varied phenomena and processes associated with trading activities. This is perhaps particularly unfortunate at a time when purely subsistence economies are a rarity, and when all contemporary agricultural, industrial, and infrastructural change can be seen to imply mutual adjustment to the limits and opportunities set by existing trading patterns. Assuming an adequate understanding of the varied and complex forms and processes, therefore, trade can clearly be a powerful instrument of change.

Any real understanding of the implications of trade for economic development generally in the tropics, however, is limited not only by the scarcity of data and information but also by the tendency to view trade as composed of a number of distinct 'types', each with its own problems, characteristics, and opportunities. It is true that a classification of trade into a number of types has obvious analytical convenience as a breakdown of the various distributive streams between producer and consumer; yet it does tend seriously to exaggerate the differences between them. More accurately, the whole trading pattern in any tropical country should perhaps be seen as a number of interwoven and interdependent types of trade.

To bring this whole question down to the level of the individual, a farmer in Yorubaland may be involved either directly or indirectly in all types of trading. He may be growing cocoa, which moves to the export port through the Marketing Board machinery. He may also be growing kola, which goes to the local market place where it is bulked up by a Hausa trader for transport to the northern areas of Nigeria or beyond to the Niger Republic. He may also grow food crops, some of which he will consume himself, and some of which will go to the local market place, from where it may reach the final consumer, be taken on to the urban retail markets, or move through the urban wholesale markets for dispatch to the Eastern Region. But almost every pattern reveals the very great significance of the periodic market place in the whole distribution network in this area. As a producer and consumer, much of the actual distribution takes place through the farmer's wife. At the local market place she may buy his imported tobacco, a shirt from Japan, or a new farm tool from Birmingham. At the same time she may buy high-value, low-bulk imported goods so that during the next few days she can operate as an itinerant trader travelling perhaps into Dahomey, down to Lagos, or just visiting other markets in her market circuit. The possibilities and variations are infinite, and it is one of the characteristics of trading life in many parts of the tropics that exclusive patterns of trade are the exception rather than the rule.

It is equally misleading to view trade out of the context of the whole production–distribution–consumption continuum. Thus the farmer referred to above cannot but be affected by fluctuations in world demand and prices for his main export crops – even though he may be cushioned against these by Marketing Boards – as well as by changes in inter-state, inter-regional, or local demand and prices. At the same time he is affected by his own production and marketing problems, soil erosion and fertility problems, pests and diseases, water supply conditions, transport facilities, and transport costs. To the farmer these are all urgent issues of which he is uniquely aware and which he must take account in all his efforts to increase agricultural production. Consequently, just as it is misleading to think of a number of quite distinct types of trade, so it is misleading to concentrate on one part of the production–trade continuum, for each affects and is affected by the other.

.   .   .   .   .

It has been implied in the above discussion that one of the crucial problems in tropical development is concerned with markets and trading – and in particular with the dependence of the tropical world upon the commercial attitudes and trading activities of the developed world. Present international trading policies still underpin the old traditional circuit of Western manufactures in return for raw materials. Western tariffs still discriminate against processed goods. It is clearly necessary to devise trading policies which have the opposite effect: 'that of stimulating local advance, stimulating local manufacture, building up export incomes, and in fact avoiding the situation . . . in which every penny of aid that has been given has been nullified by the collapse of raw material prices and by the unbroken increase in the cost of Western Manufactures' (Ward, 1964: 63). There seems indeed to be a strong case for arguing that the trading problems of the tropical world can only be solved within the wider context of changing trading policies in the developed world. Measures for bringing about trade innovations of the kind required are, admittedly, politically difficult, even when they seem economically simple. But most tropical developing countries argue with justification that the present international trading structure permanently inhibits rapid economic advance in their economies; that commodity stabilization schemes, largely financed by the developed countries, need to be put into operation; and that developed countries can do a great deal to improve and expand trading opportunities for developing countries by accepting simple manufactures among imports, and by reducing tariffs on such goods as coffee, cocoa, and bananas. In this sense the economic development of tropical countries rests as much with such international organizations as the United Nations Conference on Trade and Development as it does with the tropical countries themselves. The next chapter underlines this point within the wider context of the political factor in development planning.

CHAPTER 12

The Political Context

Governments nowadays have almost everywhere an unquest-ioned responsibility for stimulating progress in most spheres of social and economic endeavour. In considering the role of govern-ment in economic development, Lewis (1955) distinguishes nine categories of function: building public services, influencing attitudes, shaping economic institutions influencing resource utiliza-tion, influencing income distribution, controlling the quantity of money, controlling fluctuations, ensuring full employment, and influencing the level of investment. Clearly, the way in which political changes take place has profound effects upon the direction and scope of economic development and must deeply affect future prosperity. For whatever the environmental, historical or spatial basis to development, and whatever the theoretical conclusions reached by economists, sociologists or geographers for a particular place at a particular time, in the last analysis it is commonly govern-mental action that determines the direction and scope of economic policy. Government planning appears already to have replaced the market as the engine of economic growth throughout the developed world (Kindleberger, 1966: 150; Galbraith, 1967) and must presumably eventually fill the same critical role in developing countries.

It has already been necesssary on a number of occasions to refer to the political factor. As argued earlier, the natural and human resource base for development is most realistically seen within the territorial framework of the state and its policies. The motivation for a good deal of so-called economic development – the building of roads, railways, dams and the settlement of new areas – is patently political; and much of the motivation for regional econ-omic co-operation between states may also be more political than economic. Furthermore, a whole range of political decisions referring, for instance, to the economic role of the Indians in East

Africa and the Caribbean, of the Lebanese in West Africa and of the Chinese in Southeast Asia; population policy; and the distribution of wealth within a country: all these and many other issues arise continually in any study of the economic development process in tropical developing countries. It is the purpose of the present chapter to give explicit, if necessarily very brief, consideration to the political context within which economic development occurs.

Two points must be made at the outset, however. First, while it is certainly convenient for the purposes of analysis to isolate the political factor in this way, it is to some extent a rather arbitrary procedure. For the essential interdependence of political, social and economic factors is only too clearly demonstrated in almost every tropical country today. Economic and social progress is dependent upon political stability, but so, equally, is political stability dependent on social and economic progress. The political factor, moreover, operates in varying ways and is commonly open to a great many interpretations. In Ghana, for example, it is possible to argue that the overthrow of the Nkrumah régime – with all the implications this had for economic development in the country – was due largely to the oppressive form the administration had taken; but it can equally be argued that the Ghana coup of 1966 would never have occurred had not economic distress in the country – itself partly the result of low world cocoa prices – become so severe and so apparent to the people of Ghana. In Rhodesia the 1966 imposition of mandatory economic sanctions against the government of that country was undertaken with the aim of bringing about political and social change. In Malaysia the political factor has changed the form and emphasis of economic development planning from one based on maximizing production on a national basis to one based on economic integration throughout Malaysia to achieve a better balance of wealth between Malays and non-Malays. In many of the Latin American republics, too, political instability is itself caused or fostered by social and economic backwardness.

Secondly, there is a common danger of arguing in too highly generalized terms about 'the political factor' in development. For the scale at which the political factor operates or reacts with other factors is of particular significance in most tropical developing countries where the contact between local, regional and national political structures may be but slight. Certainly the authority of the local village, village-group, clan or ethnic group may well be far more effective and significant than is the national or even regional government. Indeed, the issue of the legitimacy of a government is probably more critical in tropical developing countries than in the developed world. For in developing countries it is generally true that a government – for instance its policies, parliament or agricultural officers – has no generally accepted right to do the things it does in formulating policies for development. And the most persistent and dangerous challenge to this legitimacy comes from 'the bonds of kinship, language and locality which far outweigh the "civil ties" which govern the citizen's relationship with other citizens generally and with the "civil authorities"' (Leys, 1971: 113).

The nature of the political factor. In trying to understand the nature of the political factor in tropical development it seems useful to distinguish between the external and internal aspects.

(i) *External.* As Brookfield (1973) has pointed out, 'the impress on our thinking created by some four hundred years of European expansionism [in the Third World] is so profound that we Westerners rarely recognise its all-pervading influence' (p. 79). It is certainly of fundamental importance that most parts of the tropics have at one time or another experienced external political, usually colonial and essentially exploitative, control and thus the impact of materially advanced cultures. In Tropical Asia the British held large territories, including those now known as the independent countries of India, Pakistan, Burma and Malaysia; France controlled Indochina, Holland Indonesia, and the United States the Philippines. In tropical America the chief external powers were Spain, Portugal, France, Britain and Holland; while in tropical Africa Belgium, Germany and Italy, as well as Britain, France, Spain and Portugal, have at times played their part in the general process of colonial expansion. Differences in colonial policy between the various powers have left their mark in a number of ways;

and it is probably not too much to say that the whole extent and nature of economic development in most tropical countries has at some period been conditioned by external interests and policies. This whole external or colonial experience has been interpreted in many ways, ranging from those who emphasize the political role Europeans played in 'opening-up' or 'developing' tropical countries to those who argue that external European control or involvement was essentially exploitative and actually caused and perpetuated conditions of underdevelopment. Thus Rodney (1972) has confirmed the latter interpretation in his study of how Europe 'underdeveloped' Africa. Yet another viewpoint emphasizes the wide gap or vacuum left by colonial administrations between, on the one hand, relatively sophisticated, often Western democratic-type political systems and, on the other, the backward, under-developed dependent economies and societies with which these political systems were expected to deal.

The achievement of national independence has not usually resulted in any significant reduction of this external involvement. One can readily distinguish what has been called the neo-colonial phase of development in those tropical countries today where, without maintaining any direct presence and without interfering directly in the political system of a country, a developed state or group of states nevertheless continues to exert its influence and power through, for instance, aid and trade. As shown in the previous chapter, this is particularly true of those tropical countries whose economies are still essentially export-based or 'colonial' economies: as Nkrumah argued, an independent nation is neo-colonial if 'its economic system and thus its political policy is directed from outside' (Nkrumah, 1965: ix). To the extent that this definition is valid, independence has not yet been achieved in most tropical countries; and to this extent, too, imperialism is not dead, having changed only from colonialism to neo-colonialism. And whether imperialism, or neo-colonialism, can ever be replaced by true political, economic and social independence, and whether the growing resistance to imperialism throughout the tropical developing world can be successful without the kind of armed revolution and ideological commitment associated with, for instance, China, Cuba and Indonesia, are questions with which the literature on economic development is becoming increasingly concerned.

(ii) *Internal*. The internal implications of the above line of argument are interesting and raise a host of questions, dilemmas and choices for a state to resolve. If, for instance, a state is to cut itself off – both politically and economically – from its former metropolitan power, is it prepared to face the lack of external capital and reduced trading opportunities this may involve? Must the plantation system of agriculture continue to be viewed as a heritage of colonial exploitation, even where circumstances suggest it might be the most appropriate and effective system? Whether material, social or political development is the main aim of development policy; whether equality between groups and between regions is deemed to be more important than aggregate national wealth; whether maintaining the existing ecological balance is believed to be more critical than maximizing growth; whether full employment is valued above technological progress and economic efficiency: all these and many other questions are most commonly answered not on purely pragmatic grounds but rather on the basis of ideological or theoretical political assumptions. It is impossible to look at the processes of economic development in any tropical country today without being aware of the nature of the political context: whether it be a multi-party or one-party state, a military, democratic or authoritarian government; or whether it involves a mixed or command economy.

All this may of course be seen as part of the whole issue of national integration and development. Development planning in most tropical countries is conceived within a national territorial framework and the centrifugal forces working against political unity and so against economic integration are commonly formidable. The unsuccessful attempt at secession from Nigeria by Biafra and the successful secession from Pakistan by Bangladesh are but two clear examples of this. The former Congo Kinshasa – now Zaïre – clearly demonstrates the problems of national unity and integration for economic development within a state. Zaïre faces formidable difficulties – its vast size; the peripheral spatial distribution of the relatively healthy, mineralized and populated upland rim; the difficult and relatively empty heart of the country; the complicated ethnic structure; the many different religions and mutually unintelligible languages; and the numerous contrasting cultures. The Belgian colonial period left the country without any educated or political élite to govern the country. Wealth is very unevenly distributed, both between urban and rural areas, between the different regions of the country and between classes and social groups. The attempted secession of Katanga, as well as the troubles in Kivu, Kasai and Bakongo – all are clear evidence of the difficulties of achieving any real sense of political unity or central control in Zaïre; and the problems of achieving economic development are equally formidable.

In order to deal with these kinds of problems, the internal political and administrative structures of many tropical countries have reacted in different ways. In Zaïre the earlier seven provinces were replaced by twenty-two administrative divisions with the aim of reducing ethnic conflicts and secessionist tendencies; but this structure was subsequently, for reasons of economic and political efficiency, replaced by a division into eleven provinces. In Nigeria the attempt to create a national identity for the sake of political and economic development led, in 1968, to the creation of twelve, and later nineteen, states. There is as yet, however, no evidence that changes in the internal pattern of political administrative units can cause any fundamental improvement in deep-seated divisions within a nation. In the same way, in those many cases, especially in Africa, where national boundaries cut through homogeneous ethnic or tribal zones, there is no evidence that the re-drawing of such boundaries would facilitate social, political or economic development within a state.

It is clear from what has been said above that economic development makes necessary a whole series and complex of choices between numerous alternatives, and that the political system provides the chief arena within which these choices are made. Without clear political direction and purpose, many tropical countries appear to be trying to reach simultaneously a whole range of goals – material, political, ideological, social and educational. Perhaps the most fundamental choice relates back to one of the definitions given on p. 1: that economic development implies a perceptible and cumulative rise in the material standard of living for an increasing proportion of the population. Such a definition makes an increasingly even distribution of increasing wealth the overriding aim of development; and all social and political change is merely part of the process of development designed to achieve that end. In tropical developing countries, at least where resources are so limited, change may have to be directed at one overriding goal. And that goal may not be economic at all; it may be explicitly political, social or, more strictly, ideological.

Relationship between political systems and economic development. The variety of political systems and types of related economies has led a number of writers to search for some causal relationship between political systems or 'types of régimes' and economic development. Leys (1970), ranking countries against a political classification based on the competitiveness of political structures (competitive, semi-competitive and authoritarian) finds a suggestion of some positive correlation between the level of economic development and the 'degree of democracy' or 'competitiveness' exhibited by the political system; among developing countries, at least, it seems that the highest ranking states are the most authoritarian. Irrespective of natural resources and capital, the only countries in the world which are developed are those with a strong, central government. But this strength is exhibited in two main forms. First there are those countries which have a long history of political stability, political consciousness and independence – in North-West Europe, North America, Australia and New Zealand. The second type is that of an authoritarian or totalitarian government, the prime examples being the U.S.S.R. and China. The importance of having a strong central government in economic development makes a relatively weak and perhaps fragile democracy a real limitation in tropical countries. Bhagwati, among others, refers to the dilemma of most democratic governments in the developing world, for 'no policy of economic development can be carried out unless the government has the capacity to adhere to it, no matter how organised and systematic the opposition to it by the losers – who may well be powerful pressure groups' (1970:203) And it is here, clearly, that socialist, totalitarian structures have an appeal for developing countries in that such structures 'shield the government from the rigours and reactionary judgments of the electorate' (ibid). In this sense, democratic forms of government, notably along the lines of the Westminster model, may be held to inhibit economic development; the political economy of development poses a cruel choice between rapid expansion and democratic processes (ibid.: 204).

Other authors have attempted to correlate economic development with communism. A number of authors use data on the strength of communist party membership to show that communist party membership strength differs with different levels of economic development. Regarding communist parties in developing countries as modernizing movements, it is suggested that communist party strength is lowest at the lowest stage of economic development, rises gradually with economic development, crests at a fairly high level of such development and declines strongly with the highest level. The implication of this is that until a fairly advanced stage, developing countries are helped in their modernizing process by the growth of communism. Again, Baran and Frank believe that it is capitalism, both world and national, which produced underdevelopment in the past and still generates underdevelopment today. Their analyses focus on the metropolis-satellite structure of the capitalist system, pointing to the uneven economic development and international as well as national and regional polarization which result from the monopolistic structure of capitalism. According to Frank (1968), the only way out of underdevelopment, for Latin American countries at least, is armed revolution leading to socialist development.

Yet while some correlations can be established in these ways, the relationships are not very pronounced and they tell us nothing about the causal connections between economic and political systems. It is indeed difficult not to conclude that 'this line of inquiry is premature and tells us very little we did not know before from more casual evidence. What is of much greater importance is to understand some of the particular processes and structures through which political and economic factors interact with each other in particular cases' (Leys, 1971:8).

Conclusion. The political context of planning is a matter of fundamental and immediate significance for any study of economic development; and to attempt to comment on the problems of economic development in countries as politically diverse as Venezuela, Tanzania and Indonesia without a full understanding of the political framework of economic planning in these countries and of the ideologies or sets of priorities which determine their decision-making processes is certain to lead to misunderstanding and misinterpretation. Furthermore, the essential interdisciplinary nature of development studies means that it is clearly no use merely to point to political 'obstacles' to development, or to argue that any one political structure is the panacea for the ills of tropical development. Above all, perhaps, there is the difficulty of recognizing and re-examining the many assumptions and prejudices held by Western observers of tropical development problems.

CHAPTER 13

Economic Development Plans, Capital Resources and International Aid

Economic development plans. While it may be true that economic development does not depend upon a plan, almost all tropical countries have development plans of one kind or another. Some of these are comprehensive, covering total national targets; detailed assessments of the natural, human and financial resources available, and of the investment required; an allocation of the public and private investment among major sectors together with policies to stimulate and direct private investment; and a detailed list of projects to be financed by the public sector (Galbraith, 1963). A comprehensive development plan is a valuable policy statement and an essential document for any geographical analysis of a country's economic life and problems. Such a plan is India's Sixth Five-Year Plan. Careful reading and consideration of this plan, together with the three earlier plans, provides a centralizing, focusing point for a series of otherwise discrete studies in the geographical analysis of Indian economic development. And even a simple table showing the financial provisions for the different sectors of the Indian economy made by the four development plans suggests a number of ideas and questions which are of interest not only to Indian administrators and academic economists but also to geographers concerned with the regional study of contemporary India. The plans of many other tropical countries, however, are of relatively little value, for they comprise little more than a list of projects, with little or no mention even of priorities. In many countries, of course, there are not enough data available from surveys, maps, or statistics to make integrated development planning possible. In such cases, government planning can mean little more than deciding how to resolve the most obvious problems in a few economic sectors (Eckaus, 1966).

Economic development plans also differ widely in their motivation. In general terms it may be true that the goal of economic development in all countries is to raise *per capita* incomes, but such a statement oversimplifies the issue for those countries where the decisive criteria of a successful plan are more social, political or strategic than economic. Thus whereas in one country the overriding objective is a high rate of growth of income, in another country it may be full employment, the development of backward regions, the creation of strategic industries, or the reduction of reliance on foreign trade (Bhagwati, 1966: 105). Furthermore, investment policies depend partly on a government's attitudes to public and private investment; for a conflict can easily arise between the interests of economic equality and economic growth. Again, plans differ in the emphasis they give to the various lines of development. Certainly one of the most important features of any plan is the making of decisions about the relative importance in development of agriculture, irrigation, land reform, industry, price stabilization, roads, health, and education. A choice has also to be made about the kind of balance to be reached between those projects likely to show a profit quickly and those projects – like roads, physical surveys, and social services – which can only be expected to bring long-term and indirect results. A good deal of thought, too, has to go into the 'matching and phasing of the various segments of the plan – into ensuring that kinds and amounts of steel being produced will match requirements for steel in kind and amount and that this balance between supply and requirements is maintained over time' (Galbraith, 1963: 29). The high priority given to transport and communications in most plans reflects the general consensus of opinion in economic development planning that most other aspects of development depend on good transport, which normally fails to attract substantial private investment, especially in the early stages of development, and so provides a particularly important field for large-scale public expenditure.

Economic development plans clearly represent an attempt to look at the various lines of development within a country, not as individual strands or projects but as part of the whole problem.

Plans direct, stimulate and control against a background of policy relating to priorities, and aid from outside is often contingent upon such planning. Integration and balance – these are normally important ingredients of any development plan; and this is why the examination of the plan and development problems of a particular state often provides the geographer with a useful focusing or integrating point in his analysis. A plan represents an attempt at analytical synthesis within the framework of a particular areal setting.

Some of the requirements of a 'good' plan are implicit in what has already been said. But it is perhaps worth emphasizing here three further and, according to Galbraith, often missing elements of an economic development plan. First, it should provide a strategy for economic advance without which the plan easily becomes only 'a bit of all the things that everyone would like to have done or that anyone believes ought to be done' (ibid.: 37). Those elements that are central or vital to economic development in any particular case must be emphasized and isolated from those elements that are merely useful or passive. At first sight this is similar to the point already made about the need to choose between different sectors of investment – between agriculture, industry, or transport, for instance. But Galbraith's point goes farther than that. His point here is that the various elements of each sector need to be subjected to a decision about the distinction between the vital and non-vital. Thus in agricultural development it might be decided for any particular country that water, fertilizers and improved seed are vital; and that land-tenure reorganization, mechanization, or credit facilities are merely useful. Secondly, a plan should emphasize both the visible and invisible dimensions of industrial achievement: 'like an iceberg, much of modern industrial society is out of sight. To get capital plant – steel mills, railway lines, coal mines, aeroplanes, oil rigs – into use is the visible achievement of developing planning. To ensure that this plant is efficiently used – that management is independent and sound, that in consequence material costs are low, product quality good, cost of production low, and earnings adequate for replacement and expansion of plant – is the much larger part of the task' (ibid.: 42). This brings us back to a point made earlier in this book: that the improvement in the qualitative aspects of human resources, in management, entrepreneurial activities, and the development of labour skills – what Schultz (1964) calls 'investment in human capital' – is as much an essential part of the processes of economic development as are the more obvious or visible dimensions of industrial progress. Finally, an economic development plan should have a theory of consumption which, as the previous chapter argued, is a much ignored aspect of the problem. Without a theory of consumption related to conditions in the particular country for which the plan is drawn up, consumption patterns of western developed countries or even of other developing countries will be accepted and followed as a matter of course. Each development plan, however, needs to keep clearly in mind the consumers for whom the planning is intended.

It will be noticed that these three requirements emphasize two issues: the need to consider the human context and human problems of social and economic change; and the need to consider each problem within a specific areal setting – normally the state area – rather than attempt to apply to each area and problem blanket solutions or theoretical prescriptions based on evidence drawn from often widely differing situations. The theoretical literature on economic development now abounds with planning models and analytical schemes; but, as Eckaus (1966: 393) has emphasized, there is no single best planning theory or model. Each country and each set of circumstances requires a 'tailor-made' procedure. To some extent, the same is true of regional economic planning within each state where the problems of locational specialization, especially in industry, may be crucial (Bhat, 1964; Learmonth, 1964; Grove and Huszar, 1964). Little work, however, has yet been carried out into the characteristics and implications for economic development of regional variations in industrial or any other kind of development in a tropical country, even where a federal structure confronts the planners with pressures for evening out regionally the benefits of their development programmes. Locational analysis and regional planning within the state framework is only now receiving attention from those, including geographers, concerned with the study of development.

The plans of an increasing minority of countries contain a substantial element of regional planning between different parts of the country and rely less than do most development plans upon sectoral analyses and recommendations. The question poses itself, however, as to whether a national development plan and a regional development plan within that same country may not have conflicting aims and interests. Certainly the chief criterion of a national development plan appears most commonly to be the maximizing of total production; whereas in regional planning within a state the aims are often more dominated by social, employment, and political considerations. If this is so, then internal regional development planning may in economic terms constitute a drag on national economic progress.

Rather more information is available about regional planning in the sense of co-operation between states. Some comment has already been made in the previous chapter about co-operation between states in forming free-trade areas, customs unions, and the like. Then there is co-operation for specific projects, such as the West African project for the building of one large international iron and steel mill to serve the whole region; this failed, again largely for political reasons, several of the member states – notably Nigeria, Ghana and Liberia – deciding to go ahead with their own iron and steel works. Then there are a number of attempts and proposals to create regional units for physical planning of one kind or another. River-basin and river-valley development, for instance, is seen to be desirable where rivers are international in character. There are many striking examples of this situation in the tropics – the Amazon and Orinoco in South America, the Niger, Congo, and Zambezi in Africa, and the Indus, Salween, and Mekong in Asia. But there are numerous other small though locally highly important schemes, like the Mono River Project for hydro-electric development between Dahomey and Togo in West Africa. Assuming political agreement, co-operation between states in all these cases must result in mutual benefits in the division of water, the division of costs, and the sharing of the joint benefits. The fact that it is still impossible to point to any wholly successful international river-basin development scheme in the tropics is further testimony to the political difficulties associated with such agreements.

Capital resources. It will already be clear that one of the fundamental practical problems in formulating economic development plans is to decide on the way in which available capital resources for investment are to be shared out. Economic development plans are in effect investment plans, and it is important to emphasize the relative roles of public and private investment.

Public investment has five main sources of money: budget surpluses – some countries hope to raise much of their total current investment by this means, but in most tropical countries this is not yet a very significant source; profits from public enterprises, in which state ownership of profit-making enterprises contribute to the total public investment; public borrowing, which again is of small importance in most tropical countries, though it provides some 12 per cent of the total public investment in India; foreign assistance or aid, about which more will be said later – much of it, in fact, may be available not for development investment at all but for direct expenditure on imports of consumer goods, on imports to maintain and supply existing industries, and on repaying interest or principal on loans; and deficit financing, or drawing on reserves, or printing more money.

Private investment is significant only in the more advanced developing countries like India, Singapore, Nigeria, Venezuela, and Brazil though, as pointed out earlier, political attitudes and action often affect the size and relative significance of private and public investment. Thus in several countries development plans stress the value of public investment as a means of preventing any further concentration of economic power in a few hands; whereas in others the role of public investment is mainly to support and facilitate private investment. In most tropical countries, however, the contribution of private investment to financial resources for development planning is insignificant, and any increases in this contribution are likely to result mainly from the general processes of economic development.

Whether public or private, the form of exchange in which the investment exists may be critical. A certain proportion of the available financial resources needs to be in foreign exchange, normally accumulated through exports, aid, or foreign private investment, in order that goods and skills not available locally can be imported. Foreign exchange, of course, is characteristically scarce in many tropical developing countries, and has in many cases formed an important obstacle to development.

There is, however, some controversy over the significance of capital resources to economic development. It is sometimes argued that shortage of capital is never a critical or decisive factor in the early stages of a country's economic progress: much more important is the capacity to absorb capital and to transform the economy. During the early stages of a country's economic development, it is argued, effective government, education, and social justice are the critical barriers to be overcome. As for effective government, it is particularly true of many Latin American countries that the political problem of securing governments willing and able to make the take-off into modernity seems often to be insoluble; and many writers argue for looking upon education as the most fundamental and important single factor in the early stages of economic development. Only when these social and political barriers have been removed and a fair measure of development achieved can anything really useful or permanent come either from capital investment or from technical assistance: 'capital becomes the touchstone of development, the limiting factor, only in countries that are well along the development line' (Galbraith, 1963: 21). Other writers go even farther, arguing that financial resources are exaggerated in many development analyses in developing countries and contending that such resources receive far more attention than they deserve (Cairncross, 1962; Nevin, 1961; Lewis, 1953). This tendency to give too much weight to capital resources in development is possibly due to the fact that economics has relatively little developed systematic theory regarding the factors responsible for development but already has a well-developed capital theory (Villard, 1963).

Many authorities, however, conclude that real weight should be given to capital as occupying the central position in economic development theory. It is argued that an injection of financial resources may 'set alight' or 'prime the pump' of development. Financial resources, according to this viewpoint, are of great importance in many developing countries in enabling them to break out from the vicious circle of low purchasing power and savings capacity, leading to a low rate of capital formation, lack of capital, low productivity, low real income, and so back to low purchasing power and savings capacity. This view of the vicious circle, in which an economy is imprisoned in its own shortcomings, is regarded by some economists as central in a description of what ails developing countries (Myrdal, 1956). Furthermore, as noted earlier in this book, capital can substitute for resources and for labour. Yet the necessary degree of increase in savings and capital formation in low-income countries is very difficult to achieve. In most tropical countries annual savings rarely amount to over 6 per cent of the national income, as against over 20 per cent in the developed world. Partly for this reason, it is argued, external or international aid is an essential ingredient of the economic development planning of any tropical country.

International aid. As will have emerged from the discussion in the previous section of this chapter, the argument for emphasizing external capital is both simple and attractive. The low average income of the inhabitants of tropical developing countries enforces a low level of consumption per head and reflects a low level of productivity. This low level of real output per head of population may be caused by a number of factors, including many of a social and psychological nature; but one factor is of outstanding importance – the lack of capital, including real capital equipment such as factories, machinery, or tools. According to this traditional analysis the rudimentary equipment available to the average worker in a developing country makes it impossible for him to increase his output; and for this reason the amount of capital available is critical in all attempts to increase substantially the level of productivity (Reddaway, 1966). Only a flow of external capital can help to break the vicious circle of poverty and provide the foreign exchange required to buy necessary imports of machinery and similar sophisticated goods without running into serious balance of payments difficulties.

A number of writers, however, have argued against this emphasis on the flow of external capital to help in accelerating the development of these countries. First, there is the simple fact that the total amount of such external capital is unlikely ever to be of the scale to allow even a moderate rate of growth in developing countries. Foreign capital contributions may be of real importance as 'seed corn'; but as a major contribution to development, a much larger expansion of foreign aid than now appears probable would be needed. The World Bank is becoming more and more convinced that the problem now facing them is how to see that aid flows more freely, without tying up the poorer countries with impossible debt burdens, and how to ensure that the aid so given is used effectively. The developed countries must clearly contribute to any increased aid. One suggestion is for international agreement among the developed countries to give, say, one per cent of their gross national product each year to the developing countries on terms that do not place a heavy burden of debt on the recipient country. A figure of one per cent would represent an increase of about half over the current average level of aid giving and it remains to be known whether the developed countries with large military expenditures could do this without increasing taxation. Borrowing by the developing countries is already made easier, especially through the Development Assistance Committee (DAC) and the International Development Agency (IDA), an offshoot of the World Bank; these agencies produce 'soft' loans, a matter of great significance because very large amounts of the export earnings of the poorer countries today are being used as debt repayments. Secondly, available evidence seems to suggest that external capital should only be thought of as but one factor in a detailed overall plan. Certainly the mere provision of external capital does not automatically stimulate advance in other sectors of the economy, nor can one assume that supplies of the complementary factors will necessarily be available. As Reddaway (1966) argues, the 'shortage of capital' thesis both exaggerates and at the same time makes it appear too easy. Much more emphasis should be placed on increasing the capacity of a country to absorb aid effectively and on self-help, involving the better use of existing or new capital by the developing countries themselves; and this often means in practice that attention should be concentrated on agriculture rather than on industrialization, because it is on agricultural development – by the introduction of better methods and additional equipment – that existing capital can be most effectively utilized in increasing productivity. Thirdly, there is the common argument that many developed countries really cannot afford as a regular commitment such altruistic gestures as the giving of aid to the developing countries of the world. It is frequently held, in fact, that the most important though indirect means of assistance to developing countries is the stabilization of high levels of employment in the developed countries. This contributes to the steadiness of prices and value of exports of primary products in developing countries and to the stability of the availability of private capital, much of which is dependent for its investment in developing areas on the expansion of markets in developed areas (Kindleberger, 1966: 377).

As for aid in kind, in which the United States is easily the most important participant, this is, of course, very much bound up with the wider question of international trade. Something was said about this in Chapter 11, where it was suggested that present trading policies are slanted against the developing countries and that international action for evening out the advantages of such trade needs to be given great prominence. Assistance in kind is normally in food, and the most striking instance of this sort of aid in recent years has been the movement of grain to India from the United States. This type of movement also implies surpluses in the producing countries of the developed world. Yet even within the tropics there are many cases of surpluses being wasted or not ever being produced because the existing pattern of trade or transport facilities makes such trade or production either impossible or unprofitable.

As for aid in the form of technical assistance, this is perhaps particularly important in that any financial assistance is unlikely to be fully effective unless combined with the provision of technical experts. According to some authorities, notably Schumpter

(1949), technical change is the central aspect of economic development. Yet investment in human resources is usually a lengthy process; and to be economically effective it may require far-reaching social changes which are also likely to take much time. Kindleberger (1966: 136) has pointed out that it used to be believed that technical assistance – the transfer to developing countries of advanced technological methods and ideas such as longer hoes, row planting, improved seed, and the diffusion of agricultural techniques through extension services – would by itself result in economic development. This is now known to be untrue. No such development will take place unless technical assistance also 'sets in motion an indigenous cumulative process of innovations and capital formation . . . this implies changes in attitudes, institutions, organizations, and social relationships' (Belshaw, 1956: 103). It may be, as some writers have argued, that technical assistance to tropical countries should come primarily from those countries which have only recently reached developed status. Countries like Japan, especially, are perhaps better able to give technical assistance than America or Western Europe because of their much narrower cultural and technical gaps. Even within the developing countries of the tropics, too, technical assistance can be given – for instance from relatively developed India to Indonesia, or from Venezuela to Nigeria.

Whether aid takes the form of grants or loans, kind or technical assistance, a good deal of controversy exists over the extent and even the desirability of such aid for the developing world today. To many recipient countries in the tropics, especially in Africa, all aid is interpreted as a form of neo-colonialism, more especially when this aid is bilateral and 'tied' in a number of ways – by projects or by countries. Many tropical countries, indeed, continue to adopt a restrictive attitude towards private foreign investment to an extent that is clearly holding back development. In the donor countries, too, there seems to be an increasing reluctance to provide assistance that so often appears to be wasted, misused, or little appreciated; and certainly, private investment is not encouraged by recurrent political upheavals. In Nigeria it is estimated that the 1966–1967 series of coups and wars resulted in a loss of investment opportunities of over £100 million. Some doubt is now felt, too, about the validity of the 'economic self-interest' argument for giving aid on the part of the developed world. Most authorities now find it hard to make the case that the development of tropical countries carries economic benefits for the developed countries which justifies their assistance: 'the argument that no country can be prosperous in a world where there are countries which are not prosperous is rhetorical nonsense' (Kindleberger, 1966: 365). Certainly the whole question of aid to the developing countries has been brought under severe scrutiny where economies in public expenditure in the donor countries are being practised. It is becoming increasingly apparent that many of the old assumptions about aid do not bear examination. It seems likely that multilateral aid will slowly replace bilateral aid as the chief vehicle for expressing the developing world's concern at the low levels of production and consumption in the tropics. Nevertheless, on humanitarian and on social and political, if not economic, grounds, the arguments for international aid to the developing world are decisive. As a number of writers have emphasized, the arguments for aiding the development of the developing countries 'rest less on economic and short-run political grounds than on the long-run political. Rising national expectations must see some prospect of satisfaction, or low-income countries are likely to be prey to economic, political, and social breakdown, with convulsive results' (ibid.: 379). Without substantial and continuing aid from outside it is difficult to see how development in tropical countries can ever be achieved at the rate demanded by the circumstances. Rostow's estimate of sixty years and even Dumont's figure of twenty years before underdevelopment can be conquered refer to time scales longer than anything acceptable to the peoples of the tropical world today.

Although it may seem as yet little more than a dream that developed countries should contribute multilaterally through some international body perhaps one or even two per cent of their national income to the developing countries of the world, the urgent and obvious need for some such substantial, regular, equitable and, to the recipient countries, 'anonymous' contributions is becoming more generally accepted. A good deal of literature now exists on the ways in which the giving of aid for developing countries might most fairly be shared out among the developed countries. It is suggested, for instance, that countries with higher *per capita* incomes should give higher rather than equal percentage contributions of national income, compared with those countries with lower *per capita* incomes (Rosenstein-Rodan, 1961). Given adequate safeguards about the kind of aid to be given and about the capacity of recipient countries to absorb such aid effectively, substantial multilateral aid is now at least a practical proposition, although probably the majority of current aid to developing countries is still bilateral. Yet even a dramatic increase in aid will make little impression on the problem unless it is accompanied by trade liberalization and by the encouragement of industrial exports from the developing world along the lines suggested in the previous chapter. So long as the structural imbalance of trade exists, the gap between the rich and poor nations will continue to widen and the demands for aid will continue to mount (see Appendix).

CHAPTER 14

Three Case Studies: Brazil, Nigeria and India

This final chapter draws together many of the points made in previous chapters by examining development in the three most populous countries in their respective sectors of the tropics. The discussion in each case follows broadly the order of topics and issues as they are presented in earlier chapters of this book. It must be pointed out, however, that this chapter assumes at least a working knowledge of the basic facts about the three countries. No attempt is made here to summarize, however briefly, their physical and human geography, for such information can easily be obtained from a number of excellent regional texts, many of which are referred to below or in the bibliography.

Brazil. The period of extraordinary rapid economic growth which characterized Brazil during the late 1960s and early 1970s seemed at the time to justify the claims, made repeatedly over several centuries, that Brazil has an unusual wealth of natural resources and that rapid economic growth is, therefore, ultimately assured. Certainly the facts support the contention that Brazil is exceptionally well-endowed with natural resources. The second largest country in the world after China, Brazil lies almost entirely within the humid tropics: 'as Brazil has no barren deserts, inhospitable tundras, or lofty mountains such as set finite limits to the effective areas of the world's other large nations, practically all of it is usable' (Henshall and Momsen, 1974: 3). Brazil also has rich mineral resources, none of which is locked up in frozen wastes, with her most varied and important mining region lying in the south-east; even those mineral deposits in the north are served by the remarkable inland waterway of the Amazon and its tributaries. The forest resources, too, are immense and are only just beginning to be exploited in the Amazon Basin. As for power, Brazil has abundant and rapidly developing hydro-electric power resources, though her coal and petroleum resources are as yet less promising, some coal, especially coking coal, and petroleum having to be imported.

It is true, of course, that the natural resource base here, as anywhere else, can be viewed negatively. Thus it has been suggested that Brazil suffers from having too large an area for her population; that water supply, notably in the 'dry' north-east, is often inadequate or badly distributed; that the uniformly humid tropical conditions impose a monotonous climatic environment which is far from stimulating and indeed inhibits drive and initiative; and that many of the most valuable mineral deposits are so located that their exploitation is too expensive. On balance, however, it is difficult not to accept that the natural resource base in Brazil is of outstanding size and quality: it certainly cannot be used to explain human poverty or lack of economic growth or development.

Unlike many other Latin American countries, the Brazilian population is large enough (some 120 million) to provide an adequate internal market. Moreover, in spite of the ethnically diverse nature of the population, which includes indigenous Indian, introduced African and European elements, and many mixed peoples, the population is sufficiently unified – both culturally and politically – to provide the basis for rapid economic growth. This is not to say that significant racial and class divisions do not exist within Brazil, but the Brazilian population is probably unique in Latin America for having what is now an almost completely indigenous culture – 'a general framework of cultural uniformity, which characterizes Brazil as a nation and as a distinct cultural area' (Wagley, 1965: 130). In its distribution, however, the population is remarkably concentrated in certain areas, most Brazilians living within 600 km of the Atlantic Ocean. The causes of the very uneven distribution of population – as well, incidentally, as the mixed yet culturally relatively homogeneous nature of the population – must be sought largely in the history of settlement in Brazil. When Portugal first began to colonize Brazil, the aboriginal population was very small and the Portuguese brought in large numbers of Africans to provide the basis of the labour force for the tropical agricultural economy established in the north-east in the period 1500–50. The discovery of alluvial gold and precious stones in the early eighteenth century resulted in large-scale immigration from Portugal, an immigration which substantially changed the population geography of Brazil. Up to then the population was concentrated in the Bahia-Maranhao region, where the predominantly African population was engaged in tropical agriculture. Subsequently, however, Portuguese entrepreneurs and other European groups moved into the new mining areas further south. By the end of the century, indeed, the Brazilian population was dominated by people of European rather than African origin and the centre of gravity of population distribution had moved from the north-east to the centre-south.

With this history of settlement and colonization, it is not surprising that immigrant forms of agriculture, including the plantation, have long existed side by side with the most simple forms of shifting agriculture. Well suited to a country in which land is plentiful and population densities generally low, shifting field cultivation is still widely practised throughout the country. More sophisticated forms of farming associated with permanent settlement in Brazil vary from a traditional system of river-bank cultivation to modern, highly mechanized commercial agriculture. The latter is especially characteristic of those areas in which the most recent foreign colonization since the mid-nineteenth century has been greatest, especially in the Sao Paulo and Rio Grande do Sul states.

Of the early important export crops for which Brazil was noted – sugar, coffee, and rubber – rubber has declined most drastically. But as a major world producer of tropical crops for export Brazil is still important – for coffee, cocoa, sugar, and cotton. Moreover, with the exception of some wheat which has to be imported, most of the basic food requirements – rice, beans, cassava, and maize – are provided from within Brazil's own agricultural sector. Yet the problem of how to increase productivity in agriculture has long been a serious matter in Brazil. After independence, changes in land ownership were made to produce a more varied pattern, including the emergence of large estates employing wage-earning labour and, in the southern states, a system of medium-sized farms. As late as the decade 1960–70 the number of farms increased from 3·3 million to almost 5 million and the number of agricultural workers increased by 2·5 million. Improved agronomic practices have also helped to bring about improved productivity, especially in some of the export crops and in market garden crops. Improved varieties of maize, cotton, and wheat have also contributed to higher yields. And the spread of new government-backed farming technology, notably the use of tractors, has also been an important contributory factor. However, much remains to be done. In the livestock sector productivity is particularly low, and throughout agriculture the scope for the increased use of fertilizers is immense, especially outside the relatively advanced eastern regions of the country. Agricultural extension services and agricultural marketing systems, together with better farm access roads and storage facilities are only now beginning to be satisfactorily provided. Minimum prices guaranteed to farmers for such crops as cotton and the basic food crops are also being introduced in an effort to increase productivity.

But one of the major problems in increasing productivity in Brazilian agriculture is, perhaps, the simple fact that, with her vast land resources, Brazil always has the option of increasing production by colonizing new land – by extending the cultivated area. As we noted in an earlier chapter, it is always a temptation, where circumstances allow, for increases in agricultural production to be sought by expanding the area of land farmed rather than by intensification through changes in agricultural systems or by the application of better agronomic practices and new inputs in existing areas of production. As will be seen, this whole issue is central to the question of planning in Brazil, both nationally and regionally.

It was only quite recently (in 1967) that the contribution of agriculture to the national product was overtaken by industry. Up to independence in 1822 Brazil's industrial development was held back, even prohibited, by Portuguese mercantilist policies, though some cottage industry was introduced by European immigrants, especially in textiles. This cottage industry provided the basis for Brazil's industrial revolution which began to take hold in the latter half of the nineteenth century, assisted by favourable terms of trade and tariff protection and, in 1888, by the abolition of slavery, which disrupted the traditional agrarian system and led to considerable migration from rural areas into the growing urban centres. But industrialization as a modernization process never really took off in Brazil until she ceased to be a supplier primarily of raw materials to the industrial nations of the world: up to then most of the industry was dependent on export agriculture. With the collapse of the world coffee market in 1929 industry finally escaped from this dependence. By 1958 Brazil had displaced Argentina as the leading industrial nation of Latin America. Even so, the real take-off in industrial growth was to occur only after 1964 with the change to a military government which introduced new economic policies to reduce inflation, attract foreign investment, reform the fiscal and monetary system, and so provide a proper environment for renewed industrial growth: 'Industrial production was stimulated by the expansion of the domestic market through the recovery of real wages, the organization of the credit market and government incentives to exporters of manufactured goods' (Henshall and Momsen, 1964: 157).

Today, then, Brazil can claim to be one of the major industrial nations of the developing world. Its mineral and power resources, its large domestic market, its relatively large pool of skilled and semi-skilled labour and its capacity for attracting investment – all these factors have played their part. Nevertheless, industrialization is geographically very concentrated in Brazil. Even more than in any other major economic activity, such concentration is very marked: over 50 per cent of all industrial employment is in Sao Paulo and another 9 per cent in nearby Guanabara (Rio) in the south-east. The locational factors are diverse. The location of several steel plants in Minas Gerais can be explained largely by accessibility to local iron ore; the location of the new integrated steel works near Santos depends largely on imported raw materials; and the Volta Redonda works between Rio and Sao Paulo are located near their markets. Clearly, modern industrial development and, incidentally, the associated rapid urban growth, emphasize once again the overriding importance of the south-east in development.

With such a vast land area in relation to population, both agriculture and industry continue to depend to a great extent on the provision of transport facilities. The application of a well-known transport model to Brazilian railways by Haggett (1965: 81) emphasizes the essentially colonial, exploitative origin and purpose of these lines of transport. But the great railway era, begun when Brazil's raw material exports were the foundation of the economy, lies in the past and, with the development of the national economy, the era of road transport is now firmly under way. Attention is focused on the need to integrate the interior with the rest of the country and on the poor condition of many of the roads. Of particular importance today are the developments associated with the great new pioneering roads, especially in the Amazon Basin. These have obvious social and economic as well as political benefits, though increasing concern is being expressed about the possible ecological damage such road-building projects might be causing and about their effects on the Amerindians. Conflict of opinion about the trans-Amazon roads, indeed, is an important issue in Brazil today, many authorities arguing on the one hand that they place too great a burden on the exchequer and that they entail diverting funds away from other, perhaps more worthy, programmes. On the other hand these roads – especially the transcontinental and trans-Brazilian roads – could dramatically change the whole geography of the country by accelerating international economic integration, by increasing the rate of land colonization and by enabling new mineral resources, such as iron, to be exploited. The question is whether these aims are best achieved by large-scale programmes of road-building (Gilbert, 1974).

Part of the reason for the decline of the railway in Brazil has of course been the reduction in the importance of raw material exports. The classical pattern of foreign trade with so many developing countries in which raw materials form the bulk of the exports and manufactured goods are imported has now largely disappeared, though coffee still accounts for about a fifth of the total value of Brazil's exports. As a corollary to this, the Brazilian economy has now largely ceased to be what it once was – a classic case of a country affected by a series of trade cycles for over four centuries, including cycles of trade in sugar, cotton, gold, rubber and, to some extent, coffee. Moreover, the foreign trade component must now increasingly be seen within the context of the Latin American Free Trade Area (LAFTA) and the Central American Common Market (CACM) – larger regional groupings for economic co-operation and trade.

But the significance of such wider regional groupings, as well as many of the changes referred to above, can only realistically be considered against the realities of recent political history in Brazil. This is certainly very different in many ways from that found in most parts of the African and Asian tropics. Brazil has had over a century and a half of independence, it has a population which is largely of European stock, and it has experienced many different types of government, with different priorities and philosophies. Another important factor is that Brazil is Portuguese-speaking in a continent of predominantly Spanish-speaking states. Also there are several centrifugal forces at work within Brazil: the country has common frontiers with no less than ten neighbouring states; the wealthy regions of the east and south-east contrast vividly with the relatively poor and backward regions of the country; and the gap between rich and poor in the major urban centres of the south-east is probably as great as anywhere in the world. To create a sense of national unity has of course been a major concern of all governments since Brazil's independence in 1822, though the same can be said of all governments everywhere. And, as noted earlier, Brazil does have the advantage of a certain cultural unity: the various ethnic elements have mixed well to the extent that the sense of ethnic identity in Brazil is probably now less powerful than the growing sense of national unity. The major divisive factor today is probably regional inequalities and it is an important plank of the present government's policy to try to reduce these inequalities.

Yet exactly how far regional income disparities are increasing or decreasing is largely a problem of how one interprets the available statistical data. By some criteria the inequalities seem to be lessening. On the other hand, there seems little doubt that the absolute differentials between the richest and poorest states have increased, Maranhao in the north-east being the poorest and Guanabara in the south-east being the richest. For some commentators, the continued existence of such disparities is inevitable while the government follows authoritarian, repressive policies. While change is certainly taking place in Brazil – and is taking place peacefully – criticisms of the military government are likely to increase. Only if the objectives of the present government can be achieved within a very short period of time will Brazil 'be able to take its place in world councils as an advanced country at very low social cost' (Henshall and Momsen, 1964: 22).

At its simplest, the success or failure of the government to achieve a satisfactory and acceptable level of economic development will depend on its development planning policies, not that such plans have been a feature of Brazil for very long. The first overall economic plan in the country was the Target Plan of 1956–60. Moreover, contemporary economic planning in Brazil has to take place against a rapidly deteriorating economic situation very different from that experienced in the boom decade of 1964–74 when the sheer scale and rate of growth was dramatic. Of the many measures examined and issues discussed in contemporary Brazilian planning for development there is space to deal here with only two.

The first is regional planning for development. From what has already been said, it will be apparent that there is a great concentration of people, urban centres, economic activity, and wealth in the south-east. No government can afford to ignore the obvious implications of such a fact. Attempts of various kinds have been and are being made to reduce this geographical concentration of wealth and economic activity. In the case of industry, particularly, attempts have been made to tempt industry to the north-east by instituting a financial scheme permitting all companies registered in Brazil to halve their income tax on condition that they invest their money, together with fresh funds, in approved projects in the north-east and, more recently, in the Amazon region (Gilbert, 1974). As yet, however, success has been limited, though within the south-east region manufacturing has tended to disperse from Rio to nearby cities (Niteroi and Petropolis) as well as from Sao Paulo. In agriculture, too, the desire to spread modernized agriculture, including livestock farming, more successfully into the relatively undeveloped parts of Brazil has formed some justification for the colonization policy. Certainly the expansion of agricultural settlement is still important in Brazilian planning, and the establishment of Brasilia itself has already brought about some change in the regional structure by giving focus to colonization and road-building programmes; and this, as Gilbert (1974) has pointed out, has created a new frontier spirit. The rapid movement of settlers is likely to continue, for after all the trans-Amazon road network is designed partly to open up the Amazon region; to encourage settlement there road construction sites are built on a semi-permanent basis to act as market and service centres, and strips of land 10 km wide are reserved for colonists on each side of the new road.

Aside from industrial and agricultural policy aimed at reducing regional inequalities, perhaps the most publicized measure – or at least the measure that has captured the imagination of many – has been the setting up of a new capital and Federal Territory in Brasilia. While this can be termed a largely political measure, it must affect the development of new transport and urban systems, both of which are probably the necessary preconditions for any successful regional development in Brazil. Then organizational solutions to the problem of regional inequalities have been sought with the establishment of regional administrative entities such as SUDAM (Superintendency for the development of the Amazon), SUDENE (for the north-east), and SUFRONTE (for the south-west frontier); other administrations deal with the west, with Ceara, with the central-west, with the free port zone of Manaus, and with the Sao Francisco valley. Most attention, however, has been focused on the north-east and north (Amazon). What captures the imagination is not so much the nature of the problems of these two regions as their vast scale. The north-east, of course, includes the 'drought polygon', an area roughly coincident with the *caatinga*. The north includes much of the Amazon Basin, and interest here has focused increasingly on the environmentalists' concern over the large-scale destruction of the Amazon forest by ranching and other interests.

A second and related issue is poverty – much of it extreme – in the urban centres, including especially that found in the large cities of the south-east. Numerically this is a most important problem because over a quarter of the Brazilian population now lives in cities of over 100,000 and some one-third of the total population in Brazil is said to live in poverty in slums, shanty towns, and squatter settlements. Attempts to deal with urban poverty have been made, though there is some difference of opinion on the part of many scholars over the role of squatter and shanty town settlements in the economic development process. One measure is to provide public housing on a very large scale. A new city like Brasilia consists very largely of public housing already, but elsewhere such a policy usually involves destroying squatter settlements in the city centre and rehousing the population in new areas distant from the city centre, with obvious repercussions on the city centre and on transport facilities.

One of the fastest growing economies in the world during the decade 1964–74, Brazil has subsequently been forced to face the problems both of that period of rapid growth and of the much more restricted growth now characteristic of most countries, whether developed or developing. By some criteria, Brazil is no longer a truly developing country; and at worst it must be classed as one of the most wealthy of the developing countries of the world. But whatever its level of development, Brazil has serious problems to face. Apart from regional and social class income inequalities, sectoral differentials have recently increased to the advantage of industry and infrastructure and to the disadvantage of agriculture. How far Brazil is successful in coping with her development problems it is impossible to predict. But certainly it is important, not only to Brazil but also to other countries in the continent, for whom Brazil is now seen as a pace-setter.

Nigeria. Nigeria has acquired a status in Africa similar to that of Brazil in Latin America for substantially the same reasons:

Nigeria has easily the largest population of all African countries and, ostensibly at least, it is one of the wealthiest. Smaller than several other countries in the continent, Nigeria nevertheless has a good natural resource base, including land. There are striking changes of environment from south to north: a belt of hot, wet rain forest and swamps is succeeded by seasonally dry open woodlands, grass savanna and, finally, sandy scrublands on the borders with Chad and Niger. This ecological variety occurs over a predominantly low plateau country, even the Jos plateau (1,500 m) in the north-centre of the country being no real barrier to movement. Forest resources are substantial in the south, but more important are the mineral resources. Tin and columbite are located well inland on the Jos plateau, but the early development of these resources means that their locational disadvantages have long been largely overcome. The major mineral resource today – petroleum – is, however, the most important single reason for Nigeria's wealth and it is located in the more developed south near the coast. As for other minerals, these include coal and iron. Apart from petroleum the major source of power in the country is hydro-electricity, derived from numerous rivers, but especially from the Niger-Benue system. Altogether, and in spite of negative interpretations sometimes made of Nigeria's natural resource base – interpretations which echo in a remarkable way those made of Brazil (too large a land area, seasonality and inadequacy of much of the water supply, and an 'uncomfortable' climate) – there seem to be no firm grounds for arguing that Nigeria suffers from an inadequate natural resource base.

The same can broadly be said of Nigeria's human resources. While it is easy to point to low levels of education, literacy, and health – factors which undoubtedly cause greater problems in Nigeria than in Brazil – the population of Nigeria is substantial in size and of high quality. The some 80 million population is about one-fifth of the total population of Africa, providing a domestic market large enough for a thriving industrial economy. And while the large number of ethnic groups, with their different languages, religions, and cultures, can be interpreted as a divisive force in the human resource base, which is certainly far less homogeneous than in Brazil, it can equally be interpreted as primarily a rich and varied population of immense value to a rapidly developing nation. Moreover, it is worth noting that the British in Nigeria were never present in large numbers. They never 'colonized' the country in any strict settlement sense – there was no European settlement here – and there was no mixing of European and indigenous peoples as happened in Brazil. Nigerians, for all their ethnic complexity, are all Africans.

But again, as in Brazil, the distribution of population in Nigeria is very uneven, there being strong concentrations in certain areas. From the point of view of development prospects, it may well be that the nature of polarization in Nigeria is even worse than in Brazil; for in Nigeria there are two east–west bands of population – one in the north (predominantly Muslim, Hausa/Fulani) and one in the south (predominantly Christian, Yoruba/Ibo) – with strongly contrasting cultures, attitudes, economies, and levels of education and development. Such a distribution means, of course, that there is a relatively empty, undeveloped 'middle belt' separating the two bands of population. Whether this middle belt can be explained in historical or environmental terms, it is nevertheless a most important problem in the development of Nigeria as a unified and integrated social, economic, and political system. Certainly the middle belt has resulted in glaring regional disparities, it has acted as little more than an expensive in-between zone, and until recently it contributed very little even to agricultural production, though it has provided the important minerals of tin and coal. Now, however, the potential of the middle belt for producing crops of both the north and the south is beginning to be tapped; and population nuclei are likely to emerge as a result of carving out in the centre of the middle belt the new Federal Territory near Abuja – a project which is very reminiscent of Brasilia.

While there is no European settlement in Nigeria, the influence of European colonial control on the pattern of agricultural development is nevertheless very clear. The plantation system was limited primarily to rubber in the south and south-east. But the colonial government always emphasized at all levels – marketing, research, and investment – the importance of cash crops for export. This emphasis on cash crops for export like cotton and groundnuts in the north, together with the hides and skins from the livestock industry, and cocoa and palm oil in the south, meant that little basis was created during the colonial period for increasing productivity in the basic food crops of mainly root crops (yams and cassava) in the south and grains (sorghum/millets, maize, and rice) in the north. An important plank of agricultural development in Nigeria has clearly been to stimulate productivity in such crops. This is now a critical issue. The extent to which agricultural development in Nigeria has been disappointing since independence in 1960 is evident from two facts: that some of Nigeria's major 'export' crops – notably cotton and palm oil – now have to be imported; and that Nigeria is increasingly having to import much of its basic food requirements.

As in Brazil, part of the reason for the poor performance in Nigerian agriculture has been the emphasis on industrialization. Apart from exhortations to grow food wherever possible, expressed, for instance, in the Operation Feed the Nation programme, most government interest and support has been directed at large-scale, capital-intensive schemes for agricultural development, including those associated with irrigation and water-control projects. While there is clearly scope for all forms of 'industrialized' agriculture in Nigeria, there is equally need for much more emphasis to be placed on the individual, small-scale or peasant farmer; agricultural credit, extension work, improved knowledge about and access to scientific farming methods, improved marketing, and transport facilities – all are necessary if agricultural output is to grow even as fast as the overall growth of population of about 3 per cent. And even that rate of growth of production will barely maintain the current average food intake at 2,000 calories per head.

There has long been a vigorous craft and small-scale industrial structure in Nigeria, especially in textiles, pots, and many leather goods and efforts have been made since independence to support and further stimulate such craft industries. Far more important today, however, is modern industrial activity which is concentrated in three widely separated areas. One, in the Kano area of the north, reflects the dominant position of that ancient city as the centre of the large market of northern Nigeria. The second, largest, area is based on the import–export trade of Nigeria's main port and present capital, Lagos. The third is in the Port Harcourt area of the south-east and is clearly based on the production and refining of Nigeria's major source of wealth – petroleum. Industrial projects in the country include, of course, petro-chemical industries, pulp and paper, sugar, salt, cement, oil-refining, and an iron and steel industry now essential for a rapidly industrializing country like Nigeria; this last industry, however, still has a long way to go and industries such as motor car manufacture are unlikely to emerge in the near future, though both Volkswagen and Peugeot started assembly plants in 1974.

Industrialization still faces many problems, in spite of the pre-eminence given to it in much central and regional planning: it still contributes far too small an amount to the total economy, though some improvement has already been achieved in raising the figure from only 8 per cent in 1975. While the domestic market is large in theory, in reality purchasing power in the country is still far too low. Another problem is the lack of skilled labour and entrepreneurial skills, and this may to some extent have been created by a too rapid programme of indigenization.

Severe problems also face the development of transport in Nigeria. The most common form of transport is still headloading at the local farm level, and the lack of feeder roads to the regional and national roads is an important inhibiting factor in rural development. The Federal Government has now taken over the secondary roads as well as the trunk roads, and it is hoped that state governments will now be able to concentrate on the rural link and feeder roads. Certainly there is no doubt that the road has now become the major means of overland transport in the country. The railway, so important in the development of Nigeria's export-based economy in the early part of the century, now plays but little part in the movement of goods. Compared with Brazil, the Nigerian railway network was never a close or effective network.

Of all the transport problems in Nigeria, perhaps the greatest public attention has been directed at port congestion. For so large a country, Nigeria has a short coastline, much of which suffers from serious physical limitations. These problems have certainly stimulated new ports and the improvement of existing ports, access facilities, and storage capacity. But they have also encouraged road routes to develop across the international boundary, especially in the north, where exporters and importers have begun to turn their eyes northwards across the Sahara as a practicable route for moving their goods.

Internal water transport in Nigeria has considerable potential but as yet little has been done to use the immense Niger–Benue system for the movement of goods. More progress has been made in the use of pipelines, not only for petroleum, but also for natural gas, vegetable oils, and water.

Another critical matter about which a very great deal needs to be done in Nigeria is communications. While it has frequently been argued that bottlenecks in telephone, cable, and postal services are the price that has to be paid for rapid economic advance, the fact remains that these bottlenecks are the source of gross inefficiency, frustration, and waste. The rapid movement of information is perhaps of more immediate importance to development than is the rapid movement of goods in the present state of Nigeria's infrastructural development.

Turning now to trade, the internal sector must depend for improvement not only on the improvements in transport and communications already referred to but also on better marketing and distribution institutions. At the very local level in rural areas, too, attention is beginning to focus on the value of the periodic market system's role in stimulating and facilitating rural development. As for foreign trade, as already shown this has undergone a dramatic change over the last decade or so. At independence Nigeria's colonial pattern of foreign trade involved the export of cocoa, palm oil and palm kernels, cotton, groundnuts, rubber, hides and skins, and tin – all raw materials for export to developed industrial nations. Now, however, petroleum easily dominates the export trade, and several of the former raw material exports have actually to be imported, not necessarily because of reduced production but because of increased domestic consumption. In this sense,

Nigeria's economy has certainly developed rapidly: it is very much less dependent on the rest of the world and on fluctuations in the terms of trade.

This last fact has greatly eased the Nigerian government's ability to control the kind of development it wishes to encourage. But serious political difficulties remain to face the new 1979 civilian government. As already noted, problems arise from the complex composition of the population and from the regional disequilibrium expressed in the distribution of population, main urban areas, and centres of industrial growth. A greater sense of national unity and integration must be achieved as a necessary prerequisite for further economic advance.

It is true, of course, that the present state structure of nineteen states already provides the administrative framework for regional development, diffusing the excessive power of certain groups and regions. It may well be that additional states will eventually be added to the present nineteen states; after all there were previously only twelve, and claims for up to three more states are already strong. The use of these states as planning units for many purposes is logical on many grounds. Spatial integration is certain to be facilitated by the state structure, the state capitals giving new orientation to transport and to economic and population flows within the country. Indeed, in this sense Nigeria 'stands a unique chance of escaping the blighting effect of urban primacy' (Mabogunje, in Oguntoyinbo *et alia*, 1978: 3). The attempt to create regional linkages and national integration has also been reflected in the establishment of the new Federal Territory near Abuja in the middle belt. The central location of the new capital will, so it is hoped, 'induce development to become more inward-looking, encourage more intensive exploitation of the under-utilized food productive capacity of the middle belt and impose a new radial pattern on the system of transportation and communication' (ibid.: 4). Putting it another way, the new capital should, as with Brasilia, reduce too great a concentration of wealth, activity, and investment in the major growth poles – Lagos, Port Harcourt, and Kano; it will also help to integrate the various discrete and often conflicting interests in different parts of the country. Whether all these measures will in fact do much to increase the authority and efficiency of the central government, however, is open to doubt. Conflicts of interest between the national government and state government interests seem likely to remain chronic, especially in the democratic multi-party system Nigeria has chosen to operate.

Mention has already been made of the division of responsibility between the federal centre and the states in certain specific fields. In theory state planning has to fit into an overall national plan for development. Apart from major trunk roads, the federal government has acquired power to control the marketing boards. But most important, the federal government retains in its hands the oil wealth – really the key to development in the country. However, apart from the conflict of interests already referred to, a problem about the present structure of planning is one of particular importance to Nigeria – certainly much more than to Brazil. This is the problem of data. Even basic population data are unavailable, and data on production, prices, and almost every other aspect of social and economic life are either unavailable or discredited. As one authority has put it, 'the problem of data is perhaps the single, most important weakness in the present effort of Nigeria to develop' (ibid.: 12).

The last word about Nigerian development must refer to oil. Nigeria has been dramatically affected by the enormous boom of the post-1973 oil price rise period. As a result, Nigeria has become much less dependent upon foreign aid: in her first plan the country looked for 50 per cent of investment expenditure to come from foreign sources, and in the second plan 20 per cent; but her third plan, completed in 1980, was financed entirely from her own sources. But at the same time oil wealth has brought with it problems with which Nigeria is finding it very difficult to cope. Nigeria is now a classic example of too much money chasing too few goods, as a result of which so many things that are demanded have to be imported. Thus while Nigeria clearly has all the preconditions and resources for breaking out of her traditional poverty and of bringing development to more than just her élite, she at the same time is facing many urgent problems: 'maldistribution of incomes and rewards with their accompanying political and social complications; rising living costs; widespread corruption; violent crime; and a spirit of indiscipline that may easily arise when a country thinks it can overcome all its problems with money' (Arnold, 1977: 63).

India. The enormous scale of the problem of development in India derives largely from the size of its population rather than from the size of the country: its some 700 million people live in a country less than four times the size of Nigeria and only one-third the size of Brazil. For its population, clearly, India is a rather small country. In considering the country's natural resource base, therefore, one must start from the fact that although it is the seventh largest country in the world, India does not possess the luxury of vast open lands available for colonization or development. And indeed, probably not more than half the land area is available for cultivation. Ecologically the country is as varied as either Brazil or Nigeria and, like these two countries, contains many heterogeneous regions. The low semi-desert country of Gujarat–Rajasthan contrasts not only with the massive Himalayan ranges of the north but also with the wet lands of Kerala and Assam. Seasonality of rainfall, mostly resulting from the changing monsoons, is everywhere a factor of great importance for water supply. Much of the water used for agriculture in India is provided from irrigation of one form or another; but water supply from rivers is best in the northern plains where the great Indus and Ganga river systems flow down from the Himalayas; otherwise rivers flow eastwards across the Deccan plateau towards the Bay of Bengal. About half of the country relies heavily on the annual rainfall for agriculture. Most of the rain arrives with the south-west monsoon during the growing season – the summer months. For small areas in the south there is a second (winter) monsoon. But the rainfall is not only unevenly distributed, it is also un-reliable both in amount and in timing. This fact inevitably affects the hydro-electric potential these rivers represent, though there is scope for considerable development along these lines.

India's mineral resources cover a reasonable range, though the country has to import such essential items as petroleum, of which only about one-third is derived from domestic sources, and copper. But of perhaps equal importance in a heavily populated agricultural country like India is the soil resource. The extensive level or near-level areas have for the most part soils which are naturally good, though there has been considerable impoverishment of soils in the Ganga–Brahmaputra lowlands. Indeed the real soil problem in India is not so much one of inherent poverty as one of soil exhaustion through bad management and failure to maintain fertility. Topographically India does not suffer from important barriers, except in the extreme north; but the mountains here contribute to the wealth of India by providing the sources of so many of the country's major river systems which have formed the basis of the early great civilizations of this part of Asia, located, it will be noted, on the very fringe of the tropics, for about one-third of India lies outside the strict boundaries of the tropics.

The natural resource base of India, then, is reasonably large and varied, though this must always be set against the huge population base. Above all, 'land is *par excellence* the scarce means of production, on which the lives and livelihood of the majority of the population depends' (Chauduri, 1979: 13).

The statistical data on which to base development planning in India are good by the standards of most developing countries: they are certainly better than in Brazil and incomparably better than in Nigeria. This is fortunate in a country with problems the scale of those to be found in India. The overriding fact in any study of India's development is, of course, the size of its population – greater than the population of tropical Africa and tropical South America combined. The case of India is commonly cited in any discussion on the relationship between population size or rate of growth and development, it being held that the population problem is critical and central. How, it is frequently asked, can a poor country like India cope with the addition of some 15 million to its total population every year? On the other hand, the rate of population growth in India is now not especially high (about 2 per cent per annum) and a demographic solution to the demographic–economic problem as stated in Chapter 5 is not now seriously considered as either sensible or practicable.

Of relatively less importance in development planning is the distribution of population in India. The above-average densities are found mainly in the alluvial lowlands – the Ganga and Brahma-putra plains – and in the deltas and coastal plains of the peninsula and in their extensions inland, especially in Tamilnadu. The low densities are associated with the arid lands beyond the present reach of irrigation schemes or with mountainous areas. The distribution of urban centres fairly closely reflects the distribution of higher densities of population. Urban centres are defined fairly precisely in India as having municipal administrative status *or* with over 5,000 inhabitants, living at a density of over 1,000 to the square mile, and supporting themselves by mainly non-agricultural activities. The distribution of urban centres in India does not demonstrate the same regional concentration of the extreme kind found in Brazil and Nigeria. To this extent, then, India already possesses a reasonable basis for regional spatial integration in development planning.

As for the composition of the Indian population, this is probably more varied than in Brazil but less heterogeneous than in Nigeria. Though India contains many ethnic groups, or tribes, with different languages and cultures, this variety is used much more than in Nigeria as the basis for state identity, rather than state identity being used as a basis for destroying ethnic identity. The same principle was of course used in the partitioning of former British India into independent India and Pakistan, the eastern wing of which subsequently became independent Bangladesh. But while ethnicity, language, culture, and religion are significant forces in India today, perhaps of even more importance is the division of Indian society on the basis of class and caste, though the latter is beginning to break down, especially in the larger urban areas. Viewing the Indian population qualitatively as a human resource, indeed, India probably suffers more than either Brazil or Nigeria from certain difficult and inherent social and cultural, especially religious, constraints on development. The quality of Indian labour is also affected adversely by diseases of the kind found especially in Nigeria. But more than either Brazil or Nigeria, India suffers from under-nutrition and malnutrition and so from certain specific deficiency diseases like kwashiokor and anaemia, all of which lead to low resistance to infection and low energy.

Operating as it does against a background of the peculiar problems of the natural and human resources of India – dominated as always by the shortage of land and the huge size of the population – agricultural development in the country faces many serious, perhaps intractable, problems. Predictably, the Indian peasant farmer is still predominantly a subsistence farmer, following ancient and traditional practices, many of which are, at least by Nigerian standards, sophisticated and intensive. The permanent-field cultivation of the Indian peasant is very different from the shifting-field systems of Nigeria, now found in India only among some of the hill tribes of Assam and in isolated pockets elsewhere. The preferred cereals in India are rice and wheat, though *jowar* millet comes second to rice in area sown, and *bajra* millet and maize are also significant food crops. Cash crops are mainly cotton, groundnuts, sugar-cane, jute, coconuts, tea, rubber, and coffee. Plantations are not of great significance except in the north-east and south-west, where tea, rubber, and coffee may be grown under plantations.

With an emphasis on intensive, permanent-field cultivation – the only possible policy where land is scarce and population numbers so great – and in an environment with a seasonal and generally unreliable rainfall, irrigation has long been a central feature of agriculture in India. About a quarter of the cultivated area is now irrigated, canals accounting for 40 per cent, wells for 28 per cent, and tanks for 18 per cent. In development planning, the essentially local and small-scale nature of tanks and wells means that the greatest capital outlays have been for major canal irrigation schemes. Many of the larger canal irrigation schemes, however, are not only for water for agriculture, but are also designed in some cases to control floods and are part of larger complexes of dams and power stations.

The generally low output *per capita* in agriculture, together with the existing permanent-field nature of most farming, means that much greater intensification of production is not only necessary but also possible. Particular problems constraining increased productivity in agriculture, however, include first, the subdivision and consequent fragmentation of holdings. As a result, holdings are often uneconomic in size and their scattered distribution may be extremely wasteful and an important constraint on technological change. Second, the system of land tenure is still restrictive in many ways. In northern India the *zamindari* system of rented plots in large estates has now been eradicated, the Government taking over the estates of the zamindars. But another system known as *ryotwari* has led inevitably to heavy mortgaging and indebtedness. Third, techniques of cultivation are frequently constrained by lack of tools and other equipment on the farms. Finally, there is a great need for improved seed, stock, and fertilizers. These are all necessary, indeed crucial, for increased productivity, but for the most part they are beyond the reach of the rural poor. It is easy to point to cultural constraints. For instance, it is often stated that the Indian peasant wastes an important natural manure by either removing animal dung from the field for use as fuel or by leaving the dung where it is but not working it into the soil. On the other hand, such practices may well be logical where the quality of the dung from emaciated cattle is poor, where the need for fuel may be seen as more immediately urgent than the need for fertilizer, and where in some cases there are caste scruples about handling dung. Another point often made is the Hindu prohibition on the slaughter of cattle, which has led to a vast but low quality animal population which competes with work animals for food on the farm. But whatever the difficulties, something must be done about the provision of better seed, stock, and fertilizer at a price that farmers can afford and after adequate demonstration work has been effected. Several large fertilizer plants have now been constructed in India.

Related to this last point about seeds and fertilizers is the whole issue of the Green Revolution, on which a great deal of attention has been focused over the last decade. This 'revolution' refers to the rapid increase in agricultural productivity since the early 1970s in India. High-yielding varieties of rice and wheat, together with increased use of fertilizers and pesticides and the expansion of irrigation led to substantial increases in food grain production. Clearly the Green Revolution involved the application of scientific knowledge and methods to basic food production. Opinions differ over its results. Certainly its effects have been patchy, some parts of India having been quite untouched by it. Moreover, there is no doubt that its major advances have been with the larger, wealthier farmers with sufficient capital to take advantage of the new methods and materials. The Green Revolution has also focused primarily on only two crops – rice and wheat – and has yet to make its impact on other food crops, market gardening, stock breeding, and dairying. A final problem is that the cost of applying Green Revolution methods makes any failure of crops – caused, for instance, by failure of the rains or by floods – that much more disastrous.

The emphasis on modern large-scale industry which so characterizes Indian economic development today tends to obscure the importance of small-scale or cottage industry in the country. While much of this is believed to have been destroyed by cheap imports from Western Europe, especially Britain, in the nineteenth century, some 20 million people are still engaged in small-scale, labour-intensive, cottage industry of one form or another. National and state planning now takes this sector into account, supporting and encouraging it by various means. Part of the reason for this support is the conviction in India that such cottage industry, especially the making of *khadi* cloth, has 'a respected place in Indian culture, reinforced by Gandhi's insistence on the dignity of creative craftsmanship in village life' (Johnson, 1979: 64).

Modern large-scale industry is now expanding rapidly in India, and the basic heavy industries, including iron and steel, dating back to 1911, are now well established, though textiles (jute and cotton) still tend to dominate, except in the Chota Nagpur industrial region. Labour is a major problem in Indian industrialization, which may seem odd in a country of some 700 million people, but manpower training for skilled technicians is still quite inadequate, in spite of the large number of unemployed arts graduates. Moreover, the domestic market is still remarkably narrow in that the purchasing power of the mass of the population is still very low. Yet another problem is capital and the continued dependence for this on foreign sources. Nevertheless, industrialization is firmly believed to be the *sine qua non* of Indian development. It is certainly believed to be inevitable in the face of large-scale rural unemployment: 'to absorb the excess rural population' has long been the rationale for rapid modern industrialization.

At first sight the road and rail transport network of India seems impressive, especially compared with that of Brazil and Nigeria. Once again, however, comparison is meaningless without taking fully into account the huge size of the population. Though India's transport network is perhaps the best in Asia – largely a legacy of British rule in India – it is very uneven and is certainly quite inadequate for the purposes of modern development. The large railway system, which is almost all government owned, is the most important means of movement as far as both long-distance goods and passengers are concerned. It suffers to some extent from the dismemberment consequent upon the partition of British India, and some new lines have had to be built. But perhaps the most important need is for more up-to-date rolling stock and better track maintenance. The road system is relatively poor, due partly to the difficult physical, especially climatic, conditions. There is a shortage of building material and the need for frequent bridging over the streams of the dissected Deccan plateau is particularly serious. Some two-thirds of the roads are still unsurfaced and so are very difficult to use in the wet season. The trunk roads, the responsibility of the central government, are certainly inadequate in number and quality. But perhaps of even more importance is the need to improve the state-controlled feeder and local roads in the countryside.

With a long coastline for her size, India is fortunate in her port facilities, the three major ports – Calcutta, Madras, and Bombay – being well spaced out and all in easy contact by rail with the capital, Delhi. But with her exports amounting to only two-thirds of the value of her imports, India suffers from a serious balance of payments deficit. Her exports are either foodstuffs and other raw materials (tea, raw cotton, leather, skins, groundnuts, iron ore, and mica) or manufactured goods (especially jute products and

232 · ECONOMIC DEVELOPMENT IN THE TROPICS

cotton piece goods). Imports include petroleum and petroleum products, food, especially wheat, and machinery. To deal with her trading deficit as well as to encourage import-substitution industries, India has followed, from time to time, policies of domestic protection by various tariff measures. In this way, for instance, the Indian car industry has been protected very successfully.

It has been said that population and politics dominate every problem in India. We have already seen how central the issue of population is to almost every aspect of development in the country. But the same is largely true of politics. The conflict between the Centre (at Delhi) and the States has become one of India's most intractable problems. The present division of the country into eight territories, including Delhi, and seventeen states is logical on many grounds, including the fact that the states, at least, are based primarily on language and so reflect cultural differences. But within what is usually called 'the largest democracy on earth', such a structure seems to place too great a premium upon responsibility. All kinds of decisions, including the most effective way of utilizing resources, are much more difficult to make than in countries like China, with similarly large populations but with a totalitarian government.

To some extent, the virtues of Indian democracy are seen at their best at the village and district levels within states. Here efforts have been made through the establishment on democratic lines of the traditional system of village government known as *Panchayat Raj*, to encourage a greater sense of participation. The *Panchayat* constitution requires that there be at least two women members and that two members from the *Harijan* or 'untouchable' castes be included as well.

The Centre-States problem is of course central to the problems of national economic development planning in India, as it is to a rather less extreme extent in Nigeria. With her national objectives to produce a socialist pattern of society, a reduction in inequalities of all kinds, and self-sustained economic growth – consistent aims over the past two decades at least – the Government of India nevertheless has to operate against a background of certain firm realities. India has a mixed, and not a centrally-planned economy;

India has vast resources of land, materials, and manpower but a minimum of capital and technology; India must continue to look mainly to the West for capital and technological help as well as for markets for her exportable surpluses; manpower planning is both critically important and yet impossibly difficult in a country with 700 million people; and the ballot box makes long-term economic planning a dangerous luxury for any government to attempt. Putting it at its simplest, it is worth noting that no other country of comparable size and population has ever attempted to plan for economic development with a largely free and democratic society. Perhaps the task is beyond any government.

Conclusions

The dangers of generalizing about tropical development. Much of the current thinking about tropical development is characterized by a tendency to oppose tropical and non-tropical lands in a most misleading way. Thus it is sometimes suggested that there are specifically 'tropical' problems or that the tropics have their own peculiar – and usually, by implication, inferior – physical and human geography. It is to be doubted, however, whether any useful generalizations of this kind can be made about the tropics and their development problems any more than they can be made about the temperate lands. Indeed, it will have become apparent that to write about 'tropical' as quite distinct from any other kind of development may be misleading; and very little of what has been written here about the processes of economic development could not also be written of developing countries in the arid topics, sub-tropics, or temperate lands of the world. Furthermore, in their natural and human characteristics tropical countries differ widely from one another, and each country embraces that unique complex of natural and human circumstances which provides the only realistic territorial framework for development planning. In this sense the resource bases of Brazil, Nigeria, and India differ as widely as do those of Great Britain and Ghana. Whether they occur in tropical or in non-tropical areas, almost all applied problems of economic development are regional or local problems; and the specific areal setting in which they occur is likely to reveal a unique combination of natural and human conditions.

It is similarly misleading to generalize rigidly about the whole developing world, of which the tropics forms by far the largest part, as if it were a separate and opposing entity for which a whole new set of concepts, ideas, and principles needs to be developed. As Brookfield (1973) has argued, research in the developing or Third World should lead to an enrichment in our understanding of the First and Second worlds, where exist the same phenomena of dualism, centres and peripheries, and institutional and behavioural contrasts that underly varying receptivity and reaction in the face of change. The Third World merely exhibits those things more strikingly, suffers more from innovation and gains less (p. 16). There is no single theory of economic development for any major part of the world, or for the whole world; nor can any one variable – capital, natural resources, scale, technology, human skills, or birth-control measures – ever provide the key to development. The processes of economic development are always immensely complicated. Moreover, the various countries of the developing world are clearly at different stages along a development line or even pursuing quite different lines; and any attempt to devise a general formula on the basis of an economic theory that assumes otherwise is bound to lead to failure.

There is, then, as much variety in environments and in existing levels of achievement in the tropical developing world as there is in the developed world as a whole; and the distinction between developing and developed is as arbitrary and misleading in applied economic development studies as is the distinction between tropical and non-tropical lands.

Grounds for optimism. Seen in this light, there seems to be every reason for optimism about the *potential* for economic development in tropical countries. It is accepted as a necessary working hypothesis that the tropics possess no inherent disadvantages in natural or human resources compared with any other similarly large part of the earth's surface. This holds true both quantitatively and qualitatively. To suggest, for instance, that soils are especially limiting to agriculture in the tropics, that the climate is inimical to the growth of advanced civilizations, or that tropical peoples have a relatively low innate capacity for participating in the more complex forms of social, economic, or political endeavour: all such viewpoints are rejected. Rather is it accepted that the natural and human resources of the tropics are as varied – as 'good' and as 'bad' – as in any other large region, and that these resources are certainly not especially limiting to development, given adequate knowledge about the resources and their utilization and given also a readiness to adapt economic planning to the opportunities and limitations set by them. Substantial difficulties in the understanding and utilization of the resource base do exist; but these difficulties commonly derive from a lack of information, experience, and training, and so are not of the kind to inhibit permanently the economic development of the tropical world.

Further grounds for optimism about tropical development are provided by the growing awareness among the countries of the developed world that the economic problems of tropical countries can never be understood, let alone solved, out of the context of the total world economy, and in particular out of the context of existing international trading relations. The provision of aid, whether financial, in kind, or in technical assistance, is undoubtedly important. But perhaps even more critical is the need for larger and wider trading and marketing opportunities in the developed world. Present international trading relations perpetuate the traditional exchange of Western manufactures in return for raw materials and make very difficult the kind of rapid economic advance based upon overseas markets that played so large a part in the growth of prosperity at earlier stages in the economic history of most countries in the developed world. Apart from common humanitarian motives, there are strong practical arguments for providing better trading and marketing opportunities for tropical countries, including the fact that vast potential markets in the developing world itself can never be tapped while the purchasing power of the mass of the population there remains so low: the prosperity of Great Britain as a great trading nation, for instance, must in the long run depend on the continuous expansion of world markets, and in particular on the growth of new markets for sophisticated products in the poorer countries. Furthermore, the developed countries are becoming increasingly aware that tropical developing countries now account for about two-thirds of the total voting strength of the United Nations; and the kind of political stability so urgently needed in these countries is unlikely to develop in a situation where economic instability and distress are endemic and where there continues to be little evidence of substantial improvements in living standards. While it may seem ingenuous to expect the developed world ever to indulge in the kind of economic altruism outlined in the latter part of this book, a great deal has, nevertheless, been accomplished in this direction over the last few years. Since 1964, in particular, the United Nations Conference on Trade and Development, meeting about every four years, has gathered together a body of material and initiated a movement of world opinion already much closer to agreement on wider trading opportunities for developing countries than most observers would have thought possible in the early 1960s.

The increase of production. In trying to identify the many and diverse problems of economic development in the tropical world, one central issue is taken to be what has been called in these pages the demographic–economic problem. This seems logical for many reasons, including the fact that economic development is defined, however crudely, as a rising *per capita* income and so can be considered to be a function of the changing relationship between national income and total population numbers. It is argued that in dealing with this demographic–economic problem the emphasis should not be placed upon trying to reduce the rate of population growth. While the demographic approach must have long-term implications of profound significance, to look upon birth control as a means of increasing *per capita* income is both to oversimplify economic development as a process and to ignore the role of the so-called 'population problem'. The real issue remains one of how to increase production at a rate substantially higher than the rate of growth of population.

In discussing, however selectively and briefly, some of the major issues relating to the increase of production in tropical countries, two main points have been made. First, it is misleading to isolate too sharply the supply and demand sides of production, and any applied problem of how to increase production must be seen in the context of the entire production–distribution–consumption process. Thus to increase the agricultural production of maize and cassava in an area involves considering all three aspects. At the production end there is the need to provide the appropriate fertilizers, together with information about farming methods and the cultivation cycle; and the successful introduction of such innovations implies also a host of other social, cultural, fiscal, administrative, and technological changes which are as yet perhaps little understood and require much deeper field experience and research. At the production end, too, the scope for applied scientific research into crops and their ecology – into better-yielding, disease-resistant, or pest-resistant varieties – is very wide indeed and is probably consistently underestimated in prognostications about production increases. But increased maize or cassava production in a country requires also that lines of distribution in terms of marketing organization, credit facilities, and good, cheap transport be made available. And finally, increased production cannot be expected to occur unless market opportunities are there and are seen to be there, either in the form of increased local food consumption; in new maize-processing or cassava-processing factories; or in larger overseas markets. All three aspects of the problem – at the production and consumption ends and in the distributive link – are closely related and together must always affect very deeply the individual farmer's motivation, incentives, and resistance to change.

A second point has been expressed in terms of a development continuum, in which all forms and levels of economic activity in tropical countries are seen as being at different stages along a particular development line. This is no kind of historical determinism. It is recognized that the development line followed by all countries will not be the same: the aims and methods of development are frequently widely different from country to country. Nevertheless, whatever line of development is being followed, it is contended that the problem in any particular case study is to locate the development stage and to analyse the existing tendencies to change within the economy. Only when this has been done should any attempt be made to accelerate, facilitate, or direct the economy along specific lines. This approach is likely to be more successful, and to have fewer ill-effects on indigenous societies, than the alternative approach: to consider a developing economy in the tropics as being essentially static, even stagnant; and to follow this up by trying to inject from outside a type of change which bears no relation to the spontaneous movements for improvement latent within all economies and societies. This notion also implies that the chief aim of economic policy must always be the increase of productivity by 'industrializing' all forms of economic activity, including agriculture; and by feeding back from industry into agriculture the results of applied research and technological advance.

Whether any of the measures for increasing production discussed in these pages are feasible depends a great deal upon political realities. Almost all measures for increasing production, for reducing population growth rates, for redistributing populations or wealth, for bringing about any kind of rational economic development – all such measures may never be capable of implementation except within the framework of authoritarian political structures of one form or another. As pointed out in Chapter 12, many of our assumptions about the need for or relevance of democratic forms of government may have to be examined and challenged against the realities of poverty in the Third World. Moreover, we need always to bear in mind the fact that economic or material prosperity may not be the sole, or even the chief, aim of development policy. Perhaps above all we must remain aware of the dangers of an obsession with the increase of production as an end in itself. Most countries are aware today of the environmental implications of rapid economic growth. But in a wider sense the developing countries of the tropics are becoming aware of the need to retain those qualities of life which many developed countries are in danger of losing altogether.

The Geographer and applied development studies in the tropics. It will be clear from the preceding pages that a great deal of research is now being directed into the field of tropical economic development studies. Since the early 1950s, certainly, there has appeared a spate of books and articles, only a fraction of which has been referred to in this short study. The amount of theoretical material alone is now formidable; and many physical and social scientists have greatly widened and deepened our understanding of the various countries and peoples of the tropical world.

Yet it is still true to say that one of the major difficulties with which development studies in the tropics have to cope is the paucity of theoretical and factual material. At the theoretical level, it is clear that development theory for developing countries still requires much refinement, although this is particularly difficult where the available statistical material is so limited. Existing data are usually too few and too crude to be subjected to the kind of refined techniques of statistical treatment now being adopted in the more advanced societies. There are few tropical countries, indeed, where even the basic data for development planning can yet be said to exist; and the need for more geological and topographical survey and mapping, climatological and biogeographical studies, land-use analyses, and population, settlement, and marketing studies is urgent and obvious everywhere.

But an equally urgent contemporary need is for the kind of 'grass-roots' case study of applied development in the field referred to on a number of occasions throughout these pages. In this kind of applied, essentially problem-oriented study, facts and theories are equally necessary. Furthermore, it demands an approach that is essentially interdisciplinary; and this, it has been argued, must logically result in the re-orientation of development studies to small-scale problems of micro-research (Connell, 1971; Coppock, 1969). Although the aim of economic development may be quite simply to bring about a cumulative increase in levels of consumption, it is now widely appreciated – by economists as well as by non-economists – that economic development is not simply an economic process, and that 'many if not most of the applied problems to which attention must be given if economic development is to be promoted, raise questions outside the field with which the economist is normally concerned' (Viner, 1953: 23). The range of factors operating in any specific situation in economic development reaches far beyond the confines of any one formal discipline or branch of knowledge. Especially in dealing with differences in qualities of economic factors between different regions, 'the economist is dealing with matters for whose detailed investigation other scientists – agronomists, political scientists, engineers, geographers, geologists . . . sociologists, and anthropologists – alone have the requisite professional qualifications and the economist must seek their counsel and borrow from them' (ibid.: 24).

This being so, the field study of applied problems of economic development has always to take into account the findings, methods and viewpoints of a wide range of related disciplines. Real problems of economic development are no more 'geographical' problems than they are 'economic' or 'social' problems. And this remains true whether 'geographical' is taken to mean 'physical', 'regional' or 'spatial'. The geographer concerned with development studies cannot afford to seek continually for 'the geographer's contribution', or to argue that 'our concern is with spatial relations', or to concentrate his attention on 'the spatial dimensions' of the problems of development. The spatial content in any development problem may be important. But it may equally be of little significance or totally irrelevant. And to insist on emphasizing the spatial content in a development situation may be as misleading and limiting as to focus on the 'physical environmental' or 'synthesizing' roles of the geographer. Consequently it seems logical to insist that the questions a geographer asks himself about tropical development in his field studies must be examined and answered, not within any inhibiting framework of preconceived notions about what is or is not the proper scope of geography but simply with the aim of following all relevant lines of inquiry, wherever they might lead. The value and meaning of the geographer's contribution to development studies can only be demonstrated by the way in which geographers tackle development problems and try to answer the questions these problems raise, and not by the way in which they stop their analysis every time it seems to go outside the legitimate field of geographical inquiry. In tropical development studies, as in perhaps all fields of applied knowledge, the scope of the inquiry must be defined only by the problem set.

Appendix: Notes on Some Recent Trends

The tropical rain forest genetic resources. Many authorities are now increasingly concerned about 'the long-term survival of tropical rain forest, which they see as a non-renewable finite resource that is being fast whittled away. Moreover, it is strongly believed that, simply because of the complex structure and species diversity of rain forest, its removal actually means the irretrievable loss of most of its constituent species and genetic resources' (Stott, 1978: 89). The present rapid rate of forest destruction suggests that tropical rain forest ecosystems may soon be irreparably damaged. The need for more effective exploration and conservation of tropical forest genetic resources is now urgent. The exploration, survey, classification, and mapping of rain forest present many difficulties, but even more daunting is the task of conserving its genetic resources, whether *in situ* or *ex situ*. On balance, opinion seems to favour *in situ* conservation.

However, 'the conservation of samples of rain forest depends first and foremost on the political and economic drive of governments to reserve large tracts of forest for conservation purposes. . . . In many tropical countries, the realities of short-term politics, grounded as they so often are in the desperate need to increase food production, run contrary to such measures' (ibid.: 13).

Limits to growth? During the 1960s and 1970s there has been some re-examination of the assumptions commonly held about planning for development and growth. There has been increasing concern for what is termed the 'quality of life' rather than the level of material provision, and many writers have questioned the assumption that economic growth is necessarily a desirable or feasible end: higher *per capita* incomes, more consumer goods, and greater material prosperity in all its manifestations do not, so the argument goes, necessarily add up to greater human satisfaction and happiness. The work of Mishan (1967) on *The Costs of Economic Growth* is perhaps the most important work following this line of thought, though greater popularity was achieved by the *Blueprint for Survival* (1972) and the Club of Rome's *Limits to Growth* (1972). More recently, Schumacher's *Small is Beautiful* has been very influential, and *Mankind at the Turning Point* has brought up to date much of the earlier material of *Limits to Growth*. All these and many other publications have focused attention on the dangers of unrestricted growth in the world economy, indicating that limits to growth will eventually be reached if present trends of population growth, industrialization, pollution, food production, and resource depletion continue unchanged.

These arguments and, in general, the whole anti-growth lobby have gained wide currency. At the same time these arguments have come in for a great deal of criticism, not only from international economists but also from less-developed countries, where the implications of the anti-growth movement are understandably unlikely to gain much support. At the beginning of the 1980s it is perhaps not too much to say that, while the limits to growth arguments have been helpful in emphasizing certain negative aspects of economic growth, they are now taken less seriously by a world which is increasingly experiencing zero growth as a fact of life. As one writer has put it, 'insofar as the anti-growth movement had helped highlight genuine problems – such as those of environmental pollution in general and nuclear waste in particular –. or philosophical problems concerning the relationship between needs and happiness, or ethical issues such as our responsibility for future generations, it has not been sterile and unproductive, however foolish may have been most of its arguments and however unfitted may have been most . . . of its protagonists to make useful contributions to these problems or even understand them' (Beckerman, 1979).

North–South: A Programme for Survival. This United Nations report, known as the Brandt Commission Report, has appeared at the very beginning of the 1980s and, with its particular backing and essentially realistic approach, is likely to have a more solid impact on world opinion and government policies than any of the documents referred to above in the section on limits to growth. This new report emphasizes the interdependence of nations in a period of grave recession in which peace is being endangered, not only by the arms build-up but also by mounting chaos. The report puts forward proposals for far-reaching reforms and a restructuring of the world system in order to avert global disaster. More specifically, a four-point emergency programme is put forward to include (i) a large-scale transfer of resources to developing countries, (ii) an international energy strategy, (iii) a global food programme, and (iv) a start on some major reforms in the international economic system. In spite of the simplistic nature of much of the evidence, it is difficult not to agree with much of the analysis and a good deal of the prescription. It remains to be seen, however, whether political realities will make even the Brandt Commission Report seem, in retrospect, no more than yet another document of social and economic rhetoric.

Select Bibliography

AJAEGBU, H. I. A. 1976. *Urban and Rural Development in Nigeria.* London.

ALLAN, W. 1965. *The African Husbandman.* London.

ARGAWALA, A. N. and SINGH, S. P. 1963. *The Economics of Underdevelopment.* New York.

ARNOLD, G. 1977. *Modern Nigeria.* London.

BAILEY, F. G. 1958. *Caste and the Economic Frontier.* London.

BALDWIN, K. D. S. 1957. *The Niger Agricultural Project.* London.

BALOGH, T. 1966. *The Economics of Poverty.* London.

BARAN, P. A. 1957. *The Political Economy of Backwardness.* New York.

BARBOUR, K. M. (ed.) 1972. *Planning for Nigeria.* Ibadan.

BARNETT, H. J. and MORSE, C. 1963. *Scarcity and Growth: the Economics of Natural Resource Availability.* Baltimore.

BAUER, P. T. 1957. *Economic Analysis and Policy in Underdeveloped Countries.* London.

1963. *The Study of Underdeveloped Economies.* London.

1963b. *West African Trade.* Cambridge.

1972. *Dissent on Development.* London.

BAUER, P. T. and YAMEY, B. S. 1957. *The Economics of Underdeveloped Countries.* Cambridge.

BECKERMAN, W. 1979. Small is stupid, *The Times Higher Education Supplement,* 23 November, 14–15.

BELSHAW, H. 1956. *Population Growth and Levels of Consumption.* London.

BHAGWATI, J. 1966. *The Economics of Undeveloped Countries.* London.

BLAIKIE, P. 1971. Spatial organisation of agriculture in some North Indian villages, *Transactions, Institute of British Geographers,* **52**, 1–40; and **53**, 15–30.

BLAKEMORE, H. and SMITH, C. T. 1978. *Latin America.* London.

BLAUT, J. M. 1973. The theory of development, *Antipode,* **5**, 22–6.

BOHANNAN, P. and DALTON, G. 1962. *Markets in Africa.* Evanston.

BOSERUP, E. 1965. *The Conditions of Agricultural Growth.* London.

BROOKFIELD, H. C. 1973. On one geography and a Third World, *Transactions, Institute of British Geographers*, **58**, 1–20.

1975. *Interdependent Development*. London.

BUCHANAN, K. M. 1964. Profiles of the third world, *Pacific Viewpoint*, **5**, 97–126.

1974. Reflections on a 'dirty word', *Dissent*, **31**, 25–31.

CHAMBERS, R. 1969. *Settlement Schemes in Africa*. London.

CHAUDURI, P. 1979. *The Indian Economy*. London.

CLARK, C. 1957. *The Conditions of Economic Progress*. London.

1967. *Population Growth and Land Use*. London.

CLARK, C. and HASWELL, M. 1964. *The Economics of Subsistence Agriculture*. London.

COLE, J. P. 1975. *Latin America*. London.

CONNELL, J. 1971. The geography of development, *Area*, **3**, 259–65.

COURTENEY, P. D. 1965. *Plantation Agriculture*. London.

CUKOR, G. 1972. *Strategies of Industrialisation in the Developing Countries*. London.

CURLE, A. 1963. *Educational Strategy for Developing Societies*. London.

DE SCHLIPPE, P. 1956. *Shifting Cultivation in Africa*. London.

DONALDSON, P. 1973. *Worlds Apart*. Harmondsworth.

DUMONT, R. 1966. *False Start in Africa*. London.

EHRLICH, P. R. and A. H. 1970. *Population, Resources and Environment*. New York.

EICHER, C. K. and LIEDHOLM, C. 1970. *Growth and Development of the Nigerian Economy*. Michigan.

ENKE, S. 1963. *Economics for Development*. New York.

EPSTEIN, T. S. 1970. *Capitalism, Primitive and Modern*. Canberra.

FARMER, B. H. 1957. *Pioneer Peasant Colonisation in Ceylon*. London.

1971. The environmental sciences and economic development, *Journal of Development Studies*, **7**, 257–69.

FEDER, E. 1971. *The Rape of the Peasantry*. New York.

FILANI, M. O. and ONYEMELUKWE, J. O. C. 1977. *A Geographical Analysis of Development Planning Problems in Developing Countries: The Nigerian Example*. Ibadan.

FISHER, C. A. 1964. *South-East Asia*. London.

FOSBERG, F. R., GARNIER, B. J., and KUCHLER, A. W. 1961. Delimitation of the humid tropics, *Geographical Review*, **51**, 333–47.

FRANK, A. G. 1969. *Capitalism and Underdevelopment in Latin America*. Harmondsworth.

FRANKEL, S. H. 1953. *The Economic Impact on Underdeveloped Societies.* Oxford.

FREEMAN, J. P. 1955. *Iban Agriculture.* London.

FRIEDMAN, J. 1966. *Regional Development Policy: A Case Study of Venezuela.* Cambridge.

FURNIVALL, J. S. 1948. *Colonial Policy and Practice.* Cambridge.

FURTADO, C. 1970. *Obstacles of Development in Latin America.* New York.

GALBRAITH, J. K. 1963. *Economic Development in Perspective.* London.
1967. *The Industrial State.* London.

GEERTZ, C. 1963. *Agricultural Involution.* Berkeley and Los Angeles.
1963. *Peddlers and Princes.* Chicago.
1965. *The Social History of an Indonesian Town.* Cambridge, Mass.

GEORGE, S. 1977. *How the other Half Dies.* Harmondsworth.

GERSCHENKRON, A. 1962. *Economic Backwardness in Historical Perspective.* Cambridge, Mass.

GILBERT, A. 1971. Some thoughts on the 'new geography' and the study of development, *Area*, 3, 193–8.
1974. *Latin American Development.* Harmondsworth.

GILLES, H. M. 1965. *Akufo, an Environmental Study of a Nigerian Village Community.* Ibadan.

GINSBERG, N. S. (ed.) 1960. *Essays on Geography and Economic Development.* Chicago.

GOULD, J. D. 1972. *Economic Growth in History: Survey and Analysis.* London.

GOUROU, P. 1966. *The Tropical World.* London.
1971. *Leçons de Géographie Tropicale.* Paris.

GRIFFIN, K. 1969. *Underdevelopment in Spanish America.* London.

GRIGG, D. 1971. *The Harsh Lands.* London.

GROVE, A. T. 1978. *Africa.* Oxford.

GROVE, D. and HUSZAR, L. 1964. *The Towns of Ghana.* Accra.

HAGGETT, P. 1965. *Locational Analysis in Human Geography.* London.

HANCE, W. A. 1964. *The Geography of Modern Africa.* New York.

HANSEN, N. M. (ed.) 1972. *Growth Centres in Regional Economic Development.* New York.

HASWELL, M. R. 1963. *The Changing Pattern of Economic Activity in a Gambia Village.* London.
1967. *The Economics of Development in Village India.* London.

HAUSER, P. M. (ed.) 1967. *Urbanisation in Latin America.* Paris.

HAWKINS, E. K. 1962. *Roads and Road Transport in an Underdeveloped Country*. London.

HAZLEWOOD, A. 1958. *The Economics of Underdeveloped Areas*. London.

1964. *The Economics of Development*. London.

1967. *African Integration and Disintegration*. Oxford.

HENSHALL, J. D. and MOMSEN, R. P. 1974. *A Geography of Brazilian Development*. London.

HILL, POLLY. 1970. *Studies in Rural Capitalism in West Africa*. Cambridge.

1972. *Rural Hausa: A Village and a Setting*. Cambridge.

HIRSCHMAN, A. O. 1958. *The Strategy of Economic Development*. London.

HODDER, B. W. 1959. *Man in Malaya*. London.

1965. Some comments on the origins of traditional markets in Africa south of the Sahara, *Transactions, Institute of British Geographers*, **36**, 97–105.

1978. *Africa Today*. London.

HODDER, B. W. and UKWU, U. I. 1969. *Markets in West Africa*. Ibadan.

HOSELITZ, B. F. (ed.) 1952. *The Progress of Underdeveloped Areas*. Chicago.

HUNTINGDON, E. 1915. *Civilization and Climate*. New Haven.

HUTCHINSON, SIR J. C. 1969. *Population and Food Supply*. Cambridge.

ISARD, W. 1960. *Methods of Regional Analysis*. Cambridge, Mass.

ISHIKAWA, S. 1972. A note on the choice of technology in China, *Journal of Development Studies*, **9**, 161–86.

JACOBS, N. 1971. *Mechanisation Without Development*. New York.

JACOBY, E. 1972. Effects of the 'Green Revolution' in south and southeast Asia, *Modern Asian Studies*, **6**, 63–9.

JAMES, P. E. 1963. *Latin America*. New York.

JOHNSON, B. L. C. 1979. *India*. London.

JOHNSON, E. A. J. 1965. *Market Towns and Spatial Development in India*. Delhi.

1970. *The Organization of Space in Developing Countries*. Cambridge, Mass.

JORGENSON, D. W. 1961. The development of a dual economy, *Economic Journal*, **71**, 309–34.

KILBY, P. 1969. *Industrialization in an Open Economy*. Cambridge.

KINDLEBERGER, C. P. 1966. *Economic Development*. New York.

LACOSTE, Y. 1965. *Géographie du sous-developpement*. Paris.

LEIBENSTEIN, H. 1954. *A Theory of Economic-Demographic Development*. Ithaca.

LEWIS, W. A. 1955. *The Theory of Economic Growth*. London.

LIM, J. J. 1954. Tradition and peasant agriculture in Malaya, *Malayan Journal of Tropical Geography*, 3, 44–7.

LINDQVIST, S. 1979. *Land and Power in South America*. Harmondsworth.

LIPTON, M. 1968. The theory of the optimising peasant, *Journal of Development Studies*, 4, 327–51.

1970. Interdisciplinary studies in lesser developed countries, *Journal of Development Studies*, 7, 5–18.

LITTLE, I. M. D. and CLIFFORD, J. M. 1965. *International Aid*. London.

LIVINGSTONE, I. 1971. *Economic Policy for Development*. Harmondsworth.

LLOYD, P. C. *et alia*. 1967. *The City of Ibadan*. Cambridge.

LOGAN, M. I. 1972. The spatial systems and planning strategies in developing countries, *Geographical Review*, 62, 229–44.

MCGEE, T. G. 1971. *The Urbanization Process in the Third World*. London.

MANSHARD, W. 1979. *Tropical Agriculture*. London.

MARRIS, P. 1962. *Family and Social Change in an African City*. Evanston.

MARTIN, A. 1961. *The Economics of Agriculture*. London.

MASEFIELD, G. B. 1960. *Tropical Agriculture*. Oxford.

MEADOWS, D. H. *et alia*. 1972. *The Limits to Growth*. London.

MISHAN, E. J. 1967. *The Costs of Economic Growth*. London.

MORGAN, W. B. 1978. *Agriculture in the Third World*. London.

MOUNTJOY, A. 1963. *Industrialisation and Underdeveloped Countries*. London.

1971. *Developing the Underdeveloped Countries*. London.

MYINT, H. 1980. *The Economics of the Developing Countries*. London.

MYRDAL, G. 1956. *An International Economy*. New York.

1957. *Economic Theory and Underdeveloped Regions*. London.

NASH, T. A. M. 1948. *The Anchau Settlement Scheme*. London.

NELSON, R. R. 1956. A theory of the low-equilibrium trap, *American Economic Review*, 46, 894–908.

NURSKE, R. 1953. *Problems of Capital Formation in Underdeveloped Countries*. Oxford.

O'CONNOR, A. M. 1966. *An Economic Geography of East Africa*. London.

OGUNTOYINBO, J. S., AREOLA, O. O., and FILANI, M. 1978. *A Geography of Nigerian Development*. Ibadan.

OOI, J. B. 1977. *Peninsular Malaysia*. London.

PEARSON, L. B. 1970. *The Crisis of Development*. London.

PEDLER, F. J. 1955. *The Economic Geography of West Africa*. London.

PERROUX, F. 1955. Note on the concept of 'growth poles', *Économie Appliquée*, **8**.

PIAGET, J. 1970. *Structuralism*. New York.

PIRIE, N. W. 1969. *Food Resources, Conventional and Novel*. Harmondsworth.

PREBISCH, P. 1949. *The Economic Development of Latin America*. New York.

PROTHERO, R. M. 1966. *Migrants and Malaria*. London.

RANIS, G. and FEI, J. C. 1961. A theory of economic development, *American Economic Review*, **51**, 533–65.

REDDAWAY, W. B. 1963. The economics of underdeveloped countries, *Economic Journal*, 1–15.

1966. External capital and self-help in developing countries, *Progress*, **4**, 50–7.

RHODES, R. I. 1971. *Imperialism and Underdevelopment*. New York.

RIDDELL, J. B. 1970. *The Spatial Dynamics of Modernization in Sierra Leone*. Evanston.

ROBINSON, R. (ed.) 1971. *Developing the Third World*. Cambridge.

ROSENSTEIN-RODAN, P. N. 1961. Notes on the theory of the Big Push, in Ellis and Wallich (eds) *Economic Development for Latin America*. New York.

ROSTOW, W. W. 1960. *The Stages of Economic Growth*. Cambridge.

RUTHENBERG, H. 1971. *Farming Systems in the Tropics*. London.

SANTOS, M. 1971. *Les Villes du Tiers Monde*. Paris.

SCHADLER, K. F. 1969. *Crafts, Small-Scale Industries and Industrial Education in Tanzania*. London.

SCHULTZ, T. W. 1964. *Transforming Traditional Agriculture*. New Haven.

SCHUMPETER, J. A. 1949. *The Theory of Economic Development*. Cambridge.

SEMPLE, R. K., GAUTHIER, H. L., and YOUNGMAN, C. E. 1972. Growth poles in Sao Paulo, Brazil, *Annals of the Association of American Geographers*, **62**, 591–8.

SINGER, H. W. 1964. *International Development, Growth and Change*. New York.

SPENCER, J. E. 1966. *Shifting Cultivation in South-East Asia*. Berkeley.

STALEY, E. 1954. *The Future of Underdeveloped Countries*. New York.

STAVENHAGEN, R. (ed.) 1970. *Agrarian Problems and Peasant Movements in Latin America*, New York.

STOTT, P. A. 1978. Tropical rain forest in recent ecological thought: the reassessment of a non-renewable resource, *Progress in Physical Geography*, 2, 80–95.

SUNKEL, O. 1973. Transnational capitalism and national disintegration in Latin America, *Social and Economic Studies*, 22, 132–76.

TAAFE, E. J., MORRILL, R. L., and GOULD, P. R. 1963. Transport expansion in underdeveloped countries, *Geographical Review*, 53, 503–29.

TINBERGEN, J. 1967. *Development Planning*. London.

TRICART, J. 1956. Les exchages entre la zone forestière de Côte d'Ivoire et les savanes soudaniennes, *Cahiers d'Outre Mer*, 9, 209–38.

UDO, R. K. 1965. Sixty years of plantation agriculture in southern Nigeria, *Economic Geography*, 41, 356–65.

URQUIDI, V. L. 1962. *Free Trade and Economic Integration in Latin America*. Berkeley.

VILLARD, H. H. 1963. *Economic Development*. New York.

VINER, J. 1953. *International Trade and Economic Development*. Oxford.

WAGLEY, C. 1965. *Contemporary Cultures and Societies of Latin America*. London.

WARD, B. 1964. *Towards a World of Plenty*. Toronto.

WERTHEIM, W. F. 1956. *Indonesian Society in Transition*. Bandung.

WHITE, H. P. 1959. The movement of export crops in Nigeria, *Tijdschrift voor Economische en Sociale Geografie*, 54, 248–53.

WHITMORE, T. C. 1975. *Tropical Rain Forests of the Far East*. Oxford.

YUDELMAN, M. and HOWARD, F. 1970. *Agricultural Development and Economic Integration in Latin America*. London.

Subject Index

Acclimatization, 57–8
Age structure, 73, 81, 88–90
Agriculture, 3, 37–41, 63, 82, 91, 93, 150, 196
    extension of land, 88–9, 130–3, 160–1
    increase of production, 88, 115–38
    intensification of production, 115–30, 161
    large-scale scheme, 133–8
    mechanization, 90, 136–8
    or industry? 139–50
    types, 93–114
Aid, 201–7
Automatic responses to climate, 57–9

Backward-bending supply curve of labour, 50
Balance of payments, 47, 171, 175
Big Push, 2
Birth control, 82, 84–8, 235, 237
Bride price, 49
Burning, 19, 31, 33, 95–6, 111, 121, 128

Calcium, 37
Capital, *see* Resources
Capital-intensive technology, 105, 151–2
Capital-output ratio, 7
Cash economy, 50, 100–5
Caste system, 49
Chitemene, 95
Cities, 76–7, 90–1, 172–3; *see also* Urbanization
Climate, 4–6, 11, 14–21, 31, 99, 111, 125, 181
    and human comfort and energy, 47, 50, 53–62
    equatorial lowland, 6, 14–15, 56, 99
    monsoon, 14–16, 56–7, 100
    Savanna, 6, 14–16, 56–7, 100–1

    see also Micro-climate and Eco-climate
Clothing, 55, 60–1
Colonial period, 108, 158, 175, 181, 188–9
Conscious responses to climate, 59–62
Conservation, 32–4, 41, 90, 176
Conventions, 48
Co-operative societies, 51–2
Cottage and small-scale industry, 156, 169
Credit, 118, 142
Crops, improvement of, 50, 119–21, 203–4
    rotations, successions, 42, 128–9
    yields, 19, 97–8, 109, 116–17, 127, 203–4
    see also Plant pests, diseases, populations and spacings
Cyclones, 18–19

Dams, 26, 28, 45–6, 178–9
Demographic–economic problem, 85–92, 133, 143, 238
Development continuum, 147–52, 238–9
Diet and nutrition, 54, 62, 68–72, 96, 110, 176
Disease, 3, 54, 62–8, 80, 126
Disguised unemployment, 84

Eco-climate, 20–1
Ecological factors, 30, 37–8, 40, 108
Economic development, and growth, 1
    definition of, 1, 239
    measurement of, 1–4
Economies of scale, 8, 92, 136–7, 168, 181
Education and skills, 8, 52, 150, 191
Evaporation, 22, 34
Evapotranspiration, 22